LOVE SONGS

ALSO BY JOHN DIZIKES

LOVE SONGS

THE LIVES, LOVES, AND POETRY
OF NINE AMERICAN WOMEN

John Dizikes

Animal Mitchell Publications
Amenia, New York

JUL '19   *494 2483*

Love Songs: The Lives, Loves, and Poetry of Nine American Women ©
2018 by John Dizikes

Text credits are on pages 503–506, which constitute an extension
of this copyright page.

Image credits are on pages 507–509, which constitute an extension of this copyright page

ISBN: 978-1-944037-76-5
Library of Congress Control Number: 2017946975

First edition

Book design by Colin Rolfe.
Photo research and copyediting by Susan Piperato.
Production and distribution by Epigraph: www.epigraphps.com

Jacket design by Design Monsters

Animal Mitchell Publications
POB 260
Amenia, NY 12501

AnimalMitchellPublications@gmail.com

ACKNOWLEDGEMENTS

Will Rogers, the American humorist, is reputed to have said that he never met a man he didn't like. Fortunate fellow! I confess I can't share that sentiment, but I can say that I have never met a librarian I didn't like. So it is a great pleasure to thank many librarians at the McHenry Library of the University of California at Santa Cruz for their tireless efficiency, good humor, and encouragement. In Special Collections, Christine Bunting, Gretchen Dempewolf, Luisa Orlando, and Janet Young. At the Reference Desk, Frank Gravier, Paul Machlis, Annette Marines, Karen Mokrzycki, and Debbie Murphy. Very special thanks to Laura McClanathan. As well, I am grateful for the help of the Harry Ransom Center, the University of Texas at Austin, and Special Collections at the University of California, Santa Barbara.

John Thompson typed the first version of the manuscript and the Humanities Division of UCSC made the second possible, with the assistance of Kimberly Howe and Leslie Crook. Confronted by an indifferent publishing business, longtime agent Tom Wallace worked assiduously on my behalf. Independent editor and publisher David Stanford's initiative and irrepressible determination are responsible for the existence of this book, which I hope justifies his labors. I am grateful to Epigraph for their assistance in producing the book; Susan Piperato for copyediting and photo research, Colin Rolfe for interior design and coordination, and Paul Cohen for guidance. I thank George Corsillo and Susan McCaslin of Design Monsters for the cover.

Finally, and as always, Ann Dizikes, who makes everything possible.

For
Marilyn and Dean Dizikes

Poetry is a superior amusement; I do not mean an amusement for superior people. I call it an amusement... not because that is a true definition, but because if you call it anything else you are likely to call it something still more false. If we think of the nature of amusement, then poetry is not amusing, but if we think of anything else that poetry may seem to be, we are led into far greater difficulties. Our definition of the use of one kind of poetry may not exhaust its uses, and will probably not apply to some other kind, or if our definition applies to all poetry, it becomes so general as to be meaningless.

—*T. S. Eliot*

Everything in [prose] could be said in any number of ways, while a poem is itself, inevitably, inerringly.

—*Louise Bogan*

To the Reader

I have brought together the lives and poetry of nine American women who were part of the flowering of American poetry in the first half of the twentieth century. As part of that story, I have described what brought them to New York City and what the City meant to them and to their work, how they interacted with each other, read and responded to (and sometimes reviewed) each other's poems—all this in the years when the mostly-male Modernist movement swept over the literary world. My hope is that readers (if any) will find in these pages an opportunity to read poetry which is new to them and to re-read poetry once familiar. As well I hope that if readers share my admiration for these women's art and imagination, they will join me in equally admiring their courage in expressing their independence from stultifying social conventions, courage which seems to me astonishing even a century later.

To draw the line between the creator and the thing created, between the poet and the poem, is an ancient puzzle. Poems are not things independent of the lives of the poets who wrote them, and I have associated many of the poems in this book with events and developments in the lives of their creators. At the same time, poems are not merely transcriptions of those events and those lives. They exist independently of them and are ultimately to be understood in aesthetic and not biographical terms. I leave it to individual readers to decide if I have been able to maintain this distinction.

The poems included are, with only a handful of exceptions, short poems—lyrics—a modest selection from the vast number available; and only one poem, by Edna St. Vincent Millay, appears in a much-excerpted form. The concentration on lyrics means that the broader range of poetic achievement of some of the poets is therefore unrepresented. I hope some readers will become familiar with these longer poems on their own. Of the innumerable subjects these poets wrote about, I have also selected from a relatively narrow range of subjects—poems about politics and social protest, poems about nature, both the description of the natural world and people's consciousness of it, poems which evoke a sense of place, New York City in particular, and, above all, the greatest achievement of these poets, poems about love—love of many kinds, for which no explanation is necessary.

TABLE OF CONTENTS

PART ONE

ROADS TO ROME

1. DOROTHY PARKER

DOROTHY ROTHSCHILD INHERITED New York City and therefore "it did not occur to her... that people might live elsewhere than New York."[1] Nevertheless, she too traveled a considerable cultural distance when, in 1913, she broke with her familial past and began to work in Midtown Manhattan and to publish poetry. She disclaimed the term "poet." Poets wrote literature, a very serious activity requiring talent and a commitment to art, while she wrote "light verse" because she enjoyed doing it and could make a little money. She absorbed the language and rhythm and tone of the city and the time would come when a certain kind of New York urbanity would be synonymous with her wit and her verse.

DOROTHY'S FATHER, J. Henry Rothschild, American-born of Prussian ancestry, was a hearty, industrious, and successful salesman in the New York garment business. Her mother, Elizabeth Marston, was descended from a family of skilled English gunsmiths who came to the United States in the early nineteenth century and found that guns were a means to prosperity. Henry and Elizabeth met when they were young, fell in love, and announced their desire to marry. The Marstons wanted someone other than a German Jew for their daughter and forbade the marriage. Elizabeth bided her time (as did Henry), and became a schoolteacher and, in 1880, at thirty years of age, finally married her man. Dorothy was born on August 22, 1893, when Elizabeth was forty-two and in frail health; two sons and a daughter had preceded her. Ironically, Dorothy's birthplace was not Manhattan but West End, New Jersey, where the Rothschilds had gone to escape the city's heat. She was born two months prematurely. ("The last time I was early for anything.")[2]

Going to the seashore was a summer ritual for the Rothschilds who, though not rich, lived comfortably in houses staffed by several servants. The Rothschild children took it for granted that there were always people available to serve them. It was at the seashore, in July of 1898, when Dorothy was not quite five, that her mother, age forty-eight, died of a heart condition. It was a devastating blow for the little girl and a major factor in the feelings of self-pity and self-hatred that she recognized in herself for the rest of her life but was powerless to efface. The pain of feeling abandoned became mixed up with a persistent feeling of cultural inferiority rooted in the family's mixed Jewish-and-Englishness. Dorothy often said (later) that if she wrote her autobiography (which she never did) she would entitle it *Mongrel*, a comment whose mordant exaggeration reveals how deep the feelings were.

To search the childhood and youth of Dorothy Rothschild for clues to explain the writer and her writing is to encounter the fact that Dorothy invented a childhood that was largely fictitious, the first narrative by a girl with a need and talent for storytelling. She insisted that her childhood was marked only by loneliness, shame, and anger. "All those writers who talk about their child-hood! Gentle God, if I ever wrote about mine, you would never sit in the same room with me."[3] A constant refrain in her poetry would be that life was unendurable.

In Dorothy's account, she was lonely as a child, ignored by her siblings. There was an enormous gap there. Her brothers, twelve and nine years older, could not share childhood with her but in fact were of help to her later. She spoke with envy and disdain of her six-years-older sister Helen. "She was a real beauty, my sister, sweet, lovely—but silly."[4] Actually, they spent a good deal of time together when growing up and were close throughout their later lives, visiting each other frequently. Dorothy was con-temptuous of her many Rothschild uncles and aunts—"silly stock" was the best she could say of them—but there were innumerable family gatherings in which everyone took part with uproarious pleasure. One explanation of Dorothy's contempt would be the embarrassment of a shy girl of reserved English sensibility in the presence of disorderly, boisterous older people.

In the made-up story of Dorothy's childhood, there were two primary villains. The first was her father; when she spoke of him later, which was rarely, she described him as a bully, a monster, and could not speak of him "without horror." But his greatest and un-forgivable offense was that he was the primary source of her sense of shame. It was his features, gestures and profile that she inherited. "She never forgave him for her Jewish parentage and name."[5]

The second was her stepmother. In January 1900, a year and a half after Elizabeth's death, Henry Rothschild married Eleanor Lewis, who was forty-eight years old and "the second Christian schoolteacher he liberated from spinsterhood."[6] Sadly, but not surprisingly, Dorothy could neither forgive her father for this be-trayal of Elizabeth, nor make any effort to accept or even tolerate Eleanor's presence. The three older children addressed her as Mrs. Rothschild while Dorothy treated her rudely, not even addressing her personally. "Hey, you, was about the best I could do"[7]—this at age seven! For her part, and compounding the sources of animosity, Eleanor was pious and insisted that Christian indoctrination was needed to save Dorothy's Jewish soul.

Dorothy had indulged in fantasies that she was Catholic, that Catholicism would disguise her Jewish identity. Ironically, those fantasies became a partial reality. She was enrolled in the Roman Catholic Blessed Sacrament Convent School, within easy walking distance from home and highly respected academically. It became the provocation for more acrimony. Every afternoon her stepmother asked Dorothy, "Did you love Jesus today?" and every evening made her say her prayers. As Dorothy portrayed it, the drama of the fanatical wicked stepmother and rebellious orphan was interminable. In fact, it lasted just over three years. Eleanor died of a cerebral hemorrhage in April of 1903. Dorothy was not yet ten.

Her school came out badly in Dorothy's recollections; she insisted that students couldn't learn anything there, which was untrue. The nuns recognized that she was precociously clever with words; she was encouraged to read, and did so voraciously—all the novels of Charles Reade, and, unforgettably, William Thackeray's *Vanity Fair*. Perhaps she absorbed the manner and values of another orphan, Becky Sharp, the prototypical rebel. Dorothy was determined not to fit in. "She made a special effort to criticize everyone and sought reasons to find them ridiculous."[8] She also learned something that would be extremely important to her later. She began to develop a sense of an audience. Very small, with luminous eyes, she was attractive to people, and could make them laugh. "Dottie had a dry wit that often convulsed us,"[9] a fellow student remembered.

It was at this age also that she began to think of herself as the artistic member of the family. The influence of the home, contrary to her denigration of it, was as important as that of the school. There were many books at home; books lined the corridors and filled the library. She wrote poetry and was encouraged in this by all the family. "Wonderful, to say the least," her sister said of her poetry. Perversely, she mocked such family praise by describing herself as "one of those awful children who wrote verses."[10]

Her father stimulated her to write poetry by showing her, unsuccessfully, as it turned out, that it was also a way to express affection. He wrote "pomes," verses about the family dogs, verses written down during his office day, verses scrawled quickly in letters he sent to Dorothy, mostly in the summer when he was working and the children were away from the city. He reported on one of the dogs:

> This morning Rags near' got
> a "licking"
> 'Cause he "kicked" at meat
> & wanted "chicking"
> But Mary pleased him
> with chicken hash
> And begged me to do nothing
> rash

He also wrote to say how much she was missed:

> Say, Miss Dorothy, will you kindly tell
> If the "Push" at Bellport are all well.
> All well here—but a little sad
> Your coming home will make all glad
> Rags and Bunk have got the blues
> As they seek in vain for your little (2) shoes

There were dozens of letters and cards to her father, reporting that she was well, having a good time (even when she wasn't), all written in an affectionate and easy way.

Dear Papa,
This morning I received
          your "pome."
How did you do it
          all alone?
When you come down
          on Sunday, Pa,
No, nothing rhymes
          except cigar.

In the first decade of the century, Henry Rothschild removed Dorothy from the Blessed Sacrament School and once more brought New Jersey into her life by enrolling her in Miss Dana's School for Young Ladies in Morristown. Her biographers disagree about when she entered and left the school, but they agree that its influence on her was significant. Dorothy, of course, true to the orphan-who-did-it-all-by-herself story she elaborated years afterwards, had nothing good to say about Miss Dana's. But she got on well with students there and, as a boarder, took full advantage of the school's lively (though very proper) social life, meeting boys for the first time at the school-sponsored dances. "She was most attractive," a classmate recalled. "She was small, slender, dark haired, and brilliant."[11]

As its name made clear, Miss Dana's was a "finishing" school for the upwardly mobile daughters of the middle class. But it was also much more, "efficiently run imaginative in curriculum and progressive in outlook," a school determined to turn out "well-read, well-informed, and well-spoken young women who would be effective in the world."[12] The curriculum was demanding and included Greek and Latin, classical and English literature, art history, algebra, and geometry. Instruction was in seminars. Special attention was paid to oral expression, and much of the material recited was poetry. As well, the students met as a group to discuss some of the leading questions and events of the day. Miss Dana's may have laid the foundation for the political consciousness she developed years later.

Dorothy's reading at this time, in Miss Dana's and out of it, was directed toward writers with a satirical point of view. She soon discovered La Rochefoucauld and Jonathan Swift. From second-century Rome, the Latin poet Martial spoke to Dorothy Rothschild in twentieth-century America.

> Once a surgeon, Dr. Baker
> Then became an undertaker,
> Not so much his trade reversing
> Since for him it's just rehearsing.

What most appealed to her were verbal quickness, epigrams, and paradoxes, and a prevailing tone of world-weary disillusionment, especially about the possibility of enduring love between men and women. The poems of A. E. Housman (which deeply influenced not only Dorothy but many of the other women profiled in this book), capture that mood.

With Rue my Heart is Laden

> With rue my heart is laden
> For golden friends I had,
> For many a rose-lipt maiden
> And many a lightfoot lad.

> By brooks too broad for leaping
> The lightfoot boys are laid;
> The rose-lipt girls are sleeping
> In fields where roses fade.

She left Miss Dana's without graduating. The Rothschild family was breaking up. Both sons and the older daughter, Helen, had married. Dorothy took care of her father, who retired from business and thereafter moved restlessly from one house to another. Contrary to her later retelling of the story, Dorothy's relations with her father were amicable, but no doubt the fact that the other siblings had moved away from home increased her own yearning for independence. By the end of 1913, Henry was very unwell. He died of a heart attack on December 28, 1913.

DOROTHY WAS TWENTY. Little is known about her life at this point, which was spent living with Helen some of the time, with one of her brothers and his family at other times. She always insisted that she had been left penniless, but her father had assets when he died and something must have come to her. In any event, she needed work. Circumstances had freed her from the family culture that so distressed her, but what was it she had escaped *to*? She had learned to play the piano and got a job as accompanist in a dance school, and moved into a boarding house on Manhattan's Upper West Side. She was now free from conventional restraints. She made friends with some of the male lodgers and had her first sexual experiences. One friend was particularly important; Thorne Smith, an advertising copywriter who wanted to write fiction and would become well known in a few years for his risqué "Topper" stories. "We used to sit around in the evening and talk. There was no money," she recalled, "but Jesus we had fun."[13]

She had been writing poetry from almost as early as she could remember, but she dismissed those efforts—dismissing and ridiculing things (including herself) was her way with the world, a form of self-protection—and lapsed into her "mongrel" mode when referring to it: "I was just a little Jewish girl trying to be cute."[14] Thorne Smith's example may have been influential. In any case, it was at this time that she made up her mind to support herself by writing. But writing what? And for whom? Since the age of eleven, Dorothy had read fashion magazines, had been fascinated by the sophistication they represented, and wished to be a part of it.

Wit and fashion were represented by *Vanity Fair* magazine, which was founded in 1914. Frank Crowninshield, its editor, who was born in Paris and educated in Italy and France, had quickly turned it into the most sophisticated magazine of its day, appealing to the wealthy and fashion-minded but also including avant-garde art. Its tone was clever and satirical. Its readers encountered H.G. Wells, Arnold Bennett, free verse, T.S. Eliot, and Henri Matisse. These were celebrated, or soon to be celebrated, names, but *Vanity Fair*, like most of the other popular and highbrow magazines, also sprinkled popular poetry throughout its pages. Some readers derided the poems as mere filler between articles and illustrations, but it was verse of all kinds and reached a wide audience. *Vanity Fair* was an important element in creating the culture out of which the poetry renaissance of the 1910s and '20s arose. Verse was everywhere in the air, a popular form of expression.

Realizing that she had an ear for colloquial conversation, words, phrases, and fragments of speech heard on the streets, at work, and at summer resorts, Dorothy wrote a poem in which she wove together snatches of such random talk. Here are two stanzas from "Any Porch":

> I don't want the vote for myself,
>   But women with property, dear –
> I think the poor girl's on the shelf,
>   She's talking about her 'career.'

> I've heard I was psychic, before,
>   To think that you saw it—how funny—
> Why, he must be sixty, or more,
>   I told you she'd marry for money!

She submitted this to *Vanity Fair*. It was accepted and was published in September 1915. She got a check for twelve dollars. "I thought I was Edith Sitwell."[15] Of course, she knew she wasn't Edith Sitwell and, unfortunately, had no wish to be. Had she wished it, she might have taken her poetic gifts more seriously. Instead, what she wished to be at this point was "one of those who, if only in a very minor way, were helping to establish new styles for the fashionable."[16] It might turn out that the mongrel/orphan had a smart-aleck twin.

Her verse had opened a door. She went to *Vanity Fair*'s office and asked for a job, talking to Frank Crowninshield himself. He was charmed by this dark-haired pixie. (She was an inch under five feet.) Six months later, she was offered a position at *Vogue* magazine, a lesser satellite of *Vanity Fair* in the Conde Nast publishing group—at ten dollars a week. Much of the work was drudgery and she was no more than an anonymous member of the staff. But she had decisively broken with her past and begun to invent a new person and would make a name—a new name—for herself.

2. SARA TEASDALE

SOME OF THE most memorable poems about New York City were written by a woman from St. Louis. On her first visit to the city, in 1911, this young poet, inspired by its buildings and squares, its parks and places of amusement, captured their atmosphere and, more imaginatively, conceived of them as public stages on which the often anguished drama of love between men and women was played out. She had found her theme—love—and her poetic form—the lyric. When, in 1916, she moved to New York City for good, she came as an established and widely read poet of the day, increasingly identified with that theme.

SARA TEASDALE WAS born in St. Louis on August 8, 1884 in her parents' middle age. Her father was confident enough of his family's social standing not to make a fuss about it. He was a quiet, kindly man, and his affection for Sara was uncomplicated, and she in turn adored him. Mary Willard Teasdale's ancestors were more distinguished than her husband's. The Willards settled in Concord, Massachusetts, in 1635, and later produced presidents of Harvard and signers of the Declaration of Independence. Yet, oddly, for Mary Teasdale, ancestral pride was not taken for granted but was defensively aggressive, which took the form of a single-minded insistence on social respectability. She also promoted an adherence to conventional religion, in the form of Baptist Christianity, which Sara quietly but firmly abandoned, leaving her "with all the inhibitions but none of the faith of her forebears." Psychologically very complex, "a compound of sensual feeling and prudery, of luxuriant fantasy and shrewd common sense," she struggled to conceal the disturbing conflicts which ravaged her.[1]

The most crippling of these was that from an early age she was perceived and encouraged to perceive herself as frail and sickly; activity was followed by periods of lassitude and pain. The physical causes of these episodes, if any, were never determined. Her mother's concern was heightened by the fact that she herself had been chronically ill as a child.

Solicitousness and concern were also a form of maternal dominance. Helplessness in a girl became a sign of personal superiority, a familiar situation in nineteenth-century British and American middle-class culture. One of Sara's biographers argued that, subsequently, Mary believed "good breeding proved itself in a girl by her delicacy and sickliness ... that constitutional weakness was a mark of superiority."[2] Certainly, Sara came to believe that any of her many illnesses, however trifling, might be life threatening, resulting in a lifelong preoccupation with death.

At the same time, Sara revealed independence of mind and a resolute will, which were expressed in explosions of determined resistance to her mother's dictates. A photograph of her at age five charmingly suggests this: She holds her right fist clenched in willful determination. "She lived the life of a princess in her tower," a friend later reported. She had no household chores. The family was highly selective about friends, so that she had very few of them. Not being allowed to go out on her own into the neighborhood streets, she daydreamed a good deal, amusing herself by inventing stories "of what would happen if things were very nice,"[3] and was perhaps troubled by darker thoughts about what would happen if things were not so nice.

Her mother's relentless insistence on gentility manifested itself in a curious and revealing way—she was determined that her poor little girl should play with dolls. The awkward fact, however, was that Sara did not like dolls and did not play with them. She seemingly accepted her mother's dictates, but also quietly subverted them. One of her few childhood friends observed that, passive and submissive as she usually was, away from adults "she burned up energy at breakneck speeds in her enthusiasm." And Sara herself precociously reflected on a possible connection between affluent pampering and illness. "I often wonder if I had been born into a family with no means if I would have had better health."[4]

She was not thought strong enough to go to school until she was nine and was then enrolled in Mrs. Lockwood's, a private school for girls that was only one street from home. There she quickly revealed a lively mind and a retentive memory; the children recited Longfellow's verses in a class and Sara amassed a considerable store of poems she memorized in her room at home by herself. Mrs. Lockwood was patient in helping her adapt to the presence of other young girls and Sara got on very well with them. At Mrs. Lockwood's, she was also introduced to the careful observation of nature, and retained an interest in botany all her life. She read voraciously and kept track of her reading in a note-book—over a hundred books in the next few years, from *Little Women* to Shakespeare.

At fourteen, she was placed in a prestigious girls' school, The Mary Institute, founded by T. S. Eliot's grandfather. (Tom Eliot spent the first sixteen years of his life in a house next door.) The Mary Institute was in the city. Reaching it required a daily trip by streetcar, which was thought to be dangerously exhausting. So Sara was removed after one year and enrolled in yet another highly regarded girls' school, Hosmer Hall, closer to home. Her four years there repeated the earlier pattern. She read widely and eagerly and responded to intellectual stimulation while taking little part in any of the school's social life. But there was one new development: Writing poetry became a central part of her life. She came to be recognized by her fellow students and teachers as "the poet," though she later described her verses from this time, none of which she kept, as "very bad." A number of them were sharply satirical comments on contemporary poets, a kind of poetry she didn't often write and never published. One other aspect of the emerging importance of poetry in her life was fixed now and never changed: She felt too shy to read her poems in public.

IN 1902, AT age eighteen, she graduated from Hosmer Hall. Then what? Sara never considered going to college. This was not a desire denied her. She apparently took for granted that she was not strong enough for the rigors of higher education; all her life she was uninterested in academic life and institutions and (later) skeptical of the academic criticism of her poetry. At one point, she did take two college classes, but lost interest and dropped one.

She took for granted, also, that she would live at home and that ill health would prevent her earning a living on her own. She admitted that she didn't know where money came from or how it was managed. What she could do, without quite imagining herself to be a professional writer, was to write poetry alone at home. Of course, it was taken for granted that she would leave home only when she was found by, and married, an eligible man.

However, this extreme social claustrophobia changed gradually in the next few years. Sara became familiar with other people outside her family, and she decided to be a professional writer. These were intoxicating, but also frightening, developments. Once again, achievement and exploration alternated with illness and retreat back to the security of her room in her parents' home. The crucial step was her friendship with eight young women, some of whom had been in school with her, who formed a writing and photography group and called themselves "the Potters." They met regularly to talk and encourage each other's artistic interests. The leader of the group was Williamina Parrish, who persuaded Sara to contribute poetry to the group's magazine, *The Potter's Wheel*.

The group was also a means by which its members could begin to express erotic sentiments. The members shared admiration for famous singers and actresses of the day such as Mary Garden, Julia Marlowe, and Eleanora Duse. They read popular literature associated with Medieval romance, introducing into their consciousness and discussions the sexual relationships of men and women in the form of the tragic love stories of Lancelot and Guinevere, Tristan and Isolde, stories of doomed love and of the expiation of masculine guilt through female suffering.

In 1905, Sara and her mother took a three-month Mediterranean tour on a ship with Protestant ministers. For Mary, it was essentially a religious venture, with the Holy Land as its ultimate destination. For Sara, the religious aspect was minimal and the trip turned out to be an aesthetic journey suffused with a new appreciation of beauty in many forms. In the years following, she had no formal religious affiliation. Outward bound, Sara suffered from sore throats and loss of strength, and she was frantic by the time the ship reached Greece, because it seemed she would never see the land and ancient culture she had been dreaming about—the land of Aphrodite, the goddess of love, and of Sappho, the poet of women's love for women. Typically, Sara's mother insisted on staying aboard ship to sit by Sara's bedside when they docked. But Sara found relief, roused herself, and went ashore, where two men made a basket of their hands and carried her up to the Acropolis, "the glorious Parthenon glistening yellow in the sunshine."[5]

The Holy Land for Sara was a profound disappointment, squalid and filthy, generating only "terrible memories." The return voyage took them to Rome, and her spirits lifted though she was still too weak to spend more than a few minutes in the Sistine Chapel and had to be driven by the Protestant cemetery where Keats and Shelley are buried. Paris made up for everything. She attended a performance of Wagner's *Tristan and Isolde*, "one of the most wonderful things that has ever been done by anybody," and then had an even more intense personal experience in the Louvre. At the end of a long corridor, "against a dark red curtain, beautifully lighted, stood the most beautiful thing in the world—the Venus de Milo... far more lovely than any reproduction I ever saw. The nearer I came to her, the more I loved her. Yes, I really love her—almost as one loves a real person." But of course she felt compelled to add, "It is a spiritual love."[6]

Once home, she read contemporary literature for the first time—Oscar Wilde and James M. Barrie. It was the dreamy symbolist stories of Maurice Maeterlinck and the Celtic twilight poetry of the early W. B. Yeats that had the most appeal. William Reedy, the editor of the noteworthy St. Louis magazine, *Reedy's Mirror*, knew some of the young Potters, met Sara and encouraged her to write. He published her first poem in 1906.

Sara began writing sonnets about the great Italian actress Eleanora Duse, who was concluding another tour of the United States where she had become a favorite, especially with many women who, like Sara, idealized her as the embodiment of sensuality combined with nobility of spirit. "It was as though each time she played she immolated herself upon an altar." And yet at the same time, another observer explained, it was "her force of will her mastery of herself, not her abandonment of it," which was most remarkable. For Sara, and for the Potters, Duse also represented a respectable way to understand their own sexual natures and desires. Sara wrote to a friend, "I made an altar to Aphrodite and … I used to repeat the 'Ode to Aphrodite' before it—half in fun, half in earnest … I can confess to you—tho' I'd be afraid to tell most people that she is more real to me than the virgin."[7] William Reedy encouraged Sara to collect her poems about Duse. A publisher in Boston agreed to publish them, at her expense, and her indulgent and proud parents paid $290 for one thousand copies of *Sonnets to Duse and Other Poems*, which appeared in 1907.

She was finding her compelling theme, love for a noble woman, and was now proudly launched as a professional writer. Still, she soon recognized the book's limitations: the language was forced, stilted, and sounded schoolgirlish. She promptly began a new project, one related to Duse, blank-verse monologues about celebrated women of the past. The first, "Guinevere," was published in the *Mirror* and occasioned newspaper gossip about the local "girl genius."

The next three years were pendulum swings: creative activity followed by illness and depression. She was sent to a sanatorium in Connecticut, where reading and writing were forbidden and total rest and cold baths were required for many hours of the day. The grimness of it all was mitigated somewhat by the fact that it was the first time she had ever been away from the family. She also initiated outside contacts. She wrote letters to a young male poet in New York, an exchange that continued for several years though she did not meet him in person until later. Another important acquaintance was a philosophy instructor at the University of Arizona, a married woman eight years older than she, who gave her helpful critical advice about her writing. Against her parents' wishes, she went to Tucson to spend three months with this friend, accompanied, at her parents' insistence, by a maid. Finally, she renewed acquaintance with Zoe Atkins, who had been a schoolmate at Hosmer Hall and who was writing poetry and plays and acting in a local theatrical company. Atkins introduced her to some of the suppressed erotic poems of Charles Baudelaire and to bohemian St. Louis circles, from which Sara drew back in prim disapproval. "I never feel more utterly puritanical than when I am with such people."[8]

SARA COMPLETED HER cycle of poems about celebrated women and, after the manuscript was circulated for over a year, it was published in New York City and London by Putnam's in December 1910. This confirmation of her as a writer of importance was underscored by an invitation to attend the December dinner of the Poetry Society of America.

The Poetry Society had been established earlier that year by a group of resolute women poets in New York City who, tired of

living in a culture in which "one had to be apologetic about poetry, when the poet was considered a variant from the normal,"[9]
formed their national organization to support the writing of poetry of high professional standards. The Society brought new as
well as established poets to New York City for its dinner and for
later general meetings at which these poets' works were read to the
group. Jessie Rittenhouse (1869-1948), a journalist, poet, and secretary of the Society, was one of the many women who were taking part in and shaping the growing women's poetry movement.
She was the editor of an important early anthology, *The Younger
American Poets* (1904), and it was she who invited Sara to join the
Society and proved to be a lifelong friend.

Predictably, Sara's parents, worried about her health and safety,
opposed her going to New York City, and so she was unable to be
present at the dinner. However, she overcame their disapproval and,
in January, 1911, arrived in New York for the first time, staying at
the Martha Hotel, one exclusively for women and from which she
could look out at the "marvelous skyline." With mounting excitement, Sara made a tour of some of the celebrated sights: Central
Park, "my beloved Metropolitan Tower," the Metropolitan Opera,
and the subway. In February, she attended a general meeting of the
Society. Seated just behind her that night was another poet, "a wob-
bly blond youth," who made his presence known by exchanging witticisms with others, eliciting much laughter and Sara's disapproval.
She was not pleased with Ezra Pound who, unknown to her, was
also finding freedom from provincial America and would eventually flee to Europe. Sara thought him "coarse." Though she couldn't
know it, she had experienced her first encounter with Modernism.[10]

Helen of Troy and Other Poems was published in October 1911
to favorable national reviews. It contained six dramatic monologues about those legendary tragic women whose lives meant

so much to Sara at this time, poetry in which she was "looking back and measuring the agony of their lives." The figure of Helen, in myth and poetry, would mean a great deal to a number of the women poets of the time; half a century later Hilda Doolittle would write a masterwork about her. The bulk of Sara's volume, however, was made up of poems very different in subject matter and in style from the Helen poems, and it was these other poems that made this volume a turning point.

Most striking were a half dozen New York poems. They are not primarily descriptive. There are people present, a "we" made up of a couple, a man and a woman. In the *Helen* volume, Sara grouped these poems under the heading "Love Songs." There is the possibility of love for the people present:

Metropolitan Tower

We walked together in the dusk
 To watch the tower grow dimly white,
And saw its life against the sky
 Its flower of amber light.

You talked of half a hundred things,
 I kept each hurried word you said;
And when at last the hour was full,
 I saw the light turn red.

You did not know the time had come,
 You did not see the sudden flower,
Nor know that in my heart Love's birth
 Was reckoned from that hour.

Or there is the impossibility of love:

Coney Island

Why did you bring me here?
The sand is white with snow,
Over the wooden domes
The winter sea-winds blow –
There is no shelter near,
 Come, let me go.

With foam of icy lace
The sea creeps up the sand,
The wind is like a hand
That strikes us in the face,
Doors that June set a-swing
Are bolted long ago;
We try them uselessly –
Alas, there cannot be
For us a second spring;
 Come, let us go.

In the New York City poems, the interplay of person and place is a way for the author imaginatively to explore a new degree of freedom for herself. "She had been a lifelong prisoner in her room … and New York seemed to provide everything she had been waiting for,"[11] especially the courage explicitly to declare the power of erotic love. The celebrated instance of this was "Union Square," in which a man and woman walk about, revealing to us that he doesn't really love the woman narrator. With this poem Sara achieved a degree of sensational controversy, for the woman contrasts her own suppressed desires with those of the prostitutes walking about the Square, the "girls with thirsty eyes," who are involved in an "errand each man knows."

Union Square

With the man I love who loves me not,
  I walked in the street-lamps' flare;
We watched the world go home that night
  In a flood through Union Square.

I leaned to catch the words he said
  That were light as a snowflake falling;
Ah well that he never leaned to hear
  The words my heart was calling.

And on we walked and on we walked
  Past the firey lights of the picture shows –
Where the girls with thirsty eyes go by
  On the errand each man knows.

And on we walked and on we walked
  At the door at last we said good-bye;
I knew by his smile he had not heard
  My heart's unuttered cry.

With the man I love who loves me not
  I walked in the street-lamp's flare –
But oh, the girls who can ask for love
  In the lights of Union Square.

In the months between writing "Union Square" in the winter of 1911 and the fall publication of the book, Sara was well aware that the poem would disturb readers. Some friends urged her not to include it in the final volume. Jessie Rittenhouse, by contrast, boldly advised her to stand behind it, saying that it wasn't "so very wicked after all," and was, in fact, "exceedingly strong and beautiful" and would actually be a boost to her reputation to be identified as a "new" and "liberated" woman. As it turned out, many reviewers did concentrate on "Union Square." The *New York Times* reviewer singled it out, asking, "Has the woman who speaks in that very unusual poem ... been always with us but inarticulate?"[12]

The New York poems mark Sara's abandonment of longer poetic forms, her embrace of the lyric, especially the love lyric, and the emergence of subjects that would preoccupy her for the rest of her life. A very personal one was acceptance of the absence of love.

But Not To Me

The April night is still and sweet
With flowers on every tree;
Peace comes to them on quiet feet,
But not to me.

My peace is hidden in his breast
Where I shall never be,
Love comes to-night to all the rest,
But not to me.

The lyrical poems in *Helen of Troy* revealed the future for her; brief, conventional in form, precisely controlled and, before

Modernist poets advocated it, simpler diction. She had found her true voice.

SARA WAS ALSO now certain where she wanted to live. "I feel quite like a New Yorker ... I am simply wild with the joy of life and with the most wonderful city that ever existed."[13] Nevertheless, the truth was that she couldn't live in New York City, or anywhere else except St. Louis, because she could not live alone and support herself. National magazines paid, on average, ten to twelve dollars a poem. Even a successful poet's income from his or her poetry might be as little as $200 a year. To leave St. Louis meant to escape from her parents, but now a crisis loomed for her. In 1914, she would be thirty, on the verge of becoming an old maid and pushing the outside limits of childbearing, her parents' example to the contrary notwithstanding.

For the next two years, she moved restlessly about, cultivating friendships with men. She went to Europe with Jessie Rittenhouse; to Chicago, where a lively poetic renaissance was underway; and again to New York City. In Chicago, she made contact with Harriet Monroe, of *Poetry* magazine, whom she (at first) dismissed as a "sour old maid," a feeling "perhaps arising from her own fear of that fate."[14] She got to know Floyd Dell, then editor of a progressive literary journal, who introduced her to Chicago's bohemia, where people lived and slept as they wished, which marked the narrow limits of her adventurousness. "You see SEX written over every inch of it," she grumbled disapprovingly, and thought Dell a weak person.

In New York City, she befriended John Reed, about to launch himself on a short, spectacular career in radical politics. Walking about the streets of the city, they made an unlikely pair. Reed admired her verse. "There is no better writer of delicate lyrics," he said, and, to her surprise, dismissed the notion that she should write about social questions. "Why should you bother with injustice and dirty things? The merest drudgery machine can tend to that."[15] Their time together was brief, and then he went out of her life.

By chance and by design, she became seriously involved with three men, responding to them with a mixture of awkwardness, self-doubt, and guile, primarily by means of many letters and with occasional face-to-face encounters. All through 1913 and 1914, she was absorbed in a delicate minuet, moving from one partner to another.

In this male trio, John Hall Wheelock represented New York City. A poet whose work Sara admired, he would have a successful career as an editor, and was working in a bookshop when she met and fell in love with him. "Though I could never forgive him if he stopped to love me even in the remotest," she wrote to a friend, and then added perceptively: "The chances of my ever having to do any forgiving are small."[16] When she visited New York, she looked him up and they spent many evenings walking about the city. Her own feelings were never in doubt, but from the beginning, she could not make out whether his feelings for her went beyond friendship.

Ernst Filsinger represented St. Louis, where his family was part of the intellectually lively German community. He owned a shoe manufacturing company; had traveled; spoke Spanish; had written a book, *Trading With Latin America*; was interested in the arts; and, more than Sara, was open to new forms. He was far from wealthy, and not as articulate as her poet-admirers. They were introduced to each other by a mutual friend and got on amiably. He fell immediately and unfalteringly in love with her. She found him appealing, but said that his most attractive quality was that he reminded her of John Wheelock.

Vachel Lindsay represented Springfield, Illinois (where he lived with his formidable mother), the Midwest, and America, in ascending order. He despised New York City and cast himself in the guise of a national troubadour whose mission was to infuse poetry into the soul of the common people, which he did in public readings. When he met Sara, he had become famous for "General William Booth Enters into Heaven" (1913), and "The Congo" (1914). Determined to save Sara from the taint of New York City and to make her his poetic soulmate, which didn't necessarily mean his wife, he was adamant in saying that he coveted "a fellow warrior in the Middle Western fight." He refused to join the Poetry Society. "I want them to join my gang. I want Rome to come to Camelot."[17] Sara realized that his primary aim was to evangelize for the muse of poetry.

Lindsay, of whom Sara was very fond, seemed like he would be impossible as a mate. Wheelock, when more or less confronted with her feelings, advised her to get married—to someone, but clearly not to him. That settled it. Ernst came to visit the Teasdale family in August 1914, proposed marriage, and was accepted. This meant Sara would remain in St. Louis. Ernst was genuine in saying that Sara was "the ideal for whom I have hoped since boyhood." She vowed, also genuinely, to submerge her life in his.

They were married in December 1914. "Now, for the first time in years, St. Louis seems a good sort of place,"[18] she wrote to a friend. However, she wanted no part of conventional domestic life, so they lived in a hotel, where she suffered an attack of illness as well as back spasms, but as proof of their happiness they composed a poem together. She meant what she said about Ernst, but not long after the marriage she wrote a poem about a triangle of lovers that, if we take Colin to be John Wheelock, puts things in a different light.

The Look

Stephon kissed me in the spring,
  Robin in the fall,
But Colin only looked at me
  And never kissed at all.

Stephon's kiss was lost in jest,
  Robin's lost in play,
But the kiss in Colin's eyes
  Haunts me night and day.

THROUGH IT ALL, poems had been flowing through her, five or six a month, and she collected them for a book that she was confident would be "far more vital" than *Helen of Troy*, while maintaining her lyric form. The result was *Rivers to the Sea* (1915); the title came from a poem by Wheelock, but the volume was dedicated "To E." Her publisher mounted an energetic publicity campaign and printed a first edition of 1,640 copies. The poems form a cycle about the natural world and the people in it, and grew out of her immediate personal experiences. She was self-consciously reaching for something deeper than what she had so far accomplished, while retaining the deceptive simplicity of her style.

The reviews were gratifyingly laudatory about her "beautiful lyric touch," but more significantly emphasized that the book "reveals the soul of a woman" and presented a feminine view of the nature of love, which she never presumed to do. There was less of the sentimentality that has often been (too simply) associated with her poems. Quite the reverse. Love was understood as often perverse. The heart, in its mysterious way, was sometimes most deeply touched not by loyalty but by indifference, a theme that she often returned to and which we may associate with her unrequited love for John Wheelock.

Debt

What do I owe to you
  Who love me deep and long?
You never gave my spirit wings
  Or gave my heart a song.

But oh, to him I loved
  Who loved me not at all,
I owe the open gate
  That led thru heaven's wall.

The agony of unrequited love could never be healed except by death as a form of revenge.

I Shall Not Care

When I am dead and over me bright April
  Shakes out her rain-drenched hair,
Tho' you should lean above me broken-hearted,
  I shall not care.

I shall have peace, as leafy trees are peaceful
  When rain bends down the bough,
And I shall be more silent and cold-hearted
  Than you are now.

Pain and the fear of death were so familiar to her that she imagined them at her bedside every night.

Doctors

Every night I lie awake
 And every day I lie abed
And hear the doctors, Pain and Death,
 Conferring at my head.

They speak in scientific tones,
 Professional and low—
One argues for a speedy cure,
 The other, sure and slow.

To one so humble as myself
 It should be matter for some pride
To have such noted fellows here,
 Conferring at my side.

Rivers to the Sea sold well and its success stimulated her to begin another project, an anthology of women's love poetry of the previous half century, which she called *The Answering Voice*, a title suggested by John Wheelock. The work exacted a great toll: year-long bouts with bad health. This was undoubtedly connected to her gloomy sense that, whatever her poetic achievements and however sound her marriage, she was condemned to life in St. Louis.

Ernst was under great pressure as well. His shoe company was failing and he finally decided to accept defeat and wind up its affairs, a humiliating decision for him. Bankruptcy, in addition to causing worry about their financial affairs, was a further cause of worry for Sara. Ernst realized that he would have to look for a new job, and among the possibilities open to him, given his knowledge of Spanish, was a job in Argentina. This caused Sara "frantic distress" because it would mean having to move there. Then, in November, Ernst suddenly informed her that he had found a job with a textile firm in New York. She was "wild with delight."[19] Two days after he told her of his new job, without even settling their household affairs, she took the train for New York City.

3. EDNA ST. VINCENT MILLAY

E DNA ST. VINCENT Millay would be so closely identified with bohemia and with sexual liberation that it seemed as if she had been predestined to epitomize the spirit of Greenwich Village. The four most often quoted lines of her poetry, still familiar to people who know nothing else she wrote, captured the spirit of the liberated woman:

> My candle burns at both ends,
> It will not last the night,
> But ah, my foes, and oh, my friends
> It gives a lovely light.

Dorothy Parker, who would become one of Millay's friends, reflected on the immense popularity of those words. "Miss Millay did a great deal of harm with her double-burning candle. She made poetry seem so easy that we could all do it but, of course, we couldn't."[1] Edna Millay knew the truth: that neither writing poetry nor getting to Manhattan had been easy.

EDNA ST. VINCENT Millay was born on February 22, 1892, in Rockland, Maine, the eldest of three daughters born within four years of each other. She is surely the only important poet named for a hospital, St. Vincent's Hospital in New York City. At the time of her birth, word came that the Sisters of Charity had saved the life of her mother's favorite brother and the name of the hospital was bestowed on the infant in eccentric gratitude. The family called her Vincent; for a number of years she signed herself Vincent, and was frequently presumed to be a man.

Edna's father, Henry Tolman Millay, was affable, kind, often out of work, most interested in fishing and poker. Cora Buzell Millay, her mother, was a practical nurse with intellectual and artistic interests. After eleven years, their marriage had become insupportable for Cora, though not for Henry. In 1900, Cora told Henry to leave. He did. Edna vividly remembered her father crossing a cranberry swamp to get to the railroad station "when my mother told him to go & not come back. (Or maybe she said he might come back if he would do better—but who ever does better?")[2] Henry played no further role in the lives of the four women other than to write them occasional letters.

Breaking off a marriage was a family tradition. Cora's mother, Clementine, had also felt herself trapped, with five children, in a hopeless marriage, hopeless because Clementine no longer loved her husband, though he supported them well enough. At age fifteen, knowing that her mother was miserable and had taken another man as a lover, Cora encouraged Clementine to end the marriage. "I knew it must be hell for her to have him as a husband," Cora later explained, "to wait in bed for him in mornings, when she loved this other." Clementine and Cora managed the family for four years while Clementine continued to see her lover. Clementine set up a hairdressing business; Cora quit school to help her. Then disaster came. Clementine was thrown from an open buggy and killed. The family broke up and for a while Cora was sent from relative to relative. Cousins eventually took her in, and it was there she met Henry, "as fair as she was dark, as easygoing as she was intense."[3] He was charming and made her laugh—for a few years at least.

For the next decade, after Henry's banishment, the four Millay women lived precarious lives, moved from town to town, were at times impoverished, and sank into woeful conditions; but Cora behaved—and raised her children to behave—as if their poverty didn't matter. Thrown in on themselves, they enjoyed music and poetry together. They would sing through complete operas, especially their favorite, *Aida*, or the three girls would harmonize on "My Baby Needs a New Pair of Shoes." Cora had a lively interest in the arts, played the piano and sang, helped support the family by playing the organ in local churches though she was not religious and the children received no religious instruction. Edna loved music, could read it as easily as words she learned by reading poetry. Cora recited poetry to the girls—Longfellow's *The Song of Hiawatha*, Whittier's *Snow-Bound*—and somehow managed to acquire a library of the collected works of famous poets. Cora also wrote poetry, some of which was published in obscure New England magazines. As well as the major English and American poets, the girls heard and read popular contemporaries: Eugene Field, Felicia Hemans, James Whitcomb Riley. Edna grew up with the idea of poetry as something available to all, whatever social class or economic condition.

Aggressive, "common sense mixed with earthy humor," Cora was "not like anyone else's mother." Unconventional and wholly indifferent to respectable opinion, the Millays were thought of as a harum-scarum gypsy household. Cora smoked and joked and didn't hesitate to leave the girls alone for several weeks at a time, and it is likely that they understood that these were also sexual affairs. Meeting Cora for the first time in the early 1920s, Edmund Wilson saw a bespectacled schoolmarm who had a "raffish" air about her. He acutely sensed that she "anticipated the bohemianism" of her daughters. Cora put it with characteristic bluntness, "I was a slut myself so why shouldn't my girls be?"[4]

Edna and her sisters inherited a family culture sharply divided between aesthetic tradition and social anarchy. They absorbed the example of their mother as a woman who did as she wished, not as a rebel self-consciously defying social convention, but matter-of-factly. Having survived the harsh environment of the Maine towns in which she lived, Cora felt that she had earned the right to behave precisely as she pleased, constrained only by lack of money. While she "scoffed at domesticity," Cora "encouraged her daughters to be musical, artistic, and poetic."[5] She respected artistic forms and artistic conventions while ignoring social ones.

At age five, Edna wrote her first poem, a song, in three rhymed couplets. Poetic language came naturally to her. At eight, she read Elizabethan poetry with surprising ease. Poetry became the center of her mental and emotional being; nothing else—mother, sisters, or music—rivaled it. She sensed that poetry might help her escape the claustrophobia of Camden, Maine, where the four Millays eventually settled. *St. Nicholas Magazine*, a monthly illustrated journal with a national circulation to which distinguished authors—Mark Twain, Rudyard Kipling, Louisa May Alcott—had contributed work, accepted a poem of Edna's for publication. Three more poems were published by it in 1907 and again in 1908 and 1909. She won prizes and medals from *St. Nicholas*. By the age of sixteen, she had finished forty poems to her satisfaction and, as a tribute, presented her mother with a handwritten volume, *The Poetical Works of Vincent Millay*. At about fifteen years of age, she had written her first sonnet, which is not a precocious age for a first sonnet by a poet for whom that form would be extremely important in later years. It is suffused with awkward adolescent melancholy about the past, about loss of faith, which is made tangible to her by old letters burning in a fireplace.

Old Letters

I know not why I am so loath to lay
Your yellowed leaves along the glowing log,
Unburied dead, that cling about and clog –
With indisputable, insistent say
Of the stout past's all inefficient fray–
The striving present, rising like a fog
To rust the active me, that am a cog
In the great wheel of industry today.
Yet, somehow, in this visible farewell
To the crude symbols of a simpler creed,
I find a pain that had not parallel
When passed the faith itself, – we give small heed
To incorporated truth, let slack or swell;
But truth made tangible, is truth indeed.

She was establishing a critical standard and had learned that she must write and rewrite to reach it. Her schooling did little to enrich her literary culture except in one respect that would be important later on. She learned to read Latin and began to become familiar with Latin literature, reading Caesar's *Commentaries* in the original. True to the abiding anti-intellectualism of American secondary education, her fellow students often mocked her musical and poetic interests and she didn't disguise her disdain for them and for their philistinism.

Relations with boys, as she achieved sexual maturity, were complex. A diminutive five feet one inch, and barely 100 pounds, she had become very pretty and boys both competed with her and were attracted to her, and she to them. Her private notebooks are filled with dreams and imaginings of erotic young men. "The boys don't like me because I won't let them kiss me,"[6] she said, quite inaccurately since she had many young men who took her for long walks, to dances, canoeing; what she really meant was a profoundly important discovery she made about herself: that she desperately needed to feel loved and sought after, while at the same time she had to remain in complete control of any situation. She developed a great fondness for theater and for acting, and one of her biographers is astute in emphasizing that her theatrical temperament extended far beyond actual theatrical performance: One must know the actress to know the lyric poet and woman. Her academic record, however, was mediocre. What was the point of dedicated formal study when the Millays were too poor ever to be able to send her to college? In her senior year she was made editor of the school paper, and at the end of the year won ten dollars for writing the class poem, though the students spitefully didn't choose her as class poet.

Edna St. Vincent Millay

HER LIFE AFTER graduation in June 1909 was a mixture of frustration, sadness, and new adventures. She took over for her mother, who was away so often, in managing the house with and for her sisters. She got a part-time job. She wrote innumerable diary entries about an idealized male lover. There seemed no way she would ever escape from this deadening routine. She had been an avid reader of Edgar Allan Poe and his theme of being buried alive struck a deep and terrifying chord. In the winter of 1912, there was a brief period of escape. She received a telephone call from Kingman, Maine, informing her that her father was dying. She rushed to be with him. She stayed for weeks while he gradually recovered, enjoying both him and her new found freedom from Camden. It was a freedom that made possible her first sexual experience, with the daughter of her father's doctor, with whose family she was staying. This began an important avenue of sexual liberation for her in the following years.

In 1911, Edna began a long poem, a dramatic dialogue in the first person. It was a kind of poem she had not attempted before and offered a way to express powerful spiritual feelings that found no outlet in any church. Her form of spirituality was intensely personal and conveyed a pantheistic sense of God in nature—a pantheism that approached ecstasy. She finished the poem in May 1912. Cora, ever alert for the welfare of her girls, spotted a notice inviting contributions to a national poetry competition. One hundred winning entries would be included in an anthology, *The Lyric Year*, to be published later that year. The best three poems would receive cash prizes. Edna submitted her long—214 lines—poem. Eventually entitled "Renascence (Rebirth)," it is deeply autobiographical, the work of a young woman longing to escape from the claustrophobia of small town life and express the free human spirit. It begins with the poem's narrator hemmed in between the mountains and the sea of Camden, Maine, on Penobscot Bay:

> All I could see from where I stood
> Was three long mountains and a wood;
> I turned and looked another way,
> And saw three islands in a bay.

She begins to experience a sense of suffocation:

> Over these things I could not see,
> There were things that bounded me;
> And I could touch them with my hand,
> Almost, I thought, from where I stand.
> And all at once things seemed so small
> My breath came short, and scarce at all.

She looks up. The sky seems to offer an escape:

But, sure, the sky is big, I said;
Miles and miles above my head;
So here upon my back I'll lie
And look my fill into the sky.

But when she reaches up to touch the sky, it seems low after all:

The sky, I thought, is not so grand;
I 'most could touch it with my hand!
And reaching up my hand to try,
I screamed to feel it touch the sky.

I screamed, and – lo! – Infinity
Came down and settled over me;
Forced back my scream into my chest,
Bent back my arm upon my breast,

This leads to a new ordeal, which will extend through the first half of the poem—she understands and feels all human suffering:

I saw and heard, and knew at last
The How and Why of all things, past,
And present, and forevermore.
The Universe, cleft to the core.

All sin was of my sinning, all
Atoning mine, and mine the gall
Of all regret.

She feels human hate and greed and lust. A man was starving in Capri, two ships collide in a fog bank:

Ah, awful weight! Infinity
Pressed down upon the finite Me!
My anguished spirit, like a bird,
Beating against my lips I heard;
Yet lay the weight so close about
There was no room for it without.
And so beneath the weight lay I
And suffered death, but could not die.

All this suffocates her once more and, craving death, she sinks six feet into the earth and feels the "pitying rain" begin to fall. She savors the sound, but to never again see the magic of spring and of autumn is too much to bear, and she refuses to accept this claustrophobic fate:

O God, I cried, give me new birth,
And put me back upon the earth!

And, in the last half of the poem, the fullness of life returns:

A fragrance such as never clings
To aught save happy living things;
A sound as of some joyous elf
Singing sweet songs to please himself,

And as I looked a quickening gust
Of wind blew up to me and thrust
Into my face a miracle
Of orchard-breath, and with the smell, –
I know not how such things can be! –
I breathed my soul back into me.

Ah! Up then from the ground sprang I
And hailed the earth with such a cry
As is not heard save from a man
Who has been dead, and lives again.

The poem was accepted—and awarded fourth place. Disappointed not to win any prize money, Edna could not anticipate how much attention *The Lyric Year* would receive. Neither could she have known how frequently "Renascence" would be singled out for praise that was often ecstatic. "Without a doubt, the surprise of the volume," wrote Louis Untermeyer, a rising young critic, in the *Chicago Evening Post*. Two well-regarded and established young poets, Witter Bynner and Arthur Davison Ficke, whose poems were also in the collection, wrote to her. "You should unquestionably have had the prize—all three prizes." Jessie Rittenhouse, in the *New York Times*, stressed that the themes of "Renascence" were "so personal a vision of humanity, nature and God, such a sense of spiritual elation, of mystical rebirth."[7]

A remarkable foretelling of important themes in Edna's future poetry, "Renascence" freed her imagination and liberated her. The summer before the publication of *The Lyric Year*, Edna went to work as a waitress at a Camden hotel and one night took part in entertaining the guests, singing songs, playing the piano, and reducing the room to stunned silence by reciting "Renascence." Present that evening was a New Yorker named Caroline Dow who was the dean of the New York YWCA Training School and a Vassar College graduate with wealthy friends. Tuition and board at Vassar were five hundred dollars per year, a sum far beyond the Millay family resources. Caroline Dow approached a Vassar supporter, Frank Babbot, whose wife had been Caroline's roommate at Vassar. "Frank, you've got to send her. She is superb and Vassar will be proud."[8] He agreed, and Vassar accepted Millay for admission the following fall on condition that she do remedial work—a semester at Barnard College in New York City.

IN FEBRUARY 1913, just before her twenty-first birthday, Vincent Millay got her first look at Manhattan:

> ...buildings everywhere, seven and eight stories to a million
> and billion stories, washing drying on the roofs... Children
> on roller skates playing tag on the sidewalk, smokestacks
> and smokestacks, and windows and windows, and signs way up
> high on the tops of factories and cars and taxi-cabs, –
> and *noise*, yes, in New York you can see the *noise*.[9]

There was music of all kinds: a symphony concert, then an opera, *Madame Butterfly*. Women in the audience cried in sympathy with Cio-Cio-San. Not Edna. Her response to theatre, which meant so much to her, was different. "I never cry at the theater. It seems to me that I feel things far too deeply, too deep down in my heart, to—to splash on top." Then she saw Sarah Bernhardt in *Camille*: "I'm all gone to pieces, but, oh, my soul." People in the arts, in publishing, other poets, were welcoming. Sara Teasdale was especially generous to the newcomer, asking her to tea. "Whatdoyouknowaboutthat," Edna exclaimed in surprised delight. After tea, Sara gave her a copy of *Helen of Troy*, they rode about the city on the top of a bus, had dinner together and "talked and talked." They met several times and exchanged poems. "I called her 'Sara' and she me 'Vincent,'" she wrote home. "I love her ... Here's one of Sara's little things," and Edna copied Sara's "The Kiss" for her mother.

I hoped that he would love me
And he has kissed my mouth,
But I am like a stricken bird
That cannot reach the south.

For though I know he loves me,
To-night my heart is sad;
His kiss was not so wonderful
As all the dreams I had.

"All her little songs are like that," she explained. "You think they're going to be like something else you've read, but they never are."[10]

Sara wrote candidly to Edna about her forthcoming college entrance. It was a fine opportunity of course, "to learn a lot of things that I daresay are of value." But Sara admitted that "in some ways" she was sorry about it but confident that Edna had "enough sense and humor" not to be hurt by Vassar, and she then added, "I am so ill-educated myself that colleges are always a bit of an affront to my self esteem."[11]

They remained on polite terms, but their friendship never deepened, and they saw little of each other in the years following when they were rival love poets. Sara could not have sympathized with Edna's emergence as the symbol of free love, which was deeply repugnant to her. Edna was now extraordinarily erotically attractive to both men and women, fragile looking, with a deep contralto voice. Men lined up to adore her. She wrote candidly to her mother about this, confident she would understand. There was Frank Babbot, her financial angel, "who just simply fell in love with me," adding with coarse candor, "I guess you needn't worry about the money giving out;" Ferdinand Earle, who had conceived and edited *The Lyric Year*, whom she met at a poetry reading for the first and only time, and who wrote her late that same night: "You are truly charming and lovely enough to eat—slowly and cautiously, lest one atom escape."[12]

Such attentions were flattering, but they came to nothing more. It was very different with two other men. Arthur Ficke (1883-1945), who had written her immediately upon reading "Renascence," lived in Iowa, was handsome, talented, thirty—and married. Edna fell in love with him and stayed in love for the rest of her life, though at this point it was love carried on entirely by correspondence: flirtatious, suggestive and, finally, indiscreet. They would meet in person in 1918. Arthur Hooley, an Englishman, was educated at London University, came to the United States in 1908, and became editor of *The Forum*. She fell in love with him. They became lovers, furtively and occasionally, for he was elusive and mysterious, a bachelor who would never marry. Edna insisted that she had not fallen under his spell, writing to him "No memory that any man could leave me could really touch me," and "Faithfulness is not in any way a virtue; it is oftener a stupidity."[13] She insisted too much. Hooley personified romantic love to her and his emotional remoteness only inflamed her desire.

At the same time, Edna needed and accepted the love and support of older women: her mother, Caroline Dow, and many other generous women who admired her talent and "needed her to dream upon." Not surprisingly, with all this whirling about her, she couldn't concentrate on her Barnard studies, though she did read a great deal of literature. When Vassar evaluated what she had accomplished, they doubted that she was ready. Nevertheless, she managed to convert Dean McCaleb of Vassar into an enthusiastic supporter so that, in September 1913, Edna St. Vincent Millay became a member of the Vassar class of 1917.

"I DON'T KNOW where I'm going but I'm on my way," Edna wrote to her mother; and later: "It's all right. I belong here and I'm going to stay." Vassar wasn't so certain. She failed entrance exams in Algebra and in American history; her answers for the latter "did not bear any relation to the questions asked." Dean McCaleb came to her rescue, which earned Edna's approval: "She's a darling and and I love her." Throughout her four years at Vassar, students and faculty regarded Edna with a mixture of pride and exasperation, interest and annoyance. "She was one of the celebrities… she had done something. She was special."[14] That was why she had been admitted in the first place. She was immediately taken up by *The Miscellany*, the college magazine, and she wrote poems for it while at the same time she was publishing poetry in *The Forum* and in *Poetry* magazine. She added to her notoriety by taking part in the numerous plays and pageants that were a featured aspect of Vassar culture. She was Marchbanks in George Bernard Shaw's *Candida* and wrote a play, *The Princess Marries the Page* in which, of course, she played the princess.

Vassar had high academic standards, as did the other first-class private women's colleges. They had been founded to refute the idiotic notion that women were intellectually inferior to men. As a consequence, the women's colleges were more academically serious than the comparable men's colleges, where sports and the "Gentleman's C" were firmly entrenched. The elective system introduced at Harvard in 1869 was still wreaking havoc with the curriculum at men's colleges. Vassar and the "Seven Sisters" resisted this innovation so that Edna was confronted with formidable requirements: yearlong courses in English, classical languages, a modern language, French or German history, mathematics, physics or chemistry, and half a year of philosophy. She performed superbly in modern languages, taking every course Vassar offered. She also "stood for the classics," and her advocacy gained her another old admirer and supporter, Elizabeth Haight, associate professor of Latin who, years later, wrote a memoir about Edna which began, "Once I taught a genius and she became my friend."[15]

SOME OF MILLAY's characteristic poems date from her college years when she gained command of a technique adequate to subjects and themes that would not vary greatly in the years ahead, remembering also that she was four years older than her peers. Given the demands of study and of her extracurricular activities, this was not easy, and she often complained about it. "I am going crazy with the poems that I simply don't have time to write. It isn't a joke, I can't study now. I'm too old. I ought to be through college at my age."[16] Somehow, she managed. One important theme was pervasive melancholy. There was a good deal of this in "Renascence," but in the following poem the futility of human endeavor is marked by being utterly banal:

Sorrow

Sorrow like a ceaseless rain
  Beats upon my heart.
People twist and scream in pain, –
Dawn will find them soon again;
This has neither wax nor wane,
  Neither stop nor start.

> People dress and go to town;
> I sit in my chair.
> All my thoughts are slow and brown:
> Standing up or sitting down
> Little matters, or what gown
> Or what shoes I wear.

Her central subject, with which she would be widely identified, was the power of erotic love, with mockery for those who pretended to be impervious to its power. Her poetry became fixed in the mind of contemporaries as being entirely traditional, in form, meter, images and symbols. Her years at Vassar were those that marked the advent of Modernism in poetry, but there was no one on the Vassar faculty who might have introduced it to her, unlike Marianne Moore's experience at Bryn Mawr. Actually, Edna experimented with free verse, was a superb technician, and her late poetry is stripped of any of the traditional devices; but by then it was too late to change her image and what she represented.

EXCEPT FOR BRIEF visits at Christmas, leaving Camden meant separation from the family and produced conflicting emotions. Edna wrote home infrequently, describing her hectic college life, visits to New York City to stay with the families of classmates, letters entirely about herself. Cora wasn't annoyed or disappointed at this, but Edna's sisters, who were isolated in Camden, which was "dead, worse than it ever was before," took her to task for her self-absorption. Vassar was now the center of her life, not her family, despite Edna's mixed feelings about college, fluctuating between admiration and resentment. Given her upbringing, she was bound to hate the kind of order imposed upon her, dismissing Vassar as "an orphan asylum."

"I hate this pink-and-grey college. If there had been a college in *Alice in Wonderland*, it would be this college." She didn't restrict her disdain to words. She cut classes, didn't go to chapel, blithely ignored regulations of all sorts, and she smoked (off campus but in plain sight). Faculty were outraged at her insouciant defiance, a fact which didn't bother or impress her. "I run in my rut now like a well-directed wheel. Sometimes, it is true, I feel that I am exceeding the speed-limit. But I seldom skid, and when I do there is very little splash."[17]

Henry Noble McCracken, the President of Vassar, young (thirty-five), progressive, patient, had a very high opinion of Edna's talents. "She could do whatever she liked with the world." But he hoped to persuade her that she could not do whatever she liked with Vassar. Nevertheless, he made clear that he would never expel her. "I know all about poets at college," (he taught English drama), "and I don't want a banished Shelley on my doorstep," to which she replied: "On those terms I think I can continue to live in this hell-hole." She wasn't always so harsh. After her first year she wrote: "I love my college, *my* college, *my* college."[18] She made friends. Many classes were absorbing. She took part in a great deal of theater, appearing in seven plays, at a time when theater appeared to her to be as important as poetry.

If the source of her unhappiness with life in a women's college was the absence of men—"They trust us with everything but men ... a man is forbidden as if he were an apple"[19]—there was ample erotic compensation in affairs with other women. She had her first experience of this kind in Camden, but the situation in Poughkeepsie was almost overwhelming in its intensity. She was older, exceedingly attractive, and very talented with a reputation beyond college. Younger women clustered around her, followed her about campus, had crushes on her, and competed for her attention. She reciprocated and had numerous, often concurrent affairs, which gave her a great sense of power, demonstrating her appeal by playing off one woman against another. They played various sexual roles; some classmates dressed as men, "tucked their hair in their collars and posed with chocolate cigarettes stuck jauntily in their mouths." She was a source of appeal and of misery. With her growing sense of power over men and women, she gained confidence in her ability to manipulate and torment while remaining in control. Many years later, one of her lovers reflected on this: "Millay was a seductress. Oh, I should think so! You have only to look at those poems." She might have been referring to:

Witch-Wife

She is neither pink nor pale,
 And she never will be all mine;
She learned her hands in a fairy-tale,
 And her mouth on a valentine.

She has more hair than she needs;
 In the sun 'tis a woe to me!
And her voice is a string of colored beads,
 Or steps leading into the sea.

She loves me all that she can,
 And her ways to my ways resign;
But she was not made for any man,
 And she never will be all mine.

"I see nothing wrong with that in her," the ex-lover went on, with remarkable detachment. "She drew people to her. She liked to draw people to her." But, finally, "Vincent always had an eye for herself ... Her first love, and perhaps her only one: her poetry."[20]

Edna's Vassar years ended in controversy. She violated a college rule which prohibited staying away overnight without permission. The faculty, at the end of their patience, voted to suspend her and forbid her presence at commencement (though she would receive her degree). Over a hundred students protested this decision. President McCracken pondered, vacillated, and relented. On June 12, 1917, Edna St. Vincent Millay graduated with her class and, at last, immediately moved to New York City.

4. Marianne Moore

MARIANNE MOORE'S REASONS for coming to New York City were not typical. She did not come to escape from anything. She came for reasons of family solidarity. And once there, she never left.

THE LOSS OF a parent and the breakup of the family marked the Moore-Warners. Marianne's father, John Milton Moore, was an engineer; her mother, Mary Warner, was a graduate of a small college, Mary Academy. The Moores lived in Newton, Massachusetts, where John Milton failed in his attempt to man-ufacture a smokeless furnace. As a result, he suffered a nervous breakdown that coincided with the breakup of his marriage, and was sent to his parents in Ohio, who for a time committed him to a mental institution. Mary Warner, pregnant, and with her seventeen-month-old son, Warner, went to her father's home in Kirkwood, Missouri, where, on November 15, 1887, Marianne Craig Moore was born.

Marianne's grandfather, John Riddle Warner, was a Scotch-Irish Presbyterian minister who lived with his wife, Jennie Craig Warner, and baby daughter in Gettysburg, Pennsylvania. In September 1863, two months after the famous battle, Jennie died of typhoid fever contracted in tending wounded soldiers. One year old at the time, Mary Warner Moore never knew her mother. Reverend Warner never remarried, and in 1866 accepted a pastorate in Kirkwood, Missouri. Mary Warner grew up there and, after her marriage ended and she returned home in 1887, kept house for her father while raising her two small children. Reverend Moore died in 1893. His religious faith exercised a great influence on his daughter and through her, on her children. Marianne's memories of him were pleasant ones—of his generosity of spirit, of many books in the house, and of a most affectionate person playing the flageolet.

Marianne never saw her father. Marital reconciliation was either impossible or unwanted by Mary Warner, who also did not wish any contact with the Ohio Moores. Mary, Warner, and Marianne were, therefore, on their own, but with advantages. The Reverend Warner had left Mary a modest annual inheritance of two thousand four hundred dollars, which, supplemented by her ingenuity and determination, meant they could maintain middle-class values and expectations and, above all, an emphasis on literacy and education. They moved first to Pittsburgh to live near a sympathetic paternal uncle for two years, but when Uncle Henry died, Mary Warner confronted the prospect, for the third time in a decade, of finding and organizing a home for herself and her two young children.

A formidably strong person, Mary Warner was quiet, reserved, undemonstrative, very conventional in manner, and deeply religious. In the face of any and every disappointment her spirit responded *sursam corda*: "I will rejoice forever." Her college had been a Presbyterian seminary. She loved books, instructed her children in French and taught them the piano. She stressed impatience with imprecision, and her views and values gained force by being understated. Mary Moore had a Presbyterian faith in providence and the goodness of God, and so she not only faced the world, "she prevailed."

The Moores were intensely absorbed in each other, inward looking, seeing their iron-clad unity as protection, keeping the family circles safe from external intrusions. Like other such closely knit families—like the Millays—they had a personal code of reference. Drawing on Kenneth Grahame's *The Wind in the Willow*, Marianne was "Rat," Mary was "Mole," Warner was "Badger." Marianne sometimes signed letters to friends as "Pterodactyl" or just "Dactyl." Warner and Marianne were exceptionally close all their lives and never exchanged an unpleasant word.

At seven, Marianne was already writing poetry. Her mother matter-of-factly spoke of her as being a poet from early childhood. And, not quite eight, Marianne wrote:

> The shadows now they slowly fall
> Making the earth a great dark ball

and

> Pussy in the cradle lies –
> And sweetly dreams of gnats and flies.

In 1896, Mary Warner and the children moved to Carlisle, Pennsylvania, where she had a close friend, Mary Norcross, also the daughter of a Presbyterian minister. The friendship of the Norcross family was important in helping the Moores settle permanently, and enabled them to meet a larger circle of families who combined religious faith with sophisticated intellectual life. Carlisle was also a fortunate choice academically. Dickinson College, the Metzger Institute for Girls, and the well-known Indian School were located there. In 1899, Mary got a teaching job at the Metzger Institute, and in that same year, Marianne entered it.

In the next few years, Marianne's intellectual horizons broadened. Among more worldly friends were the Benét family, who came to Carlisle for the summer and whose three children, William Rose, Laura, and Stephen Vincent, would become well-known poets and friends for life. Carlisle was neither isolated nor provincial. Philadelphia was not far away for concerts, museums, and theatre; Harrisburg, the capital, with its large library, was visited regularly. Marianne learned about contemporary painting, exchanged journals and books with friends, participated in local theatrical productions, and combined these with church and missionary social events and with suffragist rallies.

She was well prepared for college—Warner had entered Yale in 1904—as Mary Warner had always intended. Mary Norcross tutored her. Bryn Mawr college was the obvious choice, near at hand, and with a splendid academic reputation. Mary Norcross, an alumna, was strongly supportive of it. In the spring of 1905, Marianne took the formidable entrance examinations and passed thirteen of fifteen. Of the one hundred and seventeen women who would make up the class of 1909, Marianne was one of thirty-seven who entered without any conditions.

Bryn Mawr was a self-consciously intellectual college. M.

Carey Thomas, Bryn Mawr's celebrated president, had gained notoriety in the first years of the college's founding by refusing to allow a Phi Beta Kappa chapter, on the grounds that all Bryn Mawr students would aspire to Phi Beta Kappa standards. Thomas fostered an atmosphere of disciplined hard work, one that continually increased demands on students. She stressed the notion of college education as means of giving "service" to society. Her influence extended into every corner of life at Bryn Mawr while Marianne was a student there. Only her mother surpassed Thomas as a person to be emulated. Bryn Mawr was an ideal place for Marianne, but her first few weeks were difficult. She was ill and could not eat. Intense homesickness was one cause of this, anxiety about whether she could cope with the demands of the college's social and intellectual life was another. Her mother's response? Discipline and a greater effort. An academically successful first semester brought this situation to an end, and for the rest of her three-and-a-half years, Marianne delighted in Bryn Mawr's rich cultural and academic life—concerts, plays, parties, ceremonies, and the beginning of several lifelong friendships.

English seemed an obvious major for her, but surprisingly, the English department advised against it. Marianne later said that she was "too immature" to do English. Equally surprising, she didn't excel in languages, doing only moderately well in French, German, and Latin, and twice failing an Italian course she took so that she could read Dante. Her final choice of majors was history and politics, subjects in which she did well enough but which were not the center of her interests.

Marianne's intellectual interests were diverse and did not form a conventional pattern. Science and scientific thinking fascinated her and biology was an especially absorbing subject. "The professors in the department were very humane and also exciting, detailed, and pertinacious," she commented. Explaining what it was she found most exciting about it, she said, "Biology and its toil (were) a pleasure and like poetry, 'a quest.'" She came to a realization that would be fundamental to her development as a poet, that science and poetry occupied common ground. "Eye and mind could come together in harmony." Laboratory science was a form of thinking deeply sympathetic to her: "Precision, economy of statement, logic employed to ends that are disinterested, liberate—at least have some bearing on—the imagination."[1]

At the same time, one class and one instructor in the humanities were also indispensable in shaping her ideas about poetry. The class was seventeenth-century English literature, the instructor was Gergianna Goddard King. In the class, students were required to copy out and imitate passages from the prose of that century. "People say, 'How terrible.' It wasn't at all, the very thing for me."[2] It concentrated her mind on sentence structure. In addition, Miss King also lectured on comparative literature and the history of art. An acquaintance of Gertrude Stein since the 1890s, she introduced Marianne to modern French painters and to Modernist literature and photography. This was during the same years when Alfred Stieglitz was introducing these things to New York City and to America, the consequences of which would be crucial to Marianne's writing and imagination.

She understood this. In thinking about her college years she concluded that Bryn Mawr was "particularly adapted to my special requirements." There she had learned that "intellectual wealth can't be superimposed, that it is to be appropriated," and there she gained "security in my determination to have what I wanted."[3] Her poetry did not begin immediately, but she started to clarify in her mind what it was she wished to write. She had begun reading the college literary magazine, *Tipyn O'Bob*, before she got to Bryn

Mawr. It was a means by which she began to find out if she could gain readers. Between 1907 and 1909, the magazine published eight of her poems, the first of which was this lively verse:

Under a Patched Sail

"Oh, we'll drink once more
When the wind's off shore,"
We'll drink from the good old jar,
And then to port,
For the time grows short.
Come lad – to the days that are!

Another, written in 1909, her final Bryn Mawr year, is far removed from such jollity. The sparseness of image, as well as of language, might be described as Imagist, but that Modernist movement would not come into being for another half-decade. It conveys that detached, objective tone that would become familiar:

A Red Flower

Emotion,
Cast upon the pot,
Will make it
Overflow, or not,
According
As you can refrain
From fingering
The leaves again.

In January 1909, her final Bryn Mawr year, Marianne had a memorable experience, her first visit to New York City. She stayed at the Upper West Side home of a college classmate, four years before Edna St. Vincent Millay's similar experience. "In New York I flourished like a bay tree." She excitedly recounted details of two days in five different letters home, letters of two, six, forty-two, forty-nine, and fifty-three pages! She attended a performance of James. M. Barrie's *What Every Woman Knows*, and heard a talk by Judge Benjamin Lindsey, notorious in his day as an advocate of "plural marriage," who made references to the Bible in "simple (not goody) fashion," and was cheered by the audience as if it were a football game. She went to Tiffany's and indulged her passion for objects of all kinds. "The place is a marvel... a maze of jewels and necklaces, vases, and silverware to beat Aladdin."[4]

There were pictures and music. At Montross Gallery she saw two paintings by Childe Hassam, "wonderful work, so definite and brilliant and yet so imaginative," then the MacBeth Gallery which specialized in paintings by American impressionists. At Carnegie Hall she heard a recital of Schumann and Strauss songs and on her final day a piano recital by Ignace Paderewski, described by her in terms of animal imagery: "What a fox hound ... a certain captious animal whimsicalness... that tiger temperament." After seven encores: "My state of mind when we went out you can imagine."[5]

Also during that final Bryn Mawr year, again at the direction of Professor King, Marianne became aware of contemporary photography associated with Alfred Stieglitz and shown at his gallery. Then the splendid Bryn Mawr years came to an end.

Graduation was a culmination followed by anti-climax. Marianne returned to Carlisle. She took a yearlong business course at

Carlisle Commercial College, and in 1910 began teaching typing, stenography, bookkeeping, commercial law, and commercial arithmetic at the Carlisle Indian School. She liked her students, and they liked her. She worked hard, and had little time for writing. Nevertheless, she made up her mind to be a professional writer, "to turn an honest penny by my writings." But what kind of writer? Journalism wouldn't suit her. Newspapers and magazines wanted popular writing; she was interested in "fine distinctions" and "meditative comment."[6]

So, poetry it would be. *The Lantern*, Bryn Mawr's alumnae magazine, served well as the place where she could publish the kind of poetry germinating in her mind. She began to experiment with visual patterns, not necessarily connected with meter, and when she reflected on the nature of art, she found it synonymous with the precision of science.

Qui S'Excuse, S'Accuse

Art is exact perception;
If the outcome is deception
Then I think the fault must lie
Partly with the critic's eye,
And no man who's done his part
Need apologize for art.

Her temperamental affinity for the unconventional made traditional verse unappealing, and she became aware that traditionalists found her poetry disconcerting. She submitted poems to various American magazines. They were rejected. In 1915, *Poetry* published five of her poems in one issue, which might have represented a step toward more general public acceptance had she continued along that path; but she soon became disenchanted with Harriet Monroe's editing and choice of poems for the magazine and never again published her work in its pages.

She was searching for fresh, innovative art, and she vividly recalled where and when she found it—in the first number of *Blast*, a little magazine published in London in 1914-1915, and edited by Wyndham Lewis, who was the originator of a new movement called "Vorticism." Marianne thought *Blast* "a wonderful publication—compilation of curses and blessings. Bless *Blast*."[7] It had gone the way of most little magazines by the time she found it, but in this spirit of eager, hopeful exploration Marianne had also made a second exciting discovery—Ezra Pound wrote a new kind of poetry.

Marianne became so absorbed in this new poetry that her old friend, William Rose Benét (an utterly conventional poet), felt compelled to warn her not to be too influenced by it. Marianne would have none of that. "I'll have to tell Billy that it's like getting married. I am sorry to disappoint him, but it is not possible to meet his views on the subject and please myself."[8] She expressed her excitement in a poem that she never published in her lifetime. She thought Pound's poetry admirable for its vigor and ardor, not simply its newness.

Modernist poetry captured her attention not her allegiance. She was never a joiner, but since the beginning of the decade several things came together to increase her interest in advanced verse and in Pound. In 1911, Marianne and Mary went to Britain and the Continent for several months. Among the highlights of the trip were visits to two bookstores. In Paris, they went to Sylvia Beach's Shakespeare and Company, which was then publishing James Joyce and was a gathering place for the *avant garde*. Marianne was too shy and modest to walk in and say, "Here am I, I'm a writer, would you talk to me awhile." In a bookstore in London, Mary and Marianne were shown photographs of Ezra Pound, "which we were very much pleased to see."[9]

Direct contact with Modernism came in 1915 when Marianne submitted her work to a London magazine, *The Egoist*, edited by Harriet Shaw Weaver (1876-1961). *The Egoist* accepted seven of her poems in 1915, four in 1916, and three in 1918. Several of the poems were about British and Irish artists, among them Gordon Craig, a writer, editor and theater designer; Robert Browning; and George Bernard Shaw. The artists' achievements were taken for granted; it was personal qualities that most interested her, values or manners that qualified them as heroic, as in her tribute to Shaw, whose candor and courage were imagined as attributes of a bird or animal.

To A Prize Bird

You suit me well, for you can make me laugh,
nor are you blinded by the chaff
   that every wind sends spinning from the rick.

You know to think, and what you think you speak
with much of Samson's pride and bleak
   finality, and none dare bid you stop.

Pride sits you well, so strut, colossal bird.
No barnyard makes you look absurd;
   your brazen spurs are staunch against defeat.

A different order of work, fully accomplished and enduring, appeared in *The Egoist* of October 1915, one of her most frequently reprinted poems. Its background reference is to Lawrence Gilman, a contemporary New York music critic who had written an essay—a quotation from which is embedded in the poem—on a theme of central importance to Moore: the difficulty confronting any artist who attempts something new. The poem works on two levels, the description of a formidable piece of machinery that also represents a conventional, close-minded art critic.

To A Steam Roller

The illustration
is nothing to you without the application.
 You lack half wit. You crush all the particles down
  into close conformity, and then walk back and forth on them.

Sparkling chips of rock
are crushed down to the level of the parent block.
 Were not "impersonal judgment in aesthetic
  matters, a metaphysical impossibility," you

might fairly achieve
it. As for butterflies, I can hardly conceive
 of one's attending upon you, but to question
  the congruence of the complement is vain, if it exists.

IF CONTACT WITH *The Egoist* brought Marianne and other American poets in touch with Imagism, the most important of the new developments in Anglo-America Modernism, it also reconnected Marianne with Hilda Doolittle, whom she had known at Bryn

Mawr and who, in the decade since their college time together, had become the most eminent of the Imagists. In the decades that followed, she would become one of the most important Anglo-American poets of the century, and she would be a central figure in this narrative except that, like Ezra Pound and T. S. Eliot, she would achieve her eminence across the Atlantic.

Born in Bethlehem, Pennsylvania, in 1886, into an academic and artistic family—her father was an astronomer, her mother an artist—Hilda was a rebellious young woman who wanted to escape from the oppressive conventions represented by her family and national culture. She went to Bryn Mawr, but its academic demands did not suit her. Her father wished her to become a scientist but she had no aptitude for it, did not do well in her other classes, and left college after a year and a half. Poetry appealed to her as a way to find independence through self expression and she began writing poems by splashing ink from her pen all over her clothes "to give her a feeling of freedom and indifference" to any convention.[10] But she soon realized that serious poetry required the acceptance of order and self-discipline.

Two friendships shaped her future. The first was with Ezra Pound, then a student at the University of Pennsylvania. He became a frequent visitor to the Doolittle home, though Hilda's parents disapproved of his bohemian ways. Ezra and Hilda read poetry together and discussed their own poetry. Ezra called her "Dryad," the wood spirit muse of his poetry. She fell in love with him and they came to a tentative and unofficial engagement. Pound went away for the year in 1908 to teach at Wabash College, Indiana, and eventually the engagement came to nothing. Pound left for Europe.

A more unorthodox and passionate relationship with a young woman named Frances Gregg, whom Hilda met in 1910, replaced the one with Pound. Gregg too had a troubled relationship with her family, wrote poetry, was a mystic, and seemed to Hilda a "twin soul." Hilda wrote love lyrics to her and they became lovers, defying family and beginning a lifetime, for Hilda, of open rebellion against social conventions and respectable opinion. Bisexual love would remain one of the centers of Hilda's later life; for her, lesbian and male love each embodied "the visionary, the erotic, and the aesthetic."[11] In 1911, Frances and Hilda traveled to Europe where, their love at an end, they agreed to separate. Hilda persuaded her parents to let her stay in England.

In London, Hilda renewed her friendship with the ubiquitous Pound—"Ezra was so inexpressibly kind," she wrote, "to anyone he felt had the faintest spark of submerged talent"[12]—and became part of the group of poets associated with *The Egoist*, marrying one of its co-editors, Richard Aldington. All of the poets in the group were impressed by the special qualities of Hilda's poetry and actually shaped the principles of Imagism to fit these. Hilda didn't think Doolittle was a suitable name for a poet and it was Ezra Pound who bestowed on her the appropriately Imagist name "H. D." by which she was known thereafter.

What were the principals by which the Imagists challenged traditional poetry? Language must be spare and precise, stripped of any words not necessary to achieve the desired effect; rhyme was not required but was allowed; rhythms would be sequences of musical phrases not metronomically determined; no subject, however mundane, was forbidden. In 1914, Ezra Pound edited the first Imagist anthology, *Des Imagistes*, which included contributions by eleven poets, among them another American, Amy Lowell. But H. D. was the undoubted star. In 1916, H. D. published her first book of verse, *Sea Garden*, which appeared in both England and America. H.D.'s archetypal Imagist poetry emphasized crystalline images of nature, razor sharp language, an impersonal tone, as in the following:

Sea Rose

Rose, harsh rose
marred and with the stint of petals,
meagre flower, thin,
sparse of leaf,

more precious
than a wet rose
single on a stem—
you are caught in the drift.

Stunted, with small leaf,
you are flung on the sand,
you are lifted
in the crisp sand
that drives the wind.

Can the spice-rose
drip such acrid fragrance
hardened in a leaf?

Imagism in general, and H. D.'s poetry in particular, didn't provoke much publicity or outrage in the general reading public; it was poetry for poets. Neither did she receive personal attention in America, since she lived abroad and would always remain distant and little known.

In the August 1916 issue of *The Egoist*, H. D. wrote a review explaining the grounds for her admiration of the kind of poetry Marianne was now writing. She recognized that some readers found Marianne's "curiously wrought patterns, quaint turns of thought, and concealed half-playful ironies" to be odd and different, but she insisted that the poems were only initially baffling. Careful, repeated reading released the poetry's secrets and its power. "It catches us, holds, fascinates, and half paralyses us." That was saying a good deal, but her admiration went beyond that. Poets on both sides of the Atlantic were united in a common task. "We in England should be strengthened. Miss Moore helps us. She is fighting in her country a battle against squalor and commercialism. We are fighting the same battle. And we must strengthen each other in this one absolute bond—our devotion to the beautiful English language." When Marianne read these comments, she immediately wrote to express her gratitude, saying that she regarded Doolittle's approval as "the chief recommendation" of her poetry, that it meant "everything" to her and that she was especially pleased that "anything I have written ... sets itself in opposition to mediocrity."[13]

THE SAME YEAR as her contact with *The Egoist*, 1915, Marianne made a second visit to New York City, which added to her interest in and knowledge of Modernism. Her mother must have found this worrying, and Marianne, while responding to these anxieties by writing a four-part sequence of very long letters describing in detail what she had been up to, also gently mocked those anxieties by calling her letters a "sojourn in the whale," Jonah's journey to the shores of Nineveh/New York. She stayed at the YWCA National Training School, the institution run by Edna Millay's patron, Caroline Dow, attended lectures and spent most of her time in museums and galleries.

She visited Alfred Steiglitz's 291 Gallery and met the great man. "He was exceedingly unemotional, and friendly and after telling me how he was hated," showed her some paintings—Picabias and Picassos—"standing with their faces to the wall in a back room, and also a beautiful painting by a man named Marsden Hartley."[14] She saw some Van Goghs at a modern gallery and ancient Chinese rugs at an Armenian wholesale rug shop. Late that afternoon, she was called on by Alfred Kreymborg (1883-1966), poet, playwright and editor, now remembered as editor of *Others*, an advanced magazine which, from 1915 to 1919, published poetry by William Carlos Williams, Ezra Pound, Wallace Stevens, T. S. Eliot, and Marianne Moore. A Modernist poet, Kreymborg in 1916 published *Mushrooms: A Book of Free Forms.* "I never was so surprised to see anyone," she wrote of their meeting. "He is middle height, quiet, dignified, unpuffed up, very deliberate and kind." She went to dinner at the Kreymborgs' home in the Village on Bank Street—"Anyone there knows where Bank Street is"—where she saw photographs of Bernard Shaw and of Anatole France by Steiglitz and by Edward Steichen and "a magnificent photograph of Whitman."[15]

Another afternoon she traced Guido Bruno to his "lair," a gallery over a drugstore on Washington Square. He was the editor of yet another little magazine, *Bruno's Weekly*, and he too was exceedingly friendly At the end of their very pleasant visit he urged her to submit poetry to the *Weekly*, saying he would pay her "not much but something."[16] These people and places, ideas and works of art, illuminated the path that lay ahead of her as a writer.

Six months later, her life took a surprising turn but one that would bring her back to where she had just been. In the summer of 1916, her brother Warner moved to Chatham, New Jersey, to take up his first pastorate. Marianne was able to spend a good deal of time in New York City, making numerous short train trips in what she called her "Middle Pullman Period." In 1918, there was another surprise. Warner resigned from his church to be commissioned a chaplain in the U. S. Navy, serving aboard a battleship during convoy duty in the Atlantic. Marking time to wait and see what would be the next step in Warner's career, Mary and Marianne moved to the most convenient, and affordable, location available to them, Greenwich Village.

5. LOUISE BOGAN

I N EARLY 1919, Louise Bogan was living in Hoboken, New Jersey, with her soldier husband and child. She had occasionally taken the ferry to Greenwich Village, where she made friends with painters and writers, and where she found, like many others, a kind of life she had only dreamed of. That summer she made a decision, painful but final, left her husband, took her daughter to live with her parents in Massachusetts, then went back to New York City and rented an apartment at 24 West Ninth Street. "She was a New Yorker on first sight."[1]

LOUISE'S BOGAN'S ANCESTORS on both sides were Irish. Her father, Daniel Joseph Bogan, was the son of an Irish emigrant who settled in Maine and became a prosperous sea captain. Daniel never spoke of his childhood except to recount that he had accompanied his father on a sea voyage that lasted several years. Louise's mother, Mary Helen Murphy Shields, never knew her parents. She was the only child of an immigrant father killed in the American Civil War and a mother who disappeared soon after her child's birth. Mary Helen Murphy was adopted by the Shields family, who pampered her and sent her to be educated at Mount Saint Mary Academy in New Hampshire, a "select" school where she learned genteel manners and to play the piano. The Shields were very disappointed when Mary Helen, age seventeen, married Daniel Bogan, nineteen, as it was not the upward step on the social ladder they had anticipated. That was in 1882. Two years later, a son, Charles, was born to the Bogans, then another son, who died after four or five months. It wasn't until August 11, 1897, that Louise Bogan was born in Livermore Falls, Maine.

Daniel Bogan was a good and steady provider who was never out of work. The family was not poor and Mary could afford to hire help with the housework. But Mary and Daniel were disastrously unsuited to each other. Daniel bored Mary and she was unrestrained in letting him know it. She wasn't interested in anything Daniel had to say or in what he did, and she wasn't interested in anything to do with Livermore Falls. After four years, the Bogans moved to Milton, New Hampshire, where they lived in a hotel for a period. Louise shared a room with her mother, and Charles shared one with his father. Innumerable scenes of marital disharmony became scenes of screaming fury: an enraged Mary shrieking at Daniel; Daniel "groaning as if he had been hurt;"[2] the children—terrified.

Most destructive for Louise was her growing awareness of "secret family angers and secret disruptions." The secret was that Mary Bogan had lovers—doctors, lawyers, mill town professionals—men she called her "admirers." On one occasion, she disappeared from home for several weeks; on another, she traveled across the country with a female friend and an "admirer" for almost a year. Louise saw things that were "unspeakable, horrifying." As she wrote in a journal years later: "I see the ringed hand on the pillow. I weep by the hotel window as she goes down the street with another ..." Mary sometimes took her daughter with her to her trysts. By age eight, Louise Bogan was "an exile from conventional life," a person in whom "illusion had been early assassinated: shot dead."[3]

What of Daniel? He was extraordinarily forbearing and over and over again forgave his wife, entertaining no thoughts of divorce, which perversely reinforced his family's feeling that, though kind and supportive, he was essentially weak. "He simply didn't matter." And Charles? Mary favored Charlie and he adored her in return. Loving a mother and knowing of her illicit erotic life meant that he had been from a very early age "set apart from normal love," which his sister believed accounted for his ferocious temper. He would "knock down doors and smash windows with chairs, and be brought home, beaten to a pulp." Victim of a "paralyzed will," Charles never wanted to leave home and live on his own.[4]

Louise had great difficulty in learning how to read, staring at pages of print, unable to make out what the letters meant. At seven, she was ill with scarlet fever and, after her recovery, returned to school to discover that she could now read. It was "the beginning of a new life." In 1906, she was sent to Mount Saint Mary Academy, her mother's school. She felt out of place and lonely there and became aware of class feelings; most of the students came from well-to-do families and looked down on her Irishness. She came to understand that the social world was made up of "malice, gossip, insult, cliques, cruelty, pettiness, and preferment."[5] She wanted to become an opera singer, and appeared in one of the school's operettas, which exploded that fantasy, though music would remain important to her all her life. She did extremely well in her studies. She achieved Rank 1 and, in her second year, was awarded the Cross for Excellence. She stayed at Mount Saint Mary for two years, then was taken away and lived at home for a year, reading voraciously. The no-school year may have been connected with the fact that in 1909 the family, after a period of particularly horrendous quarrels, moved to Boston.

BOSTON WAS WONDERFUL, Boston was escape from the small towns and the family turmoil. Its buildings, Venetian, Romanesque, Gothic, excited her, gave her "that sensation in the pit of the stomach which heralds both love and an intense aesthetic experience."[6] The long period of solitude at home, reading on her own, allowed something to grow up inside her. She began to imagine herself as someone important, began to nourish a larger ambition. A benevolent teacher in her Boston elementary school suggested that Louise be enrolled in the Boston Girls' Latin School, one of the most outstanding schools in the nation. There, for five wonderful years, she received a first-class education: English composition, classical languages, mathematics, and science. She took Latin, Greek, and French; she joined a literary and debating society; and once again was fortunate to be taken up by an imaginative and supportive teacher, Caroline Gervish, head of the English Department.

At fourteen, "the life-saving process then began"—she started writing poetry. "Her natural gifts were extraordinary," and could not be squelched by domestic turmoil or by ignorant prejudice. She wrote poems for *The Jabberwock*, the school literary magazine, despite being told that she should never think of being its editor since "no Irish girl" could achieve that position. "It was borne in upon me, all during my adolescence, that I was a 'Mick' no matter what my other faults or virtues might be."[7] Such comments, however insulting, were not, for whatever reason, as deeply wounding for Louise as anti-Semitic ones were for Dorothy Rothschild, and didn't become a perpetual source of pain.

Once Louise began writing, the flow of poetry and prose was incessant. Every day she went home and wrote a sonnet or a prose composition, fiction and nonfiction. Her reading of poetry of the English late Victorians was avid—Dante Gabriel Rossetti, William Morris, Algernon Swinburne—but that wasn't enough, and she sensed the need to move in some other direction. She "stumbled through half-formed tendencies and intuitive leanings"[8] to French symbolist poetry, and, having discovered the enchanting ambiguity of Debussy's *Pelleas and Melissande*, played scenes from it over and over on the piano, intoxicated by its ravishing harmonies and elusive meanings. The contemporary poet whose work was most important to her was W. B. Yeats, who combined delicacy of perception with everyday speech.

She also discovered American women poets—Edna St. Vincent Millay, Elinor Wylie, and Sara Teasdale—who, in their different ways, had a great deal to say to her about love and women's experience of men. She frequented the Boston Public Library, where she read Harriet Monroe's *Poetry* from its very first issue and in whose pages she encountered Marianne Moore. Fortunately for Louise, Caroline Gervish read A. E. Housman aloud to her classes at a time when he was still regarded as "far out." And all along Louise was studying the techniques of poetry: prosody, rhyme, and form. "By the age of 18 I had a thick pile of manuscripts, in a drawer in the dining room, and had learned every essential tool of my trade."[9] Writing was a way of escape from the terrors of family life. Almost every week she published a poem in *The Jabberwock*, and a number of her poems also appeared in the *Boston Evening Transcript*.

A theme that would become central in Louise's life in the next few years would be the situation of a young woman confronting obstacles and responsibilities which suppress her artistic and sexual power. What are the claims of everyday life and what should be their relation to a woman's aesthetic gifts? The theme can be seen in "The Gift," the last poem she printed in *The Jabberwock*, in November 1914.

Louise graduated from Boston Latin School (as class poet; her fellow students well aware of and admiring of her talent) and entered Boston University in 1915. She did brilliantly there, and in the course of the year won a scholarship to Radcliffe College for the fall of 1916. She continued to write poetry and had two poems published in the Boston University literary magazine *The Beacon*. But to the dismay of her parents, she did not continue at Boston University and did not take up the scholarship offer from Radcliffe. Sexual passion and the desperate need to escape from her family (she would have lived at home had she gone to Radcliffe) shattered all those plans, and her life took a dramatically different turn.

Sometime during the year at Boston University, Louise met and fell in love with Curt Alexander. A German, born in 1888, blond, handsome, trained as an architectural draftsman, he had completed military service in Germany and emigrated to the United States where, unable to find architectural work, he joined the U.S. Army, rose quickly through the ranks, and became a captain. Louise's parents strenuously opposed the possibility of marriage and insisted that Alexander convert to Catholicism. He did. That didn't reconcile them and their opposition only reinforced Louise's desire to escape from her parental past. The appearance of this virile and appealing man must have seemed to her a gift from heaven.

They were married on September 4, 1916, just past her nineteenth birthday. Free to be free, they went to New York City. We know almost nothing about the next few months. Louise continued to write poetry and began to get to know other poets in the city; in particular, the group clustered about Alfred Kreymborg's *Others: A Magazine of the New Verse*. Six months later, Alexander was sent by the army to Panama. Pregnant, Louise went with him and in October 1917, Mathilde Alexander was born, named for Curt's mother, at his insistence. Louise hated Panama, the army, the weather—everything. She had nothing in common with the other army wives and was angry that she now had so little time to write. Nevertheless, she did manage to write two poems that were published by *Others*, her first poems composed in free verse, perhaps as a concession to the magazine's advanced interests. She was exploring various forms to find which would be most sympathetic to her.

She was quickly disillusioned with her marriage. Alexander had no interest in the arts, and soon after the baby's birth, ceased to desire sexual relations with his wife. Bitterly aware that she was repeating her parents' desperate experience, that she had only exchanged one trap for another, she left Alexander in Panama and went back to New England to live with her mother and father. A few months later, Alexander was transferred back to the United States and, in an attempt to salvage something from the marital ruins, Louise joined him in New Jersey. That effort also failed. With "clear-sighted selfishness,"[10] (her term) she took Maidie to live with her parents and be brought up by them, one more irony in a situation replete with ironies, and in the summer of 1919, moved to Greenwich Village.

6. ELINOR WYLIE

I N DECEMBER 1920, Elinor Morton Hoyt Hichborn Wylie
came to Manhattan to address the Poetry Society, an address
so successful that she was immediately invited to return the
next month to speak at the Society's annual dinner. Her spectacular appearance that night, in a white gown with a gold cord at the
waist, and gold leaves in her hair, provoked much comment. At
age thirty-six, she had decided that living in Manhattan was indispensable for a career as a professional writer, a decision confirmed
by her moving into an apartment in the Village, at 2 University
Place. Her two visits marked her introduction to New York City
literary life, but they didn't mark the city's introduction to her.
Known for a decade, not as a poet but as a notorious woman, the
subject of storms of unfavorable publicity, Elinor Wylie had come
to Manhattan trailing clouds of scandal.

Elinor Hoyt's background and upbringing didn't suggest scandal—or poetry. On her father's side she was descended from a Pennsylvania family dating from the eighteenth century and proud of their English ancestry. Henry Maryn Hoyt, Elinor's paternal grandfather, was a governor of Pennsylvania; her father, Henry Martyn Hoyt, Jr., Yale-educated, was a lawyer and banker. On her mother's side, the McMichaels were Irish immigrants who succeeded in banking and publishing. One ancestor was mayor of Philadelphia, and on both sides there was interest in books.

Henry Morton Hoyt and Anne McMichael were married in 1883. The next two years were spent in luxurious living in New York City. Things were not as stable as they seemed, however; losses in the stock market forced the Hoyts to economize and leave New York City. They moved to Somerville, New Jersey, where their first child, Elinor Morton Hoyt, was born on September 7, 1885. In later years Elinor knocked two years off her age and, regretting that New Jersey had no romantic associations, hoped people would think of "Paris or Persepolis as her birthplace."[1] (She may not have been joking.) The New Jersey embarrassment was mitigated when, in 1887, the Hoyts moved to Rosemont, a Philadelphia suburb, where the family's fortunes were soon restored. They were again able to live in comfort, with governesses and servants, spending summers in Bar Harbor, Maine.

Elinor had four siblings, Henry, Constance, Morton, and Nancy, spread out over fifteen years. All of Anne Hoyt's pregnancies were difficult and added to her chronic hypochondria and hypertension. Neither fiercely supportive, like the mothers of Edna Millay and Marianne Moore, nor emotionally destructive, like Mary Bogan, Anne Hoyt was subtler in exercising influence. The Hoyt children remembered her spending most of her time in an upstairs bedroom, issuing commands. Her control expressed itself in an obsessive desire for their social advancement, which she attempted to achieve by bestowing or withdrawing allowances. Henry Hoyt, handsome and affable, served three Presidents—McKinley, Roosevelt and Taft—and eventually became Solicitor General of the United States. He deferred to his wife's social ambitions for the children but managed a more personal relationship with them, especially with Elinor. However, Henry, too, had his problems—"his peccadilloes and love of rye whiskey were part of family lore"—and he suffered from attacks of mental illness that resulted in two protracted breakdowns. Emotional instability ran through the entire family. The four younger children, perhaps in reaction against their mother's obsession with social respectability, behaved oddly or were prone to self-destructive acts, which led their mother to characterize them as "a generation of vipers."[2]

Elinor seemed free of family foibles and instability. She was placed in Miss Baldwin's School for Girls in Bryn Mawr, Pennsylvania, where she flourished. She revealed a talent for drawing, and painting remained a lifelong interest. For several years she considered becoming a painter, like her younger brother, Henry. Her poetry would be very visual. She read voraciously, and the school stimulated an interest in languages. A governess had taught her German and French folk ballads, a poetic form she would draw on later.

Her father's first government appointment in 1897 meant that she had to be removed from Miss Baldwin's. The move from Philadelphia, with its lively and varied intellectual life, to Washington, D.C., the nation's dreary cultural backwater, was a long-term misfortune for the impressionable young girl. She was, however, enrolled in another superior school, Mrs. Flint's School for Girls. There she worked hard at history, political economy, Shakespeare, and French, read Greek and Latin classics in translation and became familiar with the major British poets, of whom Shelley was to become a lifelong preoccupation. She took a life drawing class at the Corcoran Museum.

In her last year or two at Miss Flint's, Elinor began writing poetry. She was not precocious. The first poem she thought worth keeping, "To Paolo and Francesca in Purgatory," was written when she was seventeen. She read the poetry of the "Aesthetic" movement in England of the eighteen nineties—Austin Dobson, Lionel Johnson, and W.B. Yeats—but she came of age a decade before there were any alternatives to traditional verse forms, rhyme, and regular meter. She was an exact contemporary of Ezra Pound who, confronted with the same situation, found an alternative by going to Europe. Marianne Moore, two years younger than Elinor, had the advantage of Carlisle/Philadelphia and of college as a way to broaden horizons and gain a degree of independence.

College would have done that for Elinor, but the decision depended on her mother. In the culture of the social class Mrs. Hoyt belonged to, art was fine, even important, for women, but the idea of an artistic career was anathema. Two decades earlier in New York City, the mother of Edith Jones was appalled at her daughter's desire to become a professional writer. It took twenty years and a failed marriage for Edith Jones Wharton to find her vocation in these very same years. Of course, the superior women's colleges were now established, but dishearteningly it seems that little if any consideration was given to Elinor's attending one of these. A social career, perhaps a brilliant one, was the only future imaginable to Mrs. Hoyt for her lovely daughter. Elinor would follow the respectable forms, "come out" as a debutante and then be put on the marital market to attract an eligible man, produce children and sustain, or raise, the Hoyts' social standing.

So far as we know, Elinor, eighteen years old, didn't protest against this fate. It must have been intoxicating to know that she would be admired and sought-after and, after all, marriage would give her some degree of independence and the possibility of a sexual life. Either as consolation or as a reward for her docility, Elinor and Constance were sent to the McMichaels in Philadelphia, who took them on a summer's trip to Europe. They shopped in Paris and had their portraits painted. In London, they met Ellen Terry, Sir Henry Irving, and Bram Stoker, the author of *Dracula*.

Elinor's coming-out was a great success. Alice Roosevelt Longworth, the fearsome dragon of Washington society, described her as "luminous and radiant,"[3] and she soon had several admirers. Family lore had it that Elinor fell in love and had an "unhappy romance" with a young man she met in Bar Harbor, an affair that caused her intense suffering. Perhaps on the rebound from that, she rushed into an engagement with another young man who had been courting her for a year but whom she knew only superficially. Elinor revealed nothing of all this to her parents until she had made up her mind to marry. Keeping things to herself was one way to assert her independence. Marriage must have seemed a means to escape, whatever it was she was escaping to. This pattern of behavior would mark the rest of her life. An insupportable situation would produce a desperate need to escape, at whatever cost to herself and to others.

ELINOR MORTON HOYT and Philip Simmons Hichborn, Jr., were married on December 12, 1906. The wedding ceremony was held in the Hoyt family home, presided over by the Episcopal Bishop of Washington and attended by President Theodore Roosevelt. The son of an admiral, Philip had been educated at Harvard where he gained a reputation for letters, as an editor of the *Lampoon*, and for affability as a member of the Hasty Pudding Club. He became a lawyer, with a Washington practice, and was a passionate sportsman. A local gossip sheet contrasted his "silent studiousness" with Elinor's "fun-loving but difficult manner." To complete an ideal picture, a son was born on September 22, 1907. Unfortunately, the marriage had gone badly almost from the first. If Elinor had a "difficult manner,"[4] Philip had a fierce temper, behaved oddly or worse, threatening to kill himself and saying he hated the child. (This story, it should be pointed out, is one-sided, known from recollections of the Hoyt family.) With no interest whatsoever in her husband's sporting life and friends, Elinor was utterly bored with him and with their life together. Philip suffered a serious fall from a horse and doctors at Johns Hopkins diagnosed *dementia praecox*. Elinor, in turn, developed high blood pressure and suffered from agonizing headaches, conditions she endured for the rest of her life. "I felt stifled," Elinor said later. "There was no room for my mind at all."[5]

Elinor Wylie

Sometime in 1909, she found diversion and relief in the company of Horace Wylie, a well-to-do Washington attorney. He was forty-two, Elinor twenty-five. He was married and the father of four children, and once before had left his wife for a younger woman. He was well-read and interested in literature. Their friendship became clandestine, with meetings in Rock Creek Park. Within a year, the situation was spiraling toward a climax of some sort when, in November 1910, Elinor's father died suddenly. As she had never been able to turn to her mother for understanding, the disappearance of her father was a great blow. At this time the family learned that Henry Hoyt had been involved in a secret sexual affair with a co-worker. Elinor contrived to believe that this justified her desire to leave her husband. Rebecca West, the English writer who came to know Elinor later, commented caustically on this notion: "Elinor ... always expected me to take it for granted that when you found out that your father had been in love with someone not your mother, why, of course, you left your own husband; you just had to, you were so upset."[6]

On December 16, 1910, Elinor and Horace ran away—escaped—from their marriages, leaving behind one husband, one wife, and five children. People were astonished and outraged. The escapees eventually made their way to England, but for some time their whereabouts were unknown. President Taft offered to use the diplomatic corps to find Wylie and bring him back home and to his senses. For some time, both families chose to believe that this was an outbreak of Hoyt madness and not a permanent state of affairs. Efforts were made at reconciliation, with Mrs. Hoyt going to England, and Horace coming back to Washington, but the marriage couldn't be reconstructed. Philip Hichborn and Katherine Wylie refused to grant their spouses a divorce. Horace deeded his assets to his wife Katherine and the children and returned to England to be with Elinor, who then and later bore the brunt of the outrage. It was understandable, if not proper, that a woman might leave a difficult husband and an unsatisfactory marriage, but it wasn't considered acceptable to abandon a three-year-old child.

Philip Hichborn continued his law practice and wrote a book of sporting stories, *Hoofbeats*. If it was any consolation to him, public opinion was uniformly on his side. Elinor was the guilty *femme fatale* and home wrecker. Eventually, he filed for divorce and said he was going to move to Wyoming with his son and live on a ranch. But on March 26, 1912, he committed suicide in his sister's house in Washington. He left a note: "I am not to blame for this. I think I have lost my mind." He was twenty-nine.

THROUGHOUT THE TROUBLED times of her marriage, Elinor wrote poetry. After 1910, Horace was of great help to her, reading poems to her every day. "The amount I learned from him is without end," she said, and added frankly, though her arithmetic was shaky: "He was twenty years older than I, and father as well as husband to me." Horace encouraged her to collect and publish the poetry she had written between 1902 and 1911 and paid for the private publication (sixty copies) of *Incidental Numbers* at the end of 1912. It received no public recognition and Elinor soon dismissed it. "These verses are so incredibly bad it takes my breath."[7] But the book is valuable in showing us how she began as a professional writer (like Edna Millay presenting her mother with *Poetical Works*). There are poems about nature and about magical enchantment, but what is most striking is that the poems of 1909 and 1910 are inspired by her love for Horace Wylie. "I cannot help making fables and bitter fairy tales out of my life."[8] That life produced feelings of guilt and defiance.

From Whom No Secrets Are Hid

O Jesus Christ, Whose love forgives
  The sins of such as I,
Surely no other soul there lives
  Untouched, unsaved thereby?

For women who can lightly sin
  May for thy pardon sue,
Saying, "Our souls are dark within,
  We know not what we do."

And others who have sinned, who went
  With open eyes, like mine,
May afterwards be penitent
  And so their souls are Thine.

But I shall not repent me of
  My sin – the promise stands
I never shall deny my love.
  My soul is in his hands.

Most audaciously defiant of conventional views is her belief that Eve's carnal love in Paradise is to be preferred to the virginal love associated with Mary.

Eve in Heaven

Eve, the mother of us all,
  Walks in Heaven alone,
Jostled towards the outer wall.
  Shouldered from the Throne.
Souls remembering her fall
  Think upon their own.

Angels multitudinous
  Shun her steps, and so
Saints and Mary scorn her thus,
  Frowning as they go;
And, "The woman tempted us,"
  Cry the damned below.

From her side the seraphs start,
  Lest her touch defile;
Modestly she goes apart,
  Silent all the while.
What has she within her heart
  Telling her to smile?

Still she smiles, nor envies yet
  Crowns nor grace thereof
No – nor Saintly Mary set
  All the saints above.
Never shall her heart forget
  Eden and her love.

Sometimes even she will stare –
While the paeans roll –
At the Virgin crowned and fair
Whom the Heavens extol,
Thinking, "She was never there –
Ah – poor soul, poor soul!"

Elinor's escape from her suffocating marriage and way of life produced *Incidental Numbers*, but then poetic silence followed.

England was a refuge and an opportunity to read the poetry of the previous decade. Walter de la Mare's *Songs of Childhood* (1902), with its depictions of haunted worlds of reverie and magic, made a great impression, as did the mystical poetry of W.B. Yeats. Living in England in these years, Robert Frost also was struggling to find his poetic voice, though Elinor knew nothing of this. Later, his poetry would impress her. England's greatest influence was to strengthen her adherence to tradition, in poetry and in everything else. For a time, she and Horace lived in a thatched cottage in a "fairy-book" village where, unforgettably, she met Shelley's grandson. "Think of it. Shelley's grandson, and I have had tea with him frequently."[9] The outbreak of war forced them to return to the United States in 1915. Horace had very little money left by this time and they moved restlessly and aimlessly, from Maine to the South, living in cheap boarding houses. The greatest source of unhappiness was Elinor's inability to have a child by Horace. In 1914 in England, she had suffered a stillbirth; in 1916, a son was born but died a week later; in 1919, there was a miscarriage. These seem to have sharpened her remorse about her living son. She once confessed to a confidante, "I left my baby when I ran away. That was the one thing I have ever done that I think was bad. Other things, no. I would do all of them over again. But that was utterly bad. I was a bad woman."

And then she made a strange additional comment. "Now I would rather have a child that I could think of as really my own than anything else I shall ever have."[10] Phillip was not "really [her] own"? Such confusion was no doubt due to her misery mixed with guilt.

Then came a development that offered some hope for a way out of the maze. Katherine Wylie agreed to a divorce. Immediately after it was granted, Horace and Elinor were married, on August 7, 1916. Mrs. Hoyt offered them the use of a house in Washington. Horace found a job there with the U.S. Railway Administration as an accountant paid one hundred dollars per month. They tried to work out a normal social life. Horace would play golf when he could, come home to do his accounts and cook—Elinor never learned to cook—while she wrote poetry. But it didn't work. Washington bristled with unforgiving enemies. Elinor was unwelcome as the new Mrs. Wylie. She received anonymous insulting letters and she responded by behaving arrogantly and rudely in public. Horace was denied access to his children. He hid in the shrubbery outside his old home hoping to glimpse them and tried to talk to servants about them, but they were threatened with dismissal if they spoke to him.

That was bad enough, but bearable. Worse was Elinor's growing feeling that Washington was not simply hostile but a prison, as it had seemed ten years before. But even Washington wasn't the fundamental problem. The fundamental problem was Horace. He had served an earlier purpose but by now "he was a dead weight on her life." She came to believe that he was "the sole source of her isolation and that he was holding her back." Years later she would recall her indebtedness to him: "It was Horace who made a poet and scholar of me," but she now felt only that "their love was a vast structure that housed nothing."[11]

Elinor needed a new man to rescue her and she found him in William Rose Benét, whose family had been friends of the Moores in Carlisle years before. There was a further family connection: He had been a classmate at Yale of her brother Henry, and they had become the closest of friends. Bill Benét was a prolific poet of pleasant light verse; he was kind and patient, had great energy, and loved and needed women's company. His first wife had died in the influenza epidemic of 1919, leaving him with three young children. He was a very efficient literary organizer and had built up a circle of friends and an even larger one of contacts. Bill and Elinor met on several occasions at Mrs. Hoyt's house. He was then working as an editor for a business magazine, and fell in love with Elinor. When she showed him some of the poems she had been writing, he thought them beautifully fragile, and came to admire them as much as he loved their author. He set about to promote Elinor's career, jokingly referring to his activities on her behalf as those of the "Benét Literary Agency."

In 1919-1920, deciding that poetry might afford her a way out of her now hopeless imprisonment, and that nothing must stand in the way of a possible literary career, Elinor did not look only to Bill Benét for help, but on her own sent some of her poems from *Incidental Numbers* and some of her new poems to *Poetry*. They were rejected but accompanied by an encouraging note asking for more. She sent more, adding her own different note, "I do this with hesitation, as I do not consider most of my work modern enough for *Poetry*."[12] Two months later came Harriet Monroe's personal reply, "I find your poems quite 'modern' enough for *Poetry*." She accepted four, paying Elinor twenty-five dollars for them. A poem was also accepted for *Contemporary Verse*. She had left behind the juvenilia of her earlier years, and now looked directly at the harsh reality of the world.

Village Mystery

The woman in the pointed hood
And cloak blue-gray like a pigeon's wing,
Whose orchard climbs to the balsam-wood,
Had done a cruel thing.

To her back door-step came a ghost,
A girl who had been ten years dead,
She stood by the granite hitching-post
And begged for a piece of bread.

Now why should I, who walks alone,
Who am ironical and proud,
Turn, when a woman casts a stone
At a beggar in a shroud?

I saw the dead girl cringe and whine,
And cower in the weeping air –
But, oh, she was no kin of mine,
And so I did not care!

She had broken through as a poet, but what of her personal life? Benét moved to New York City to work as a literary editor on the *New York Evening Post* and to share an apartment with Henry Hoyt. Publishing some poems convinced Elinor that she probably could support herself and be truly free. What of Horace? "I will always stick to him, but the question is—should I pass up the chance to earn my own living? I should certainly like to earn my own living—Gosh how I would love it."[13]

While she dithered and pondered, there was an outbreak of Hoyt madness. In August 1920, Henry had attended the wedding of his younger brother, Morton, to the same woman for the second time. It was a riotous affair; Morton ate the bridesmaids' gardenias and then got very drunk. For his part, Henry returned to his apartment, tidied it and put his papers in order and committed suicide by turning on the gas jets. Bill Benét found his body.

Two visits to the Poetry Society and the rapturous response she received in December 1920 and January 1921 were pivotal in helping Elinor make up her mind to leave Horace. When she confronted him with this decision, he was not disconcerted. "You better remain with me. Elinor, you are a fantastic creature and I understand you."[14] She responded to his detachment with a bout of severe headaches, but gradually Horace's response came to seem a form of blackmail. He was using the past against her, not looking to the future for her. She cringed at divorce. Better a trial separation for one year; if then she didn't want a divorce they would remain separated or she would return to him, a compromise that was entirely self-interested. She expressed her sense of growing estrangement from Horace in an unpublished sonnet written at this time that describes their marriage as "strange warfare," and as a kind of "mysterious and hallowed hate." Even as Elinor hesitated about whether or when to leave Horace, she was considering which furniture and silver she would take with her to New York City. As they talked, "Horace sat passively in his chair. It was a sobering finish to eleven years."[15]

PART TWO

MANHATTAN
1917–1921

1. OVERVIEW:
THE VILLAGE AND FEMINISM

"**M**AD IRELAND HURT me into poetry," wrote William Butler Yeats. New York City's influence on the poets who appear in this book, as well as on innumerable other artists, was of a different nature. This influence was captured perfectly by one of them, Alfred Stieglitz, in his photograph entitled "City of Ambition." By the early twentieth century, New York City was unchallenged as the nation's cultural capital, the arbiter and creator of fashion in the arts, as well as in commerce. While Hollywood was establishing itself as the center of film production, New York City was supreme in radio, live theater, and publishing. There were between seventy and eighty theaters in the city in which dozens of plays and musicals were performed, and touring companies multiplied Broadway's impact by taking its successes into the provinces. Its dominance in word culture was equally unchallenged. It supported twenty-five daily newspapers, and most of the important national magazines were published there. Book publishing, centered in midtown Manhattan, was virtually a New York monopoly. "Of the ambitions of the great Unpublished," the novelist Frank Norris wrote, "the one that is strongest, the most abiding, is the ambition to get to New York ... the indispensable vantage ground."[1]

Greenwich Village was a clearly identifiable neighborhood bounded on the north by 14th Street, on the west by the Hudson River, on the south by Houston Street, and on the east by Third Avenue. It was a neighborhood known everywhere as America's pre-eminent bohemia. People, young people especially, came from everywhere in the nation to escape from the polar philistinism and isolation of small town and farm life. The Village represented youth, freedom, adventure, and rebellion.

In the first decade of the twentieth century, internal social and economic change accelerated the emergence of Greenwich Village as the best-known American bohemia. As middle-class residents moved out and up to the more fashionable uptown, real estate values in The Village declined sharply. This meant that Irish and Italian immigrants could afford to move in as permanent residents, and so too could transient renters, including artists and non-conformists of all sorts. The result was an essentially working-class neighborhood of dilapidated but still charming brick row houses, wandering streets, occasional courtyards, crooked alleyways, the site of a teeming street life and of places of informal sociability, restaurants, bookstores, bars, cafes, theaters, galleries, and clubs. Its colorful reputation obscured a sharp division; the fact that old-line inhabitants and the newer Catholic arrivals regarded bohemianism "as a menace to the decency of their neighborhood and to the morals of their children."[2]

At the same time, the Village became most notorious not for social nonconformity but for political radicalism centering on socialism and women's rights. *The Masses*, edited by Max Eastman (1883-1969), constituted the most celebrated challenge to capitalism. Born in upstate New York, Eastman held views which were a blend of Christian moralism and Marxist paganism; he achieved a Ph.D. in philosophy from Columbia University, and oversaw the growth of *The Masses*. After a faltering start, it became the leading radical organ in the country—its circulation grew from ten thousand in 1911 to forty thousand at the time of America's entry into World War I in 1917. The war and the Russian Revolution unleashed hysteria in America about supposed threats to national security. *The Masses* was prosecuted as seditious and closed down, at least two thousand socialists were deported, and the Red Scare of 1919-1920 crushed the political culture in the Village.

Rights for women, the other major political cause, was victorious, enshrined in the Nineteenth Amendment to the Constitution. However, far from marking the end of agitation for women's rights, there developed a broader movement that characterized the second great period of vigorous political village life, from about 1917 to the end of the 1920s. Feminism—the term became well known by about 1910—was led by a number of powerful and outspoken women—Mary Heaton Vorse, Emma Goldman, Crystal Eastman, Inez Milholland, and Margaret Sanger—who wanted to liberate women from the crushing weight of masculine social convention, to achieve sexual, social, and personal independence in the person of the "new" woman.

The reformer Hutchins Hapgood said, with only modest exaggeration, that "the restlessness of women was the main cause of the development called Greenwich Village." Women began to do shocking things: cutting their hair, smoking in public, keeping their own names after marriage—when there was a marriage. It is often trivial acts and gestures that most inflame and frighten conventional folk. A headline in the *New York Times*, about a woman who did not adopt her husband's name, makes the point. "No Mrs.

Badge of Slavery Worn By This Miss Wife," it proclaimed. "Separate names," the writer of the headlined article warned, "were the first step in a slippery slope that led to feckless wives of loose morals, easy divorce, and free love."[3]

Free love! More threatening even than Marxism, "Free love was the raffish accomplice to free speech and free expression."[4] Villagers publicly proclaimed their fallings-in and their fallings-out of love, their delight in flirtations, seduction and carnal pleasures of every conceivable kind. Like sex before marriage, drinking was also a sign of liberation for women, who joined men in drinking too much, wickedness especially pleasurable after it was legally prohibited by the Eighteenth Amendment.

Less pronounced and publicized, women began moving into professions, achieved a degree of freedom, as divorce laws were made less rigid, and continued to gain access to higher education. In the "word culture" of Midtown, they worked for male editors, their salaries were low, and they had only modest formal authority. Nevertheless, they played important roles and exercised influence. Mabel Dodge Luhan, who lived in both worlds, the Village and Midtown, believed that book publishing in New York City was largely run by women. "There was a woman behind every important editor in every publisher's office and in all editorial circles... and it was the judgment and intuition of these that determined many policies."[5]

Poetry—writing poetry, expressing uncommon ideas by means of poetry, reading poetry aloud to eager audiences—was an important expression of liberated and thoughtful women. The women's poetry movement of the first third of the twentieth century didn't come out of nowhere. It existed within a larger cultural context that engaged women and men to reconsider the nature of the poetic art and to value and cherish it to an extent never before seen in the United States. The art existed for its own sake, but also for the sake of a meaningful exchange of ideas. Poetry was a form of women's liberation. The all-engrossing subject was love.

There were precedents and antecedents. In 1886, Ella Wheeler, a Wisconsin farm girl, published *Poems of Passion,* which deserves the term path-breaking, as does the poetry of Lizette Woodward Reese, a Maryland school teacher whose *A Branch of May* (1887) matched emotional subtlety with technical simplicity. Constrained by inhibitions and proprieties, the poems still carry conviction; that they have long been consigned to virtual oblivion is further proof of the unhistorical nature of our culture.

The poetry of Emily Dickinson (1830-1886) gains cultural significance in this context in one specific way. *Poems* was published posthumously in 1890 and caused a sensation. It went through six printings in six weeks. While not love poetry in any ordinary sense, the originality and depth of psychological and spiritual understanding of her poetry shattered the assumption, at least for some, that poetry in America was a male domain.

The popularity of women's poetry in the 1910s and '20s underlined the difficulty American male poets had in expressing the deep emotions between men and women. This profound limitation is reflected in the poetry of Edwin Arlington Robinson (1869-1935), a New Englander who went to New York City at the turn of the century and lived an impoverished bohemian life in the Village. In 1897, he published *The Children of the Night,* a book made up of harshly realistic vignettes of men and women living and suffering together in a small New England town, their lives characterized by "fear, bafflement, ambivalence and despair."[6] But not by love.

2. SARA TEASDALE

NEW YORK CITY—at last! Sara Teasdale's first year there was packed with achievement and public recognition. Her anthology, *The Answering Voice*, dedicated to her sister, appeared at the beginning of 1917. *Rivers to the Sea* went into its fourth printing in the course of that year, and her new collection, *Love Songs*, was published in the fall. She enjoyed her literary prominence and, when interviewed, said that inspiration came from her new life in New York City. "Poems are written because of a subconscious combination of thoughts and feeling coming together like electrical currents in a thunder storm." These thoughts and feelings, she explained, "were produced by both actual and by imaginary experiences. In either case the poem is written to free the poet from an emotional burden"[1]—in her case, the burden of being trapped in St. Louis for the rest of her life.

In New York City, she took part in what was for her an active social life, the theater, meetings of Poetry Society, and taking tea with Theodore Roosevelt and Willa Cather. All the while, however shy and retiring, she displayed a worldly understanding of the elements of her success, "withholding poems that might confuse her public image or disturb her followers." She read voraciously and when asked to serve on committees to award prizes, she didn't hesitate to express her views. And, for the private amusement of a handful of friends, she wrote erotic limericks about the contemporary scene.

Love Songs was reviewed enthusiastically and, combined with *The Answering Voice*, did more than just reinforce her popularity. It established her as the leading proponent of women's poetry and of the emerging women's poetry movement. While neither a self-declared feminist nor a Modernist, she was proud to think of herself as representing all the varied aspects of the women's poetry revival, of women at last finding their voices. In her prefatory note to *An Answering Voice*, she proudly argued that the lyric poetry written by women since the middle of the nineteenth century marked "the first time in history of English literature [when] the work of women compared favorably with that of men, and in no other field have done such noteworthy work as in poetry." How to account for this? Love poems written by women, "for reasons well known to the student of feminism," were rare because women lacked economic independence and were stifled by masculine social conventions. Women had accepted these conventions in the past; but no longer and "in most cases the finest utterance of women poets has been on love."[2]

Love Songs appeared at precisely the right historical moment and defined it. The Poetry Society awarded her a prize for one section of the book, "Interlude: Songs out of Sorrow." Within two months of publication the volume was reprinted, and in May of 1918 it received another prize, an unprecedented honor for its author. Columbia University and the Poetry Society gave her a $500 prize for the best book of poems published in 1917. It was in effect a Pulitzer Prize. Those prizes had been established that year, administered by Columbia University, but had not included a poetry prize. Columbia and the Poetry Society therefore offered their prize as a supplement to the Pulitzers until 1922 when a regular Pulitzer poetry prize was established. Sara was "intoxicated" by the prize, "as near to heaven as I have been since I was in Italy."[3]

IN *Love Songs*, she refined her observations and her language as she recounted the infinite forms and sources of love. The first of these was the love of language, the poet's "house of shining words."

Refuge

From my spirit's gray defeat,
From my pulse's flagging beat,
From my hopes that turned to sand
Sifting through my close-clenched hand,
From my own fault's slavery,
If I can sing, I still am free.

For with my singing I can make
A refuge for my spirit's sake,
A house of shining words, to be
My fragile immortality

The poet gives the world her song but the passions aroused by love also demand personal surrender.

The Tree of Song

I sang my songs for the rest,
 For you I am still;
The tree of my song is bare
 On its shining hill.

For you came like a lordly wind,
 And the leaves were whirled
Far as forgotten things
 Past the rim of the world.

The tree of my song stands bare
 Against the blue—
I gave my songs to the rest,
 Myself to you

One of her most popular poems embodies the dream she had cherished since she was a young woman; the ecstatic love of all forms of beauty.

Barter

Life has loveliness to sell,
 All beautiful and splendid things,
Blue waves whitened on a cliff,
 Soaring fire that sways and signs,
And children's faces looking up
Holding water like a cup.

Life has loveliness to sell,
 Music like a curve of gold,
Scent of pine trees in the rain,
 Eyes that love you, arms that hold,
And for your spirit's still delight,
Holy thoughts that star the night.

Spend all you have for loveliness,
 Buy it and never count the cost;
For one white singing hour of peace
 Count many a year of strife well lost,
And for a breath of ecstasy
Give all you have been, or could be.

Less well known but also joyously affirmative—love of women for men.

Child, Child

Child, child, love while you can
The voice and the eyes and the soul of a man;
Never fear though it break your heart—
Out of the wound new joy will start;
Only love proudly and gladly and well,
Though love be heaven or love be hell.

Child, child, love while you may,
For life is short as a happy day;
Never fear the thing you feel—
Only by love is life made real;
Love, for the deadly sins are seven,
Only through love will you enter heaven.

These exalted notions of love were unfortunately incompatible with the reality of her marriage, which was going badly and apparently had been from the beginning. While on their honeymoon, Sara had written to her mother, "Neither of us can realize that all of this happiness for which we have longed is really ours. It is too good to be true." It was. She later admitted (to John Wheelock) that once she was engaged, she spent a good deal of the time "wondering dismally how she could have done such a thing," and later described the honeymoon as "a fiasco."[4] As a child she had never shared a room with anyone else and, once married, insisted on sleeping alone in her bedroom. Ernst apparently did not object.

Marriage bristled with contradictions. It was to have been a fortress of security, but the fortress began to resemble a prison. It was to have been the means to material independence, but initially at least the Filsingers could not make ends meet. Ernst therefore worked long hours in his new job which meant he was absent much of the time. She resented it, although she was unwilling to give up her maid or to move out of their hotel. Domestic duties were simply beyond the pale. Her parents helped them out financially, which in turn undermined her sense of independence. So she went round and round and round.

Sometime in 1917 she became pregnant. She and Ernst both said they wanted children. To be a mother was at the center of that powerful web of conventions that determined a proper woman's life. But she had increasingly come to feel that she was not strong enough to raise a child and also, frankly, she feared that being a mother would jeopardize her career as a writer. She had an abortion. This was a wrenching decision and the cause of profound feelings of guilt. In one of her notebooks there are some lines for a poem, perhaps never completed, and certainly unpublishable, under the heading "Duty."

Fool, the wrong is done.
The seed is sown.
The evil stands.

But "out of the web of wrong," she would continue her "thread of song."

The creative burst of 1917 and the abortion were followed by a period of protracted inactivity—indigestion and neuralgic pain. She could not walk for more than a few minutes at a time. She needed to be away from Ernst and went to Massachusetts for a month to recover. But she also desperately needed him. More and more reclusive, she sent him to represent her at social occasions she could not entirely ignore but couldn't attend in person. She reiterated that he was an ideal husband. When wartime conscription threatened to take him away from her, she persuaded her doctors to state that her ill health prevented her from supporting herself. He was reclassified and exempted from military service.

His firm scheduled an extended business trip to Europe in 1919. He urged Sara to go with him, but she thought Europe so soon after the war would be cold and uncomfortable, so he went alone. "I almost break down when we talk of his going. Yet I want him to go."[5] At the same time, she developed morbid fear that he was having sexual affairs with other women—though there was never any evidence for this—and would desert her.

She did go with him to Havana. The trip was not a success, but it stimulated her to write one of her psychological responses to the outside world. Previously, in a familiar Romantic way, death had been represented in her poetry as soporific, extended sleep, itself an escape from life. But here, though still responsive to exotically beautiful Caribbean nature, saturated with erotic longings, the external world is seen as menacing and, even, terrifying:

In A Cuban Garden

Hibiscus flowers are cups of fire,
(Love me, my lover, life will not stay)
The bright poinsettia shakes in the wind,
A scarlet leaf is blowing away.

A lizard lifts his head and listens—
Kiss me before the noon goes by,
Here in the shade of the ceiba hide me
From the great black vulture circling the sky.

In 1919 she was alone for six months of the year. She tried to discipline her anxieties and fears by an act of will, which took the form of a further withdrawal. When Ernst did return that year, she was initially ecstatic, but soon she was ill again and subject to the same anxieties about his absence and his presence. When his employer sent him on a four-month business trip to South America, they repeated the by now familiar pattern. He begged her to accompany him. She said "no" and went instead to Santa Barbara, California, where she thought she would be warm, undisturbed and able to write. She liked the town initially. "With sea and mountains...I've not needed people much." She didn't push herself to write. "Maybe a poem comes to me at night, maybe not." If she briefly found happiness in Santa Barbara, she also realized that happiness was not conducive to writing poetry. One poem concludes: "My heart sings only when it breaks." She soon tired of the town and its "spoiled, rich people." However, there was one high-point, the appearance of W.B. Yeats, who came to speak to a women's group. She was able to talk with him and was surprised that "he spoke of knowing my name and liking my work." Her admiration for Yeats had grown since those early years of the Potters Club in

St. Louis. "There is no other artist in the world for whom I feel the same admiration and enthusiasm."[6] Inspired by this encounter, on her return to New York City she sorted through her work, arranging her poems for a new book. In October 1920, *Flame and Shadow* appeared, its title taken from a poem by Victor Hugo and dedicated "To E." It was a great success, as popular as her previous books, and went through four printings in that year. "It is my best book and shows a stronger grasp of life as well as more flexible technique."[7] It was her most ambitious book in structure, made up of twelve sections, the last poem of each section summing up the section's theme. She wished to show that the short poems "are in reality one life poem." The overall theme was love—the effort by the artist to convey to the reader the love of beauty in its many forms.

Like all her poems, those in *Flame and Shadow* (shadow predominated) are very personal, which was why she disliked hearing her poems read in public. She intended for her lyrics to be listened to by "no more than two or three people." Because they were so directly her own feelings, "the idea of their being read or recited to a roomful of people (especially if I have to be present), gives me a longing to die at once."[8]

I Have Loved Hours At Sea

I have loved hours at sea, gray cities,
The fragile secret of a flower,
Music, the making of a poem
That gave me heaven for an hour;

First stars above the snowy hill,
Voices of people kindly and wise,
And the great look of love, long hidden,
Found at last in meeting eyes.

I have loved much and been loved deeply—
Oh when my spirit's fire burns low,
Leave me the darkness and the stillness,
I shall be tired and glad to go.

A personal favorite among her poems was

The Coin

Into my heart's treasury
 I slipped a coin
That time cannot take
 Nor a thief purloin, --
Oh better than the minting
 Of a gold-crowned king
Is the safe kept memory
 Of a lovely thing.

The year 1921 was, like all Sara's other years, a mixture of intense joy and grinding depression. She and Ernst went to western Massachusetts for one carefree weekend, "the happiest we have had since our marriage." She was "vastly enthusiastic" about Henry James's *The Wings of the Dove*, but at the same time anxieties and fearful moods piled up. The most direct cause of these was her father's worsening health; the possibility of his death increased her sense of what he had meant to her—her main source of strength since childhood and the model of honor and fortitude for her own character;"[9] and it brought home powerfully her fear of death.

3. EDNA ST. VINCENT MILLAY

I N THE FALL of 1917, Edna Millay plunged into New York City life. Letters to her mother and sisters bubbled with excitement. She savored the "beautiful anonymity" of a big city and relished "really feeling at home in New York now: the man in the information booth in Grand Central knows me & nods & smiles when I come up for a time table." It wasn't all positive. "There is no air on 5th Avenue … never one breath of pure air, nothing but gas, gas, gas." Always broke, she experienced the unromantic reality of bohemian poverty, eventually settling into a tiny apartment at 30 West Ninth Street. She invited her sister, Norma, to join her. "It's going to be hard, baby; we'll probably want money pretty bad pretty often…but we shan't starve, because we can borrow. I'm all enthusiasm & good courage about it."[1] Norma came. They spent much of the "ice-bound, dreadful" winter of 1917-18 huddled together in the apartment. In the spirit of the Village, she cut her hair, wrote poetry, and sewed costumes for the Provincetown Players. After a year and a half, they were evicted for not paying the rent.

Edna's theatrical success at Vassar led her to hope that Broadway might be her career, "for who could expect to make a living at writing poetry?" People often commented on the beauty of her voice and her dramatic power over audiences; so she gave a few readings in private homes, once making fifty dollars. Later, this would become a major source of income. In pursuit of her theatrical ambitions, Edna gained the support of another older woman, Edith Wynne Matthison, a successful Broadway actor whom she had met at Vassar. A handsome, commanding woman in her forties, she exuded confidence. "I shall ultimately be able to find something for you," Matthison wrote and arranged meetings for Edna with theatrical producers. Edna's effusive letters show her as the humble supplicant: "I know that your feeling for me, however slight, is of the nature of love…and nothing that has happened to me for a long time has made me so happy." And again, "Love me, please; I love you; I can bear to be your friend. So ask of me anything and hurt me whenever you must; but never be 'tolerant,' or 'kind.'"[2]

Unfortunately, nothing came of Matthison's efforts. Edna made her own way into theater, not popular commercial theatre but—her only contact with the artistic *avant-garde*—with the Provincetown Players, a Village theatrical collective that had recently moved from Cape Cod to a former stable on Mac-Dougall Street and was rapidly becoming one of the centers of Village cultural life. Resolutely noncommercial, the Players sold tickets only by subscription, didn't publicize themselves, sought out new and provocative work, plays by Eugene O'Neill and also by William Carlos Williams, Sherwood Anderson and Alfred

Kreymborg. Marsden Hartley and Art Young designed sets and costumes. For three years Edna was an important figure in the group, acting in several plays, writing, directing and starring in her own *The Princess Marries the Page*, which opened one of the Players' seasons, and writing and directing *Aria da Capo*, *(Repeated Song)*, in which Norma had a leading role. A fierce anti-war play, it enjoyed success in many American cities in subsequent years as well as in England and on the Continent. She never again equaled that success as a playwright. Poetry, not the theater, would be her way to fame.

In December of that first year, Mitchell Kennerley published *Renascence and Other Poems*, a slender volume, beautifully produced. He was an imaginative and adventurous publisher, eager to find and bring attention to new work. Edna was grateful for his support from the time of her first visit to New York and in the four years following, when *The Forum* published her poetry. However, he was a devious, even dishonorable businessman who managed his affairs in a secretive, slap-dash manner. Writers frequently found "someone from the sheriff's office sitting in the front office."[3] Kennerley had promised Edna an advance of five hundred dollars for *Renascence and Other Poems*, at the time of publication but was slow in sending the balance owed her. He would also prove maddeningly difficult in publishing her next book of poems, which she had promised to him.

The initial collection contained sixteen lyrics in addition to the title poem. All of them dated from Edna's Vassar years and were similar in tone and subject matter. If none quite reached the ecstatic spirituality of "Renascence," one other was singled out for its "overpowering radiance," its "rapture."

God's World

O world, I cannot hold thee close enough!
   Thy winds, thy wide grey skies!
   Thy mists, that roll and rise!
Thy woods, this autumn day, that ache and sag
And all but cry with colour! That gaunt crag
To crush! To lift the lean of that black bluff!
World, World, I cannot get thee close enough!

Long have I known the glory in it all,
     But never knew I this:
     Here such a passion is
As stretcheth me apart,—Lord, I do fear
Thou'st made the world too beautiful this year;
My soul is all but out of me,—let fall
No burning leaf; prithee, let no bird call.

Although she continued to use archaic locutions—"thy," "prithee," "oft,"—to denigrate these traditional aspects was to miss the point. Her poems were loved by many precisely because they were a familiar part of the tradition of English and American romantic poetry. Louis Untermeyer understood this in characterizing her work: "Traditional in form and unorthodox in spirit, it satisfied the reader's dual desire for familiarity and surprise."[4]

Among the other poems in *Renascence* were five sonnets about love—lost love—a subject and form she would make very much her own in the years ahead. Among them was one strikingly stoical in the face of tragic loss:

V

If I should learn, in some quite casual way,
  That you were gone, not to return again –
Read from the back-page of a paper, say,
  Held by a neighbor in a subway train,
How at the corner of this avenue
  And such a street (so are the papers filled)
A hurrying man—who happened to be you—
  At noon to-day had happened to be killed,
I should not cry aloud—I could not cry
  Aloud, or wring my hands in such a place —
I should but watch the station lights rush by
  With a more careful interest on my face,
Or raise my eyes and read with a greater care
Where to store furs and how to treat the hair.

Most of the reviews were positive, some extravagantly so, but *Renascence* did not by any means make Edna Millay a well-known name in poetry circles. The first edition was a small one and the book made its way only gradually in subsequently modest editions in 1919, two in 1921, and a fifth in 1924. Mitchell Kennerley did one thing with the first edition that would have long-term consequences. The dust jacket was a photograph taken by Arnold Genthe in the spring of 1913. "Winsome and young and fragile," it was the image of the poet come from another world.

She always took it for granted that she was writing for a popular audience—and for money. "I have a perfect passion for earning money, don't care much how I earn it, just feel I have to hurry around all the time and make money." She had no choice. She was initially inexperienced and was taken advantage of, as her dealing with Kennerley made clear. "It's so funny for me to think of the business end of [writing]." But she learned quickly and recognized her power with publishers as her popularity grew. At the same time, her deepest aspirations for her poetry went beyond money. "I want it to be read—it's that more than the disgusting money—the dirty necessary money!"[5]

She happily put her poems in *Ainslie's: The Magazine That Entertains*, which had paid little attention to poetry until Walter Adolphe Roberts became its editor. *Ainslie's* had always featured a girl on its cover—Edmund Wilson dismissed it as "trashy"—but Roberts set about changing that, paying Millay 50 cents a line and putting her poems in wherever there was an empty place below the pictures. He genuinely admired her. "Yours is a real genius, a fine and delicate gift. You are a real poet. There are not many such." He also conceived the idea that Millay write fictional pieces about young women, potboilers for which he paid more than for poetry. These appeared under the name of Nancy Boyd, never under the name of Edna Millay. And of course Roberts fell in love with her, took her out to dinner any night she was free. She didn't love him in return and he kept his balance about it all and refused to become jealous when Edna told him she was seeing other men. "I took her temperament exactly as I found it and preached no sermons."[6]

The other magazine that helped her define and reach the audience she wanted in these years was *Reedy's*, which was edited by Sara Teasdale's patron in St. Louis, William Reedy, a "crusty Midwestern editor, who published only what he liked. Luckily, what he liked was absolutely first rate." *Reedy's* published twenty of Millay's sonnets in batches of five. William Reedy had met Edna one night at the Kennerleys', had a protracted "gab-fest" with her, lost his head and, as he put it, "honestly, a bit of my heart, too, in the glorious talk." His characterization of Millay's poetry—"It's splendid work—all shot through with brightness, the air of the open world in it too"—no doubt mirrored that of his readers.[7] It was Reedy who later published *Aria da Capo*. *Reedy's* and *Ainslie's* widened her audience, but the enduring image and reputation were associated with Greenwich Village.

"From the first moment Vincent entered the Village, she was doomed to myth." She didn't just proclaim sexual freedom for women; she practiced it with exuberant high spirits. She had "so many concurrent liaisons with so many lovers" in the Village and beyond that it "makes a biographer cross eyed to look at her calendar." Her first Village lover was Floyd Dell, who had come to New York City from Chicago (where Sara Teasdale had met and intensely disliked him). A proponent of free love and of Freudian ideas, he'd written a one-act play for which Edna auditioned. He promptly fell in love with her. (She got the part.) Thirty years old and divorced, Dell was able to introduce Vincent "to many things she'd missed and didn't know about," especially to try to draw her away from lesbianism, "the enchanted garden of childhood which excluded males;" and to introduce her to Freudian thought. Dell failed on both counts. Edna regarded his ideas as a "Teutonic attempt to lock up women in the house and to restrict them to cooking and baby tending,"[8] a view many have come to share in our time. Dell wanted to marry her but Edna refused him. "Anybody can get married. It happens all the time." Dell was devastated, but Edna was undisturbed. "I shall have many lovers,"[9] she predicted.

And she was right in her prediction. Among her lovers were many of the leading Village intellectuals. Edmund Wilson, a graduate of Princeton University, who would become the greatest American man of letters of the mid-twentieth century, was just out of the army and embarked, as an editor and reviewer, on a career in journalism. He had read Millay's Vassar poems and reviewed them for the *New York Evening Sun*. After he finally met her, they spent many evenings reading and discussing Latin and European literature. He also proposed marriage. She thought about it, saying, "that might be the solution," but she declined. Wilson realized that proposals of marriage "were not a great source of excitement for her."[10]

Wilson and Millay remained friends, writing occasional and interesting letters. He reviewed her poetry and his praise was much valued by her. Many years later he wrote movingly about her "intoxicating effect on people, of all ages and both sexes."[11] More than any other man of the time, Edmund Wilson played an important role in the professional lives of the women in this story. His knowledge, critical acumen and sympathy were important to them. He was one of the few critics able to move readily between the traditional and Modernist camps.

John Peale Bishop—Princeton graduate, critic, journalist, friend and collaborator of Edmund Wilson's—also succumbed to Edna's enchantments. He suffered protracted torment and yet was also able to analyze her appeal with great insight. Erotic energy and emotional remoteness, he believed, were the source of her power. "I wonder sometimes," he wrote to her, "if you do not hurt for sheer pleasure in hurting."[12] Many of her lovers would have agreed. Arthur Davison Ficke, who had been corresponding with her since the *Lyric Year* days, and with whom she insisted she was in love, was brought round to her one day by Floyd Dell. "Tall, handsome, elegant, rich, a poet, kind, gentle"—and married—he was a Major in the army about to go to France. They had a passionate seventy-two hours. She didn't see him again for four years, insisted that she loved him deeply, but reluctantly understood that he was then essentially unavailable.

She didn't limit herself to intellectuals. There was an Italian tenor, Luigi Laurenti. And there was James Lawyer, an engineer who poured out his adoration in letters. She pursued him and said that she wished to marry him, but there was a problem. He was married. He said his wife would grant him a divorce, but instead she tried to commit suicide and Lawyer ended the relationship with Edna, who was contemptuous of his weakness, referring to him as a "poor fish," and treating him callously and angrily. It was perhaps in relation to Lawyer that Cora, who was kept informed in considerable detail by Edna about her love life, asked, matter-of-factly, "Who is Edna killing now? Is he almost done for?"[13] Edmund Wilson estimated that by the time he came to know her, Edna had had eighteen sexual affairs and once had four going at the same time. She came to make love one afternoon with John Bishop and casually told him that she had already had sex with a man that morning and was going to see a third man that evening. No wonder Wilson proposed that Edna's lovers and former lovers should form an alumni association.

Her love affairs were local and discreet, though gossip may have circulated beyond the Village and throughout publishing circles. What brought together her unconstrained sexual indulgence and her expression of it in poetry for readers outside the Village was the publication by a small Village firm in 1920 of another of her slender volumes. She had assembled a different collection as her second book, but Mitchell Kennerley was so disorganized or devious that the second book was continually delayed. So Millay went ahead with *A Few Figs From Thistles*. Its impact was explosive. It sold well, but the publicity and scandal went far beyond copies sold, and it began the process by which Millay's poems were quoted and re-quoted, and misquoted, by people who knew nothing about her actual behavior. It established her as a symbol of the new and liberated woman who was an unrepentant sexual hedonist.

Even now, ninety years later, we open to the first page and find the two "figs," boldly and briefly blazing out her defiance in six lines:

First Fig

My candle burns at both ends;
 It will not last the night;
But ah, my foes, and oh, my friends—
 It gives a lovely light!

Second Fig

Safe upon the solid rock the ugly houses stand:
Come and see my shining palace built upon the sand!

More rockets—brief, quotable, memorable—continued the mockery of the conventional people whose domestic life was so often a dead end.

Grown-Up

Was it for this I uttered prayers,
And sobbed and cursed and kicked the stairs,
That now, domestic as a plate,
I should retire at half-past eight?

Then there was the brash, matter-of-fact poem,

Thursday

And if I love you Wednesday,
　Well, what is that to you?
I do not love you Thursday—
　So much is true.

And why you come complaining
　Is more than I can see.
I loved you Wednesday,—yes—but what
　Is that to me?

Far better to embrace sex whenever you could find it, however trite that might seem:

The Unexplorer

There was a road ran past our house
Too lovely to explore.
I asked my mother once—she said
That if you followed where it led
It brought you to the milkman's door.
(That's why I have not traveled more.)

Ideas of love turned upside down, *A Few Figs* ended with four sonnets in which Millay continued to invert conventional notions about faithfulness. Words, mere "vows," were nothing. True love was faithful only to love itself; true lovers must rightly desert what is no longer appealing. To be faithful on any other basis is actually to be faithless.

Having dispensed with conventional platitudes about undy-

ing love, it was much better to recognize the determining reality
of biology.

IV

> I shall forget you presently, my dear,
> So make the most of this, your little day,
> Your little month, your little half a year,
> Ere I forget, or die, or move away,
> And we are done forever; by and by
> I shall forget you, as I said, but now,
> If you entreat me with your loveliest lie
> I will protest you with my favourite vow.
> I would indeed that love were longer-lived,
> And oaths were not so brittle as they are,
> But so it is, and nature has contrived
> To struggle on without a break thus far, --
> Whether or not we find what we are seeking
> Is idle, biologically speaking.

Not everyone applauded. Professor William Lyon Phelps
of Yale University: "These whimsies are graceful and amusing
enough but of no importance. A fig for such poetry." Louis Untermeyer: "Facile cynicism, an ignoble adroitness."[14] Innumerable
people were shocked. What most shocked them about this view of
human love, a view at least as old as the Latin poems, was that a
woman uttered it, and that she had the effrontery to do so in tones
of gaiety and amusement.

"I am becoming very famous," Edna wrote to her mother
with a touch of disbelief about what was happening. In a single
week the New York newspapers featured a photograph of her, a

page of her poems, and three reviews.[15] One newspaper verified her popularity by organizing a contest. Contributors sent in couplets and quatrains using Edna's name in the final line as if it were a limerick. After a while, when the novelty no longer appealed, she was annoyed by it all and complained that she couldn't write any more. "My poetry needs fresh grass to feed on…New York is getting too congested for me, - too many people; I get no time to work."[16] From the fall of 1917 to the end of 1920, she had published seventy-seven poems, thirty-nine of them sonnets. On January 4, 1921, after three and a half years in New York City, she sailed for Europe—alone.

4. DOROTHY PARKER

FOR TWO AND a half years at *Vogue* magazine, Dorothy Rothschild served her apprenticeship in Manhattan's word production culture, taking part in the coming of age of a distinctive New York style of humor, characterized by insolent hilarity. *Mademoiselle New York* stressed witty accounts of everyday events and adopted a tone of mild cynicism about institutions. *The Smart Set*, self-designated as "The Magazine of Cleverness," became, when H.L. Mencken and George Jean Nathan joined it as contributors in 1908, a repository of jokes against entrenched American dullness in any form. Add to this in the first two decades of the twentieth century the infusion of Jewish humor, mordant, fatalistic, verbally self-aware.

Searching for a distinctive voice, Dorothy perfected the device of biting the hand that fed her, sharpening her wits at the expense of *Vogue*. She wrote captions for advertisements with an alarming (to the editors) lack of commercial decorum. She adapted

Shakespeare for an underwear ad: "Brevity is the soul of lingerie—as the Petticoat said to the Chemise." She also wrote special features, on beauty care, weddings, dogs, and interior decoration, which she ridiculed as *Vogue's* taste for "interior desecration." "Boy did I think I was smart."[1]

Dorothy Parker

At the same time, *Vanity Fair* published three more poems in her conversational style, about mundane acts and events of middle class social life. Amiability, not satire, was the prevailing mode. Aware that these poems were experimental and not yet in the style she was working toward, Dorothy didn't reprint them in subsequent collections. She observed the contemporary poetry scene carefully, and was fully aware of the *avant-garde* verse being submitted to *Vanity Fair*. However, as a professional writer she needed whatever income she could get and therefore didn't aim exclusively at *Vanity Fair* readers. She also published a large number of her poems in *Life*, a humor magazine of the day, not to be confused with the very different news magazine founded by Henry Luce in the twenties. *Life* existed to amuse people by joking and making fun, and it was the appropriate outlet for her spoof of a contemporary fad among intellectuals—psychoanalysis. Dorothy picked up the idiom deftly even if she couldn't resist an obvious pun at the end.

The Passionate Freudian To His Love

Only name the day, and we'll fly away
    In the face of old traditions,
To a sheltered spot, by the world forgot,
    Where we'll park our inhibitions.
Come and gaze in eyes where the love-light lies
    As it psychoanalyses,
And when once you glean what your fantasies mean
    Life will hold no more surprises.
When you've told your love what you're thinking of
    Things will be much more informal;
Through a sunlit land we'll go hand-in-hand,
    Drifting gently back to normal.

While the pale moon gleams, we will dream sweet dreams,
    And I'll win your admiration,
For it's only fair to admit I'm there
    With a mean interpretation.
In the sunrise glow we will whisper low
    Of the scenes our dreams have painted,
And when you're advised what they symbolized
    We'll begin to feel acquainted.
So we'll gaily float in a slumber boat
    Where subconscious waves dash wildly;
In the stars' soft light, we will say good night –
    And "good-night!" will put it mildly.

Our desires shall be from repressions free –
    As it's only right to treat them.
To your ego's whims I will sing sweet hymns,
    And ad libido repeat them.
With your hand in mine, idly we'll recline
    Amid bowers of neuroses,
While the sun seeks rest in the great red west
    We will sit and match phychoses.
So come dwell a while on that distant isle
    In the brilliant tropic weather;
Where a Freud in need is a Freud indeed,
    We'll be always Jung together.

Wide-ranging as was her choice of subjects, increasingly the central theme of her poetry was contemporary versions of love between men and women, a wry recognition that it would not be enduring; the tone is not yet bitter, the disillusionment, mild. But the form in which this theme will be expressed evolved and became compact. There is a formulaic twist at the end of her verse, the last line turning what has preceded it upside down.

Absence

> I never thought that heaven would lose its blue
>> And sullen storm-clouds mask the gentle sky;
> I never thought the rose's velvet hue
>> Would pale and sicken, though we said good-by.
> I never dreamed the lark would hush its note
>> As day succeeded ever-drearier day,
> Nor know the song that swelled the robin's throat
>> Would fade to silence, when you went away.
> I never knew the sun's irradiant beams
>> Upon the brooding earth no more would shine,
> Nor thought that only in my mocking dreams
>> Would happiness that once I knew be mine.
> I never thought the slim moon, mournfully,
>> Would shroud her pallid self in murky night.
> Dear heart, I never thought these things would be –
>> I never thought they would, and I was right.

Her poems for *Life* began to make her name familiar among humorous writers; but it was a 1916 poem for *Vanity Fair* that attracted considerable attention. In it she began to release the furies contained within herself, the conflicts in her nature that Edmund Wilson said made her interesting. The title of the poem caught people's eye. She had submitted it under a different title and it is unclear who settled on "Women: A Hate Song." Having found a popular formula, she subsequently added seventeen "Hate Verses," as they were also called, eight for

Vanity Fair, ten for *Life*, both audiences responding positively. Other hate subjects were actresses, whom she routinely disparaged, relatives (getting even with the Rothschilds?), summer resorts, men, actors, bohemians. Also addressed were things she personally loved: drama, books, and movies. What was startling for a writer of popular verse was explicitly to call her poems "Hate Songs." This gained her notoriety but curiously, hate doesn't come through in them; the tone ranges from annoyance to animosity. And, in recognition that these were experiments in finding her true voice, none of them were included in her later collected verse.

In the spring of 1917, Dorothy Rothschild fell drastically in love. He was twenty-three, tall, good-looking, well dressed, amusing, a stockbroker, and pure Anglo Saxon with not a touch of mongrel in his background. Since the seventeenth century, generation after generation of Parkers had been protestant ministers, though he had become something of a rebel against his own traditions. Eddie was a "picture book prince," and had a "nice clean name."[2] Even as they became passionately intimate, Dorothy didn't allow herself to think that anything permanent would come of this affair. She was too absorbed in her own shortcomings to estimate his. She confessed her Jewishness; he didn't care. On the last day of June, Edwin Pond Parker II and Dorothy Rothschild were married in Yonkers, New York.

She was now and would forever remain Dorothy Parker. She might have kept her own name, as non-conformist women were now doing, but Dorothy Parker was not a Village type. Neither was she, at this time, an advocate of women's rights. She needed no instruction in the unequal terms of the battle of the genders, but she was nonetheless indifferent to politics. She was forthright. "I married to change my name from Rothschild to Parker—that is all there was to it."[3] The hateful past, especially if it's imaginary, had to be effaced.

That April, the United States had declared was on the Central Powers. Edward Parker volunteered for ambulance duty in the army and awaited assignment, which added another element of instability to what was a precarious married life. Dorothy certainly meant it when she described, in her "Hate Song," the kind of women she hated most:

> There are domestic ones
> They are the worst.

She was utterly not domestic and "would rather starve than boil an egg for herself."[4] The Parkers spent little time at home, ate in restaurants, and drank a good deal. Looming marital difficulties were postponed when Eddie was sent overseas in May of 1918. Ambulance duty meant transporting the wounded and was a nightmare for him. He became deeply depressed. Dorothy later asserted that he became addicted to morphine as an escape. After the Armistice in November 1918, he was assigned to occupation duty in Germany. She did not see him again until the middle of 1919.

Well before that, her writing career changed dramatically. In the fall of 1917, she was transferred from *Vogue* to *Vanity Fair*. Frank Crowninshield had a moment of inspiration when P.G. Wodehouse, the magazine's regular theatre critic, took a leave of absence. He gave the job to Dorothy. "Her perceptions were so sure, her judgment so unerring," he said, "that she always seemed to hit the centre of the mark." He was right. Hitting a target aptly described Parker's idea of reviewing. It was "more fun to revile than to extol." Conscious of writing for *Vanity Fair*'s sophisticated readers made Dorothy determined to show up the vulgarity of contemporary theatre. A reiterated refrain: "It was a thin month for the drama." Many of the plays were "just naturally poisonous." Or she might be in a puckish mood, saying of a play that it was "an excellent place to do knitting and if you don't knit bring a book."[5]

Dorothy first found her mature voice in prose, an annihilating voice that was cool, acerbic, ironic, its most devastating and compact expression coming in later poetry. The obverse of her popularity as an assassin has been forgotten; when the hard-boiled finally find something to admire, they often go overboard. Her positive reviews of plays and fiction were often fulsome and trite: "Mr. Rudyard Kipling is no slouch at short-story writing;" of Ring Lardner's *Round Up:* "What more are you going to say of a great thing than that it is great?"[6] It was the demolition work that excited people, but there were those who were not amused. She was often cutting about actresses (see, "Actresses: A Hate Song"). Dorothy's mockery of Billie Burke so angered her husband, Florenz Ziegfeld, the most powerful Broadway producer of the day, that he put pressure on Frank Crowninshield, who gave way and fired Dorothy as theater critic in early 1920.

She was quickly hired as theater critic of *Ainsley's*, where for three years she wrote a monthly column, "In Broadway's Playhouse." And she could turn to a very different form of expression, more influential than theater reviewing. This was a curious phenomenon, the Algonquin Round Table or Algonquin Circle, a group that met at the Algonquin Hotel on West 44th Street, close to the offices of *Vanity Fair*, to have lunch and gossip with each other. It was a shifting group, but among the regulars were F.P. Adams, Alexander Woollcott, Harold Ross, later founder of

The New Yorker, Harpo Marx, and Robert Benchley. Additionally, there were three successful playwrights: Robert Sherwood, George Kaufman, and Marc Connelly. And there was Dorothy Parker. She had been introduced to them when she attended a luncheon at the Algonquin to welcome home Alexander Woollcott, the drama critic of *The New York Times*, after his military service. Subsequent lunches followed, and she became one of the boys.

Frank Case, the owner of the Algoquin, came to realize the advertising value of this group, rather to his surprise, for he initially found them not worthy of any special attention. First he reserved a special table for them and, as they became identified with his hotel, moved them into the Algonquin's Rose Room where members sat at the table only by invitation. Instrumental in getting the Algoquinites publicity was a group of press agents who saw to it that the jokes and quips and outrageous comments appeared in newspapers and magazines. The Algonquin Circle was a publicist's dream and publicists' creation.

The Algonquin habitués didn't comment on national or international affairs, or on literature or the arts. They competed to top each other's jokes or puns, and these wisecracks were reported, repeated, and re-repeated. Soon readers looked forward every day or so to the most recent witticism. Robert Benchley, after a rainstorm, said, "Let's get out of these wet clothes and into a dry martini." More memorably, Alexander Woollcott said, "All the things I like to do are either illegal, immoral or fattening." This was New York humor, caustic, dismissive, deflating, relentlessly ironic and perverse. They promoted insult as an amusing gambit. "Hello, repulsive," was Woollcott's way of greeting people. (Kaufman and Moss Hart's play *The Man Who Came to Dinner* introduced Woolcott's rudeness to a national audience.) Spontaneous witticisms were rehearsed. All non-New Yorkers who came to the Big Town and talked as they imagined sophisticated New Yorkers talked, they were writers who didn't write: they told jokes. Woollcott, Adams, and Benchley are unread today. "It took me fifteen years to discover that I had no talent for writing," Benchley remarked, "but I couldn't give it up because by that time I was too famous."[7]

Dorothy's psychiatrist thought, as many have since, that Algonquinites and Algonquin atmosphere were the source of grief for her. "They never spoke about anything for more than a minute, and never in depth and so they were being forced to sell short on the other side of their nature, the Purposeful, striving side." And there was a more damaging aspect as well: "damaging for other people, seeing the amount of time they spent together…as an index of how insecure they all were. One of the results was a terrible malice. Nearly all of them had a terribly malicious streak."[8] This played into one of Dorothy's worst qualities. She was soon identified as a notorious hypocrite, saying one thing to people's faces, then assaulting them after they had gone.

For better and for worse, Dorothy mastered the style and soon came to personify it. She delivered her comments with a deadpan expression that owed something to a writer she admired, Ring Lardner (who occasionally came to the Algonquin and sat, utterly silent, while the others roared). In the verbal rough-and-tumble in the Rose Room, Dorothy was the quickest guy there. Small, very pretty, she too sat silently for long periods of time and then "shook wisecracks" out of her sleeve. The temptation, usually succumbed to, was to go for the immediate effect, the easy laugh. When told of the death of a young man known to her she replied, "What else could he do?" This pointless retort was thought madly amusing. A contemporary observer admired her as a "born artist" who might win an important place in American literature if only she settled down and wrote. But she did not so do. The observer reflected sadly, "All her things are asides."[9]

ALGONQUIN CULTURE CONTRIBUTED to the collapse of her marriage. Edward Parker came back to the United Stated just as Dorothy was hitting her Algonquin stride. He went back to work on Wall Street but was unwell. Making routine, albeit restless, evening tours of speakeasies, both Parkers drank heavily. They moved to an apartment on West 57th Street that became a marital battleground. Though Edward was depressed by it, Dorothy was exhilarated by this version of bohemian life. She began to deride Eddie in his presence, and in the presence of others, telling story after story of his alleged bumbling and failings, depersonalizing him, referring to him only as "he," the same way she had spoken to her step-mother. Being home alone produced the "howling horrors" in her and, when they went out, it was always in groups—the same groups of people who worked, played, and slept together. In 1921 Eddie said that he wanted to move away from New York, which was an idea that was impossible for Dorothy to accept as she made clear with a poem for *Life* magazine, a poem so successful that *Life* reprinted it.

Song Of The Open Country

When lights are low, and the day has died,
　　I sit and dream of the countryside.

Where sky meets earth at the meadow's end,
        I dream of clean and wind-swept space
Where each tall tree is a stanch old friend,
        And each frail bud turns a trusting face.
A purling brook, with each purl a pray'r
        To the bending grass its secret tells;
While, softly borne on the scented air,
        Comes the far-off chime of chapel bells.
A tiny cottage I seem to see,
        In its quaint old garden set apart;
And a Sabbath calm steals over me,
        While peace dwells deep in my brooding heart.
And I thank whatever gods look down
        That I am living right here in town.

The "Roaring Twenties" were now underway, and through the din a small but sharp and unmistakable voice could be heard, telling truths we often deny.

Song for the First of the Month

Money cannot fill our needs,
        Bags of gold have little worth:
Thoughtful ways and kindly deeds
        Make a heaven here on earth.
Riches do not always score,
        Loving words are better far.
Just one helpful act is more
        Than a gaudy motor car.
Happy thoughts contentment bring
        Crabbed millionaires can't know;
Money doesn't mean a thing-
        Try to tell the butcher so!

The varied and fluid social life of New York City obscured its cultural and intellectual divisions. The most familiar of these was the contrast between the Village and Midtown. This had primarily to do with audience. Midtown was popular and commercial, the Village, experimental and hostile to salesmanship. Large national circulation magazines were associated with Midtown, while the Village cherished its "little magazines," tiny in circulation, irregular in publication, magazines "that died to make verse free." Midtown was "middle brow," the Village, "highbrow."

Of course in reality these two cultures overlapped, differences were often blurred. Writers lived in one place and worked in the other. Edmund Wilson, for instance, didn't wish to flaunt his aesthetic purity by writing and working for marginal little magazines, so he lived in the Village but wrote for and edited Midtown journals. Poets divided along these lines as well, depending on how one wrote and for whom. Edna Millay and Marianne Moore, Villagers both, lived near each other but inhabited different poetic spheres. They had nothing to so with one another or with each other's work. Marianne never mentioned Edna in print and Edna had nothing to say about Marianne's poetry. At the same time, Edna and Dorothy Parker moved in separate social circles, but their poetry had many similarities in tone and subject matter. Both wrote for a general audience, influenced each other, and eventually became friends. But between 1913 and 1917 the Modernist Revolution in the arts transformed the old divisions and alignments, dividing audiences along new lines. Modernist art challenged traditional art, but Modernism was by no means identical with the Village's traditions of bohemianism.

5. OVERVIEW:
MODERNISM

THE MODERNIST STORY has been told and retold. The celebrated event was the Armory Show of 1913 in New York City at which for the first time a large number of people, not just artists, saw examples of the new painting and sculpture. The notorious scandal of the show was Marcel Duchamp's *Nude Descending a Staircase*. Historians have ever since stressed the obtuseness of the public in its response to this and other works of art, which is itself an obtuse interpretation. Many people, neither anti-intellectual nor philistine, liked what they saw, but were puzzled by it, and there was no one to explain the new artistic sensibility. This void was filled in part by photographer and gallery owner Alfred Stieglitz, who in his galleries didn't advise American plutocrats to buy Old Masters, but rather introduced them to and explained new art.

Among the thousands who went to the show was Edna Millay. A serious writer who understood that complexity and clarity were difficult to reconcile, she had once sent two of her poems to William Rose Benét, then with *The Century* magazine. He had returned them to her saying that he could not publish them because they contained obscurities. Edna responded by saying that "some of the obscurities happened to be the best things in them," and refused to rewrite the poems. Yet, confronted by Duchamp, and writing to her mother and sisters about the Armory Show, she lapsed into mockery of the art: "Perfectly unintelligible things done by people they call the 'Cubists,' because they work in cube-shaped shingles. I'll get some postals of the pictures, I think—especially the one called *Nude Descending a Staircase*, and if you can find the figure, outline it in ink and send it back to me." When the show went to Boston, Amy Lowell, well traveled and sophisticated, went to see it and came away puzzled and frowning. "I had a faint idea of what the idiom of Cubism must be, but I could get no clue to the other schools."[1]

For Modernist poetry, there is no single event as dramatic as the Armory Show, but the appearance of T.S. Eliot's *Prufrock and Other Observations* (1917) is useful. When it was published, few people would have known anything about him. Thomas Stearns Eliot (1888-1965) was born and grew up in St. Louis, went to Harvard and, after his 1909 BA degree, studied philosophy at Oxford and in Germany. His early poems were published in the *Harvard Advocate*. In 1914 he decided to live permanently in England. His poetry was influenced by French symbolist poets, and by Ezra Pound, whose ideas and editing were crucial to him. In the half decade between *Prufrock* and *The Waste Land* (1922), despite unrelenting denigration and derision by critics, Eliot vaulted from obscurity to preeminence as the leading representative of Modernist verse. His critical essays, in which he surveyed with immense assurance the past and the current condition of poetry, were as influential as his poetry. His followers, it must be added, then proceeded to be as ungenerous and derisive about traditional poetry as its opponents had been about Modernism.

Eliot's reflections on American poetry and poets in the early years of the twentieth century, when he began writing poetry, would come to be the prevailing view and, therefore, demand our attention. Surveying the American landscape before 1917, he characterized it as "a complete blank," asserting that "there was no poet who could have been of use." He believed that Algernon Swinburne was the last significant poet writing in English. To the question, "Where do we go from Swinburne?" he could only reply that "the answer appeared to be nowhere."[2] In his magisterial way he dismissed any poetry that was of no personal interest or use to him. The limitations of his interest and knowledge should not be allowed to obscure our perception of what actually was happening in America.

Far from being a "complete blank," the poetry of this group of American women was vital and diverse, ranging from early Modernist work (which Eliot unaccountably overlooked) to traditional verse that was itself varied in form and tone. It is important to emphasize that the work of the newcomers to Manhattan whom we have already encountered was augmented by other women poets and editors, also diverse in social class, personal values, and aesthetic aims. They, like the Manhattan poets, did not constitute a self-conscious movement but came to know each other's work and often supported each other, so avoiding the desolating sense, common for American writers of all kinds, of working alone. They did not pretend to know the direction in which poetry was tending in this wildly confusing and exciting time, but they could reply to Eliot's other observation by answering that they were most certainly going somewhere. Who were they and what were they doing?

Chicago played an important role. Harriet Monroe (1860-1935) was born there, educated in Washington, D.C., and lived for a number of years in New York City before returning to Chicago, where she wrote about theatre and architecture and published her first collection, *Valeria and Other Poems*, in 1892. *The Dance of the Seasons* followed almost two decades later in 1911, and she went on writing until her death. Her poetry was conventional in form and expression, but she was determined to broaden the range of subject matter and to bring poetry more closely in touch with aspects of everyday life.

Radio

"I caught a fella last night in the South Pacific --
He was on a freighter way beyond New Zealand.
And what do you think he said to me, that guy?"
The young radio man was talking.

"'How did the Cubs come out today?' he said --
'How did the Cubs come out?' Nothing he wanted
But that fool game! 'They got it in the neck,'
I answered him -- ten thousand miles across --
'The Pirates chewed 'em up' 'The hell they did!'
'Say, where's the sun out your way?' I ticked off --
'Here it went down an hour or two ago.'
'It'll be coming up in half an hour,' he answered,
'It's Sunday here.' 'Oh, get a move on you! --
Sunday's most over -- you're in yesterday.'

'Well, it's the same old sun coming or going --
Yesterdays and tomorrows get all mixed up;
We'll cross the line pretty soon. Where are you, buddy?'
'Oh, near Chicago. So long -- see you again.'
So I clicked off and went to bed -- and he
To breakfast probably."

"Do you often talk
So far?" I asked him, wondering.
                                    "Oh, that's nothing!
I talked with Byrd's Antarctic Expedition
The other night. Say, but it's cold down there!"

Whatever the status of her poetry, there is no question about what made her a major figure in the history of American literature in the twentieth century. She conceived and realized *Poetry: A Magazine of Verse*, the first issue of which appeared in September 1912. Its circulation was modest but not its influence, which was far reaching. It opened new vistas for many of its readers. Louise Bogan remembered, "It was a great thing to have it in the same country, to be able to read its bound volumes in the library, for a young person at once eager for and abashed by its achievements." In the two decades after its founding, almost all the important American poets contributed to it. The first issue contained two poems by Ezra Pound, who served as its European correspondent for a number of years. It was in *Poetry* that Eliot's "The Love Song of J. Alfred Prufrock" appeared in 1915, two years before its book publication. The magazine remained open to most kinds of verse, though Monroe came to dislike poetry which "did not make sense."[3]

Another advocate of the new directions in poetry was *The Little Review*, also Chicago-based and edited by two intrepid women, Margaret Anderson (1886-1973), and Jane Heap (1887-1964). Outlasting many of its contemporaries, it was published irregularly from 1914 to 1929. It welcomed any kind of poetry, its motto being "Applied Anarchism." The magazine's European editor was—who else?—Ezra Pound. Marianne Moore published some poems in *The Little Review*. Eventually she was "not heartily in sympathy with [it] though I have supported other magazines for which less could be said."[4] She never published in it again.

Her disapproval had to do with *The Little Review's* greatest aesthetic distinction, that it published James Joyce in defiance of conventional notions of obscenity. This was a complicated matter for Marianne and revealed her prudish side. She had said of Joyce's *Dubliners*: "It is pretty nearly a manual I think of the fundamentals of composition;" yet when *The Little Review* published *Ulysses*, she drew back, claiming that the novel didn't hold her attention enough to allow her to finish any section of it; but her real objections were to the novel's language and sexual candor. "I accept mongrel art but a flavor of the exceptional must be there along with the negligible."[5] Her views about these matters would come back to trouble her when she became an editor.

Of all the expatriate American writers associated with Modernism, Gertrude Stein was the most notorious, subject to ridicule and silly publicity. Born in Pittsburgh, Pennsylvania, her youth was spent in Oakland, California. She was educated at Harvard and Johns Hopkins. Emigration to France in 1904 followed and she was soon in the milieu of advanced Parisian painters centering on Pablo Picasso, whose friend and patron she became. She possessed an impressive capacity for self-dramatization, presenting herself as an oracle, the high priestess of modern art, writing in a language few others could understand. She preceded even H.D. as a Modernist poet in America. As early as 1914, a small collection of her poems was privately published in New York City. *Tender Buttons* was a puzzle. Stein's witty and playful delight in words was part of a serious effort to convert Cubist painting into words, not bothering with logical meaning.

What Do I See?

A very little snail.

A medium sized turkey.

A small band of sheep.

A fair orange tree.

All nice wives are like that.

Listen to them from here.

Oh.

You did not have an answer.

Here.

Yes.

Gertrude Stein

A Very Valentine

Very fine is my valentine.
Very fine and very mine.
Very mine is my valentine very mine and very fine.
Very fine is my valentine and mine, very fine very mine and
mine is my valentine.

She didn't return to visit and tour America until the nineteen thirties. As love was not her subject, she played no personal part in the women's poetry movement, but as newspaper and magazines writers began, as a joke, to quote from the poems in *Tender Buttons*, it became influential after all.

6. AMY LOWELL

As DIRECTOR GENERAL of Modernist poetry, Ezra Pound exercised influence in many ways, encouraging other poets, publishing his own Imagist verse in *Poetry* and in the *Little Review*; but his most important achievement in America was his forming an always precarious alliance with Amy Lowell who, even in this gallery of remarkable women, stands out as a much neglected poet, critic, biographer, advocate of poetry of all kinds, and as a vital and colorful person.

She was born in Boston on February 9, 1879, the youngest of five children (two others died in infancy)—brothers nineteen and seventeen, sisters sixteen and twelve years older. Her parents, Augustus Lowell and Katherine Lawrence, included in their joint ancestry many distinguished names—Cabots and Putnams among them, but though their families went back ten generations, it was in the nineteenth century that fortunes were made and leadership assumed in New England's textile industry, as evidenced by the two centers of cotton manufacturing: Lowell and Lawrence, Massachusetts.

Augustus graduated from Harvard, sustained interests in horticulture and science, while maintaining the family tradition by going into cotton manufacturing. Quiet and self-effacing, he had a reputation for being stern and hard, but in fact he was supportive of the children and devoted to the idea of family. He bought an estate in Brookline, where he could gather together under one roof his seven family members; he called it "Sevenels." Its garden would become famous and very important for Amy. Katherine was more literary. She supervised the children's absorption of culture in museums, theatre, and travel in Europe, and she is credited by all as bestowing on them her positive temperament.

Amy was educated in private schools and by tutors and led a lively social life as child, girl, and young woman. Between eight and nine years of age, there were two developments that shaped her later life. At age eight she began to be over-weight, due probably to a glandular condition about which nothing was known at the time. At nine she began writing poetry and, in school and at home, immersed herself in books. She could hardly have escaped awareness of literature and of writing, even had she wished to do so. The most celebrated Lowell was not a cotton manufacturer but cousin James Russell Lowell (1819-1891), poet and man of letters, whose reputation overshadowed everyone else in the family—something that she rather resented for many years. She wrote her first poem at age nine, on what was a surprising subject for a Bostonian:

Chacago

Chacago, ditto
the land of

the free.
It is on lake
Mich'gan, and
not on the sea.
It has some
fine houses
in the suburbs
I'm told
And its people
are rolling in
silver and
gold....

Little or no poetry followed from this beginning. At thirteen she turned to writing fairy stories, slowly and laboriously, and when she couldn't manage the writing, dictated them to her mother. Finally, the two of them turned this collaboration into a pamphlet, *Dream Drops, or Stories From Fairy Land*, which was printed by the family. Copies were sold to raise money for a local charity.

Of our poets, Amy Lowell had the most cultural advantages but was the least precocious. Her schools were uninspired and her reading erratic: eighteenth century prose in school and, on her own, Dickens and Thackeray. Her parents had forbidden her to read Louisa May Alcott's stories because they thought them to be ungrammatical and untrue to life. She read them (and agreed with her parents). She was positively hostile to poetry for a while. "We all hate the poetry we learnt in schools."[1] The nearest she came to contemporary American literature was Washington Irvings's *Rip Van Winkle*.

In 1891 Amy made her social debut. However, instead of making the first steps on the path, familiar to any young woman of her class and background, toward marriage and children, she turned her back to that. Though she took part in the social activities of her contemporaries, she showed no interest in marriage, then or later. There seemed to her to be an alternative possibility in scholarship and writing. Her brothers served as examples. Percival spent several years in Japan and wrote four influential and readable books about the Far East. Abbott wrote about government and embarked on an academic career at Harvard that would eventually lead to the presidency of the University. But she wanted no part of that, being determined to avoid the clutches of conventional, unimaginative academia.[2]

For Amy the real significance of 1891 was that it marked the beginning of a decade of heartache. Her mother died in 1895 and her father in 1900. She bought Sevenals from her siblings and lived in it for the rest of her life. The end of the century found her, at twenty-six, in her own estate, with a sizable fortune at her command, independent as few women were at the time, but still uncertain about what her future would be.

In the middle of the previous decade, she had taken some steps toward controlling her future. She saw a performance in Boston of Victor Hugo's *Ruy Blas* by a renowned French actor, Jean Mounet-Sully. In the months that followed she frantically began reading Hugo, "which opened the doors of poetry for me." This was followed by her discovery of the poetry of John Keats. "I surrendered completely to poetry." Another formative event came in 1902 when, like Sara Teasdale, Amy was overwhelmed by the presence of Eleanora Duse. She had seen Duse on her two earlier American tours and had been impressed, but Duse's third tour, performing the plays of Gabrielle D'Annunzio, with whom she had a much-publicized, torrid affair, was triumphant. After Duse's performance Amy went home and wrote a poem.

"What really happened was that Duse's performance revealed me to myself." Amy knew nothing about the techniques of poetry. "I had never heard of free verse…I had never analyzed blank verse—I was ignorant as anyone could be." Writing that poem "loosed a bolt in my brain and I found out where my true function lay."[3]

For the next eight years, in a fever of excitement, she studied poetry and wrote poems, bought Keats manuscripts, and wrote poems, traveled to Europe, and wrote more poems. By 1910 she was publishing them in national magazines and, the next year, set about collecting and selecting for a book, *A Dome of Many Colored Glass*, which appeared in 1912. She was thirty-three. The book was modeled as closely as possible on the first edition of Keat's *Lamia*, its title taken from Shelley's poem about Keats.

Reviewers were tepid, thought it sentimental and conventional, and failed to note the flashes of originality and vivid imagery. Rightly, she later stood up for it, insisting that "it contains certain poems which are quite satisfactory as any I have done." Among them was one inspired by Sevenels, the "dear garden of my childhood."[4]

The Fruit Garden Path

The path runs straight between the flowering rows,
A moonlit path, hemmed in by beds of bloom,
Where phlox and marigolds dispute for room
With tall, red dahlias and the briar rose.
'T is reckless prodigality which throws
Into the night these wafts of rich perfume
Which sweep across the garden like a plume.
Over the trees a single bright star glows.

Dear garden of my childhood, here my years
Have run away like little grains of sand;
The moments of my life, its hopes and fears
Have all found utterance here, where I stand;
My eyes ache with the weight of unshed tears,
You are my home, do you not understand?

At the same time she became aware of the new poetry across the Atlantic. "I had been writing poetry in accordance with my own inclination," she wrote, "and I made the discovery that what I had been writing was Imagist poetry. New ideas were descending through the air, ready to settle into whatever minds were good soil."[5] Harriet Monroe gave her a letter of introduction to Ezra Pound, and she traveled to London to meet him and his fellow Imagists. Pound was receptive, then balky, eager for a recruit (with money) and assertive, but he had met his match in assertiveness. On the whole, Amy and the Imagists got on well. She made good friends with H.D., Richard Aldington, and with an expatriate American who was sympathetic to Imagism but not one of the inner circle, James Gould Fletcher. They became very close and Amy was particularly fond of his poetry. She also established a strong and lasting friendship with D.H. Lawrence, with whom she corresponded copiously and candidly. (She also helped Lawrence financially.) The history of the fallings-in and fallings-out between Pound and Lowell has been fully written about and can be summed up for our purposes by saying that Amy returned to the United States eager to put all her time and energy into the battle "to put Imagism on the map," by which she meant *her* conception of it. A first step was to publish a poem in *Des Imagistes*, a poem both Imagist and erotic which makes a remarkable contrast with her garden poem from *A Dome of Many Colored Glass*.

In a Garden

Gushing from the mouths of stone men
To spread at ease under the sky
In granite-lipped basins,
Where iris dabble their feet
And rustle to a passing wind,
The water fills the garden with its rushing,
In the midst of the quiet of close-clipped lawns.

Damp smell the ferns in tunnels of stone,
Where trickle and plash the fountains,
Marble fountains, yellowed with much water.

Splashing down moss-tarnished steps
It falls, the water;
And the air is throbbing with it.
With its gurgling and running.
With its leaping, and deep, cool murmur.

And I wished for night and you.
I wanted to see you in the swimming-pool,
White and shining in the silver-flecked water.
While the moon rode over the garden,
High in the arch of night,
And the scent of the lilacs was heavy with stillness.

Night, and the water, and you in your whiteness, bathing!

The Imagist cause released her formidable will and orga-
nizational skills. She became a whirlwind of activity, tirelessly
promoting Imagism and her own verse, but above all, and most

generously, the cause of poetry, including lecturing before responsive (and unresponsive) audiences. When people sniffed that she was promoting "Amyism," she paid no heed. She was entirely free of any hypocrisy about equalitarianism and democracy, and contemptuous of those who tried to gain popular favor. Yet she made no distinction of class or ancestry in promoting worthy poets where she found them, was generous with her time and with her money—people were not bashful in asking for support. In 1915, 1916, and 1917 she financed and edited three anthologies of the new poetry, all called *Some Imagist Poets*. Each was eagerly read by poets and sold over 1,000 copies.

The poems came flowing through her. She published her next volume of lyrics, *Sword Blades and Poppy Seed* (1914), which commanded the attention of reviewers and established her as a poet. The reviewers observed that her poems combined the delicate clarity and precise observation of Imagism along with her own distinct voice.

The Pike

In the brown water.
Thick and silver-sheened in the sunshine.
Liquid and cool in the shade of the reeds.
A pike dozed.
Lost among the shadows of stems
He lay unnoticed.
Suddenly he flicked his tail,
And a green-and-copper brightness
Ran under the water.
Out from under the reeds
Came the olive-green light,

And orange flashed up
Through the sun-thickened water.
So the fish passed across the pool,
Green and copper,
A darkness and a gleam,
And the blurred reflections of the willows on the opposite bank
Received it.

She would never be associated with the poetry of ordinary people and of everyday life, but she would apply her Imagist inspiration to contrasting idealized images with ordinary appearance.

Music

The neighbor sits in his window and plays the flute.
From my bed I can hear him,
And the round notes flutter and tap about the room,
And hit against each other,
Blurring to unexpected chords.
It is very beautiful,
With the little flute-notes all about me,
In the darkness.

In the daytime,
The neighbor eats bread and onions with one hand
And copies music with the other.
He is fat and has a bald head,
So I do not look at him,
But run so quickly past his window.
There is always the sky to look at,
Or the water in the well!

But when night comes and he plays his flute,
I think of him as a young man,
With gold seals hanging from his watch,
And a blue coat with silver buttons.
As I lie in my bed
The flute-notes push against my ears and lips,
And I go to sleep, dreaming.

SHE BECAME A dominant much-publicized personality—"an event, a national phenomenon, a freak of nature, a dynamo on the loose"[6]—in what was popularly called the Poetry War waged between the innovators and the traditionalists. Her lectures in the East and Middle West were constantly in the newspapers. She was plainspoken, cheerful, and argumentative. She also elicited derision and resentment and provoked remarkable and surprising outbursts of anger. Her numerous forays into New York City to address the shocked and angry women of the Poetry Society were perhaps predictably regarded as a "Bostonian invasion." These lectures gained greater currency by being turned into books—*Six French Poets* (1915), and *Tendencies in American Poetry* (1917).

Part of her notoriety resulted from the portrayal of her as an oddity, with quirks of behavior that made her a "character." What could after all be more comic than that an aristocratic Bostonian woman was fostering radical verse? Journalists recounted her eccentricities—working all night and sleeping till the afternoon; mirrors in her estate shrouded in black; and most gleefully reported, the sister of the President of Harvard smoking cigars in public!

Amy fought the new poetry's battles, and won—not by herself; but she was a major influence. She succeeded in putting

Imagism on the map, but she didn't see that as an end itself. Imagism was only a skirmish in the larger war, which was between *vers libre*, free verse, which Amy preferred to call "cadenced verse," and traditional forms. She rallied the troops. "I hope young poets will follow me in opening up the still hardly explored possibilities of verse libre."[7]

Tendencies in American Poetry made this perfectly clear. It was a reasonable, readable statement of her sense of the historical situation and of her ambitions. She identified American culture as the culture of the new and therefore believed that innovation in art as in everything else was true to cherished national values. "We are no longer colonies of this or that other land," she wrote, "but ourselves, different from all other people whatsoever." In American poetry the prevailing, irresistible tendency was for change. So she identified three pairs of American poets who truly represented both achievement and promise for the future, Literary Evolutionists, Revolutionists, and Imagists, all agents of change. Robert Frost and Edwin Arlington Robinson, Evolutionists, brought to the new poetry their emphasis on realism. Edgar Lee Masters and Carl Sandburg, Revolutionists, carried change further by breaking away from conventional meters. And the Imagists, H.D. and John Gould Fletcher, represented "the full achievement of the modern point of view." Amy published Hilda's photograph over the signature "H.D." in *Tendencies in American Poetry*, and this angered Doolittle. "The initials had no identity attached," she explained. "They could have been pure spirit. But with this I'm embodied." This didn't seriously disturb her friendship with Amy.[8]

Ezra Pound had been tiresome in his skepticism about Amy's fidelity to Imagism, but beyond that he was certainly perceptive in understanding that her poetic aims were not Modernist, and, ironically, that they might come in time to be seen as traditional.

But even as the battle about the new poetry raged in the late teens, Amy moved on, true to her faith, to what were new forms of poetry for her, abandoning Imagist-influenced lyrics entirely. In 1916 she published *Men, Women and Ghosts*, followed by *Can Grande's Castle* in 1918, both of them in a form called "polyphonic prose," explaining what it was. "I have called it polyphonic because it permits the use of all the methods: cadence, rhyme, alliteration, and assonance, also perhaps true metre for a few minutes."[9]

Most people didn't bother to distinguish any difference between "new" poetry and "modern" poetry. For example, Margaret Anderson, whose *Little Review* was a leading supporter of radical departures. She said of Amy, "she wanted to subsidize modern poetry and push it ahead faster than it could go by its own impetus." Her recollection of her first meeting with Amy is no doubt not an accurate transcription, but it captures the impression of relentless power that Amy communicated. Amy said to her, "I love *The Little Review*...and I have money. You haven't. Take me with you."[10] Presumably this meant as an editor. Whatever language was used, Anderson turned down the offer.

Amy combined contradictory modes of behavior, amiability and imperiousness. There was the practical manager who made all decisions about her investments herself. At Sevenels "the 'business' of reading and writing verse went forward as though controlled by a general manager of a cotton mill." And yet there was also the self-conscious performer. "Amy was the distinguished character actress" and Edna Millay "the small red haired juvenile lead. Not unlike the public entrances and exits of Hollywood movie stars, the two women from New England in New York gave the 'new poetry' a touch of theatrical brilliance that writers of poetry seldom achieved."[11] And then, having led the battle on behalf of new directions in poetry, Amy demonstrated her adherence to the idea of new directions in poetry by once again embracing change, this time a return to traditional forms. She abandoned the "polyphonic prose" of the two previous books and went back to lyric poetry. She gathered 171 poems, from magazines and anthologies, and in 1919 published *Pictures of the Floating World*. The title referred to poems, in a "quasi-Oriental idiom," which reflected "the inspiration that both poets and painters are discovering in Oriental art." Those poems made up Part One of the work. Part Two consisted of lyrics on many subjects, deriving "from everywhere and nowhere as is the case with all poetry."[12]

The succinctness of Japanese haiku and Imagist precision combined can be seen in poems such these:

Middle Age

Like black ice
Scrolled over with unintelligible patterns
　　　　　　　　by an ignorant skater
Is the dulled surface of my heart.

Amy was not considered a "nature" poet, but evocations of the natural world often appeared in her poetry in various forms—among them, Imagist couplets.

Trees in Winter

Pine-Trees　　　　　　　　　　Cedars:

Black clouds slowly swaying　　Layered undulations
Over a white earth.　　　　　　Roofing naked ground.

Hemlocks	Almonds
Coned green shadows	Flaring needles
Through a falling veil.	Stabbing at a grey sky.
Elm-Trees	Weeping Cherries
Stiff black threads	Tossing smoke
Lacing over silver.	Swept down by wind.
	Oaks
	Twisted beams.
	Cased in alabaster.

What an amazing seven years of achievement it had been. Since *A Dome of Many Colored Glass* in 1912, she had published four volumes of poetry, three anthologies, two historical surveys and thirty-five reviews and articles in magazines and newspapers. Only Elinor Wylie would rival her in productivity over a short period of time.

7. MARIANNE MOORE

THE MAGNET OF artistic freedom and experimentation drew many Americans from small towns throughout the country to New York City, and to Greenwich Village, in these first decades of the twentieth century. Marianne Moore's arrival did not fit this pattern. It was pure chance that she and her mother found themselves in the Village in 1918, as Marianne explained in a letter. "By reason of my brother's entering the navy, my mother and I are living at present in New York in a small apartment."[1] Marianne's "at present" suggested that their stay there might be a brief one, which would have surprised none of their friends and acquaintances, for whom the idea of the Moores living in the Village was bizarre. Marianne was thirty-one years old. Her personal habits were firmly established. Organization and responsibility were the order of the day. While Edna Millay was burning candles at both ends, and Dorothy Parker was dominating the caustic crowd at the Algonquin, Marianne was working at the Hudson Park branch of the New York Public Library. She adhered strictly to a carefully worked out half-time schedule, at $30 per month, and spent much of the rest of her time at home writing poetry. Her mother admiringly noted her daughter's "grim sternness" and "monk-like severity."

The dynamics in the Moore family were changing. Warner had given up his pastorate for Navy service as a chaplain, a shock to Mary, to whom it seemed a lessening of his religious faith. And then in 1918 he married. Marianne's relationship with her mother was also changing, slowly, privately, less obviously than Warner's but in ways that produced some strain and pain. As a published poet, she began to think about worldly success and to become part of intellectual and artistic circles in the Village. She enjoyed music, the theatre and the museums abundantly close at hand. She began a poem, "Museums," never completed, with this revealing observation:

> One goes to a museum to refresh one's mind with the
> Appearance of what one has already valued.

The appearance of things and how to describe this in words was one of her central concerns, captured in a recollection of her by Louise Bogan, one of several women poets (among them Elinor Wylie and Genevieve Taggard) whose acquaintance she made at the library. Louise was supporting herself by pasting book pockets into books alongside Marianne, who was "continually comparing the small objects with which we worked—mucilage brushes and ink and stamping rubbers—two oddly analogous objects; and she smiled often and seemed happy." Marianne was kind, but distant, treating Louise almost as if she were invisible, "as indeed I probably was," Louise remembered, "being, at that time, more or less invisible to myself, as well."[2] The two of them never talked about poetry, but the time would come when they would know each other's work intimately and admiringly.

Away from the library, the city was replete with unexpected pleasures. "I like New York, the little quiet part of it in which my mother and I live. I like to see the tops of the masts from our door and go to the wharf and look at the craft on the river." That was easy, but one aspect of Village life was not—parties, like the one she described to Warner as "a jammed unsorted Mammoth gathering…the lights were dim and at the same time glaring and smoke crowded the atmosphere." She believed that "some sort of hand mask ought to be invented or hindoo veils for the city social event."[3]

She stood out from the crowd. This was not an affectation. She was a genuine nonconformist and resisted obligatory informality, dressing as she had always dressed, in lady-like clothes (Village women on the whole were not lady-like). This only made her of greater interest to people. Like Sara Teadsale, she said she disliked the custom of poets reading their work aloud; but unlike Teasdale, she took part and did it well. She was clever. Edmund Wilson believed her to be "the most intellectual woman he had ever met."[4] She found stimulating people with whom to talk. The person for whom Village life and Village parties were deeply objectionable was her mother, who intensely disapproved of most of what she saw and heard. Mary was disconcerted by Mariannes's attraction to Village culture. But what could she do? What alternative could she offer? It was a long way from Carlisle and Kirkwood. While Marianne went to parties, Mary went to Bible classes.

It was in the midst of this diverse and rapidly changing culture that Marianne established her reputation as a Modernist poet, but one who defied categorization. She never belonged to any of the Modernist movements—Vorticists, Imagists, Futurists, or others. Her Modernism was like no one else's. When Ezra Pound wrote to her, asking if she would explain her poetry and identify which poets had influenced it, she replied that her verse was an arrangement of stanzas, each "an exact duplicate of every other stanza." The form of the original stanza was due to chance or to whatever seemed suitable to the subject. The meter of her verse was not syllabic, as critics said and continued to say. As for "influences," Pound had mentioned the name of Jules La Forgue, who had profoundly influenced Eliot. Marianne replied that she didn't know the name. What writers had influenced her? Henry James, William Blake, Thomas Hardy and the "minor prophets." Did that illuminate the darkness for Pound?[5]

Marianne insisted on one thing—she was not trying to be obscure. Quite the reverse. "Anything that is a stumbling block to my reader is a matter of regret to me." She cherished precise observation and description. "Too much cannot be said for the necessity in the artist of exact science." She was a bookish person and owed much to books, embedded direct quotations from books and from magazines in her poetry. She read a good deal of literary criticism and believed that good criticism could inspire and teach poets. In this she agreed with Louise Bogan who wrote of Modernism in America that "the creative side had shot ahead with very little accompanying critical background."[6] Contemporary poets of all kinds, Louise argued, should strive to establish a "broad and deep" aesthetic criticism. Marianne Moore, Amy Lowell, and Genevieve Taggard had achieved this to some extent, but it was Louise who excelled.

Marianne's explanation to Ezra Pound about her poetry left out an important aspect: that aesthetic judgment might have a spiritual basis, a point of view alien to most writers of Modernist verse. The spiritual basis of Marianne's poetry became more pronounced in later years, but it was present in much of her earlier work. This was an aspect she did not discuss with Pound or with anyone else outside the family. (The opinions of family members in this respect meant a great deal to her.)

The picture of the straight-laced, conventional Marianne Moore in close contact with raffish Village culture and the worldly mores of the international *avant-garde* surprised observers, but not the Moore family. Mary and Warner prized Marianne's independence of mind and her determination to go her own way as a poet. Marianne often asked her mother's and brother's opinions. When she said to her mother about one of her poems, "How did you permit me to let this be printed?" her mother answered, "You didn't ask my advice." Queried about another poem she said only, "Well, it won't do;" and about another, "I like it." Warner was terse but supportive. "If your poem is not taken by the *Book News*— whatever you do, don't quit."[7]

Warner's and Mary's opinions were idiosyncratic and personal, like Marianne's poetry, but they rested on the bedrock of a firm belief that, whatever its form, Marianne's poetry was not essentially Modernist but spiritual. Warner always saw her poems in "exalted terms" and believed that Marianne was raising secular art to "a level commensurate with his religious vocation."[8]

That Marianne Moore, whose poetry many considered part of the radical Modernist movement, was concerned with spiritual values, though that disconcerted Modernists, does not seem surprising to us, who have the benefit of hindsight and are aware of T.S. Eliot's own traditional Christianity. And Marianne's spiritual values might have been apparent from one of her poems of this period.

When I Buy Pictures

or what is closer to the truth,
when I look at that of which I may regard myself as the
                                   imaginary possessor,
I fix upon what would give me pleasure in my average moments:
the satire upon curiosity in which no more is discernible
than the intensity of the mood;
or quite the opposite—the old thing, the medieval decorated
                                         hat-box,
in which there are hounds with waists diminishing like the
                                waist of the hourglass,
and deer and birds and seated people;
it may be no more than a square of parquetry; the literal
                                biography perhaps,
in letters standing well apart upon a parchment-like expanse;
an artichoke in six varieties of blue; the snipe-legged
                              hieroglyphic in three parts;
the silver fence protecting Adam's grave, or Michael taking
                              Adam by the wrist.
Too stern an intellectual emphasis upon this quality or that
                              detracts from one's enjoyment.
It must not wish to disarm anything; nor may the approved
                              triumph easily be honored—
that which is great because something else is small.
It comes to this: whatever sort it is,
it must be "lit with piercing glances into the life of things";
it must acknowledge the spiritual forces which have made it.

As confirmation of her growing achievement, 1921 saw the publication of Marianne's first volume of poetry. This came about indirectly. In the five years from 1916 to the end of 1920, she had published thirty poems in various magazines. Several people urged her to bring these together in a book so that her work could be brought into clearer focus. Ezra Pound bluntly warned her, "You will never sell more than five hundred copies as your work demands mental attention."[9] So it is not surprising that out of a mixture of modesty and anxiety about the scrutiny her poems would be subjected to in book form, she resisted these urgings.

The matter was taken out of Marianne's hands by her friendships with H.D. and their mutual respect for each other's poetry. Marianne said of H.D.'s verse that it touched "the inner world of interacting reason and unreason," which was true of her personal life as well. H.D. had become aware of Richard Aldington's numerous infidelities, left him and moved in with the composer Cecil Gray, became pregnant by him and then left him. After the birth of a daughter, and in a state of despair, H.D. met Annie Winnifred Ellerman (1894-1983), a poet and novelist who wrote under the name of "Bryher," (one of the Scilly islands). She was the heir to an immense English fortune and became an anonymous patron of the arts and of artists.

Bryher and H.D. became lovers/partners and Bryher saved H.D.'s sanity. As rehabilitation, she took H.D. to Greece, with momentous consequences for H.D.'s poetry. In 1920-1921, they came to America and paid a call on the Moores, who were charmed by both, but especially by Bryher. Marianne and Bryher began a steady correspondence, sometimes two or three letters a month, which lasted for forty years.

When they returned to England, H.D. and Bryher took up the matter of the publication of a volume of Moore's poetry. Bryher financed publication, Harriet Shaw Weaver had it printed by The

Egoist Press, and early in July of 1921 a copy of the book appeared in Marianne's mailbox. She was annoyed because she had not authorized the book, but also moved at this expression of affection and respect for her poetry and for her. She especially liked the Cretan pottery pattern on the dust jacket, and the handsome printing.

Poems had a tiny print run and was a commercial failure, as Ezra Pound had predicted and as Bryher and Friends must have assumed it would be, but at least there was now a body of accessible work for those who cared to read it. Glenway Westcott, a young novelist and critic, didn't underestimate the difficulties involved in reading Marianne's "aristocratic art." The popular mind, he thought, would avoid "paths so stony, steep and winding."[10]

The uniqueness of her voice and vision is evident in a poem about New York City. It is a description of maritime New York, its rivers and wharves and ships, its sights, sounds and smells, which expands beyond the city to consider ships and sailing as one of the oldest human activities.

Dock Rats

There are human beings who seem to regard the place as craftily
        as we do—who seem to feel that it is a good place to come
    home to. On what a river, wide—twinkling like a chopped sea
                        under some
        of the finest shipping in the

    world: the square-rigged Flemish four-master, the liner, the battleship
                    like the two-
        thirds submerged section of an iceberg; the tug
    dipping and pushing, the bell striking as it comes; the steam yacht,
                        lying
        like a new arrow on the

stream; the ferry-boat—a head assigned, one to each compartment,
            making
    a row of chessmen set for play. When the wind is from the east,
    the smell is of apples, of hay; the aroma increased and decreased
        as the wind changes;

of rope, of mountain leaves for florists; as from the west,
    it is aromatic of salt. Occasionally a parakeet
    from Brazil, arrives clasping and clawing; or a monkey—tail and
            feet
    in readiness for an over-

ture; all arms and tail; how delightful! There is the sea, moving the
            bulk-
    head with its horse strength; and the multiplicity of rudders
    and propellers; the signals, shrill, questioning, peremptory, diverse;
        the wharf cats and the barge dogs; it

is easy to overestimate the value of such things. One does
    not live in such a place from motives of expediency
    but because to one who has been accustomed to it, shipping is the
        most interesting thing in the world.

Even at this distance in time one is surprised by the fierce-
ness of the criticism of Moore's poetry. The anonymous reviewer
in the London *Times Literary Supplement* scoffed at the "lack of
inspiration under the volley of superficial unconventionality." The
American poet Mark Van Doren thought *Poems* "a product of wit
lacking all beauty or more important, sense." *The Nation*'s review,
entitled "Women of Wit," centered on Edna Millay and Marianne
Moore, recognizing that their poetry came from "independent,
critical, and keen minds. It is feminine, it is fearless, it is fresh.

For better or worse their poetry is here to stay." Better with Millay, worse with Moore. "She wedded wit, but after divorces from beauty and sense. Her manners are those of the absurder coteries, her fastidiousness is that of the insufferable highbrows." Poetry like hers, written for *Others,* made that magazine "difficult to take seriously."[11]

The harshest criticism, however, originated at 14 St. Mark's Court. When Marianne told her mother that several people were urging her to publish a volume of her verse, Mrs. Moore's lips "curled in disdain." "I wouldn't publish," she said.

"Never? You would omit all these things I prize so much?" asked Marianne.

"Yes. They're ephemeral."[12]

Mary Moore and the other critics were entirely wrong.

8. Louise Bogan

Having been lonely for much of her childhood and youth, Louise Bogan reveled in the sociability of Village life, the food and drink at parties, the exciting conversation and poetry and the life of the mind. Members of the Modernist circle around *Others* were welcoming. The studio of Walter Arensberg became a familiar place. It was on one of these occasions that she first met Marianne Moore. The advent of Modernism generated controversy but also great excitement. William Carlos Williams: "The yeast of the new work in the realm of the poem, was tremendously stirring."[1] Louise respected the Imagist desire for precision combined with sensuous feeling, and also respected the parallel effort by Marianne Moore to unite precise observation with conventional poetic stanzas.

However, she didn't limit her friendships to any one group. Her own instincts and inclinations led her away from Modernism. She would experiment with versions of free verse, but her deepest intellectual and emotional allegiance was to the English metaphysical poetry of feeling with the restraint of form. Romanticism was anathema to her, hence her belief that, while she respected Edna Millay's work, it was replete with emotional overflow.

The little magazines were not all Modernist. One that Louise found congenial was *The Measure: A Magazine of Verse*, founded in 1921 by Padriac Colum and Maxwell Anderson. The editors were not entirely inhospitable to free verse, but their general approach was made clear by their assertion that Edna Millay was "just now the most interesting person in American poetry."[2] Traditionalists controlled the anthologies. Louis Untermeyer, the leading anthologist for two decades and thus a very influential figure, wouldn't print Modernist poetry at first, but he got on the bandwagon later when it had established itself. Louise published her work in a wide group of magazines: *Vanity Fair, The New Republic* and *Poetry*. For her the exemplar in terms of understanding new ideas but absorbing them in conventional forms was W.B. Yeats. Having published *Responsibilities* (1917) and *The Wild Swans at Coole* (1921), Yeats was at this time at the apex of his marvelous career.

Ambition drove Louise, though she was assailed frequently by feelings of terror and grief. She began to understand that psychic pain would be a condition of her life, so her primary task as a writer was to work out the relationship between her personal experience and her poetry. This involved her in a paradox. Many of her poems drew directly on the injuries and anguish of her personal life, and yet she despised anything directly autobiographical in poetry because it was crudely egotistical. The answer to this dilemma was that the poet must repress the explicit narrative of her life but then "absorb it along with life itself" into the poem, but the poem reshaped by the imagination. Thus, though she often wrote down her experiences in "the closest possible detail," the "rough and vulgar facts are not there."[3]

In her first year in Greenwich Village she was beginning to write mature verse as a professional. We can follow her as she experienced three complex blows that were eventually transmuted into poetry. The first was the death of her brother Charles, who was killed in combat in France just days before the November 1918 armistice. In the winter and spring of 1919, she reflected intensely on the meaning of a life that seemed to her wasted, to see if she could find any peace of mind about it. There was none. Some things endured, resistant to the passage of time—material things, for instance "struck by the hooves of disaster." And so too did the agony of her loss.

To My Brother Killed (Haumont Wood: October, 1918)

O you so long dead,
You masked and obscure,
I can tell you, all things endure:
The wine and the bread;

The marble quarried for the arch;
The iron become steel;
The spoke broken from the wheel;
The sweat of the long march;

The hay-stacks cut through like loaves
And the hundred flowers from the seed;
All things indeed
Though struck by the hooves

Of disaster, of time due,
Of fell loss and gain,
All things remain,
1 can tell you, this is true.

Though burned down to stone
Though lost from the eye,
I can tell you, and not lie,—
Save of peace alone.

The second blow was the unexpected death of Curt Alexander. Coming to terms with what he had meant to her was a pain-filled, long-term matter. She had loved him, once, or had desired him so ardently as to be the same thing as love. He had enabled her to escape from her parents' miseries. He was the father of her child. She was not to blame for his death, but surely she shared some blame for the disintegration of their marriage. Yet she did not attend his funeral and, in fact, his death simplified her life in some ways. She didn't have to file for divorce and, as she received widow's benefits from the army, Alexander "made it possible for her to start out alone with some small measure of security."[4] Even more, "absorbing his death along with life itself" into a poem reduced the crippling effects of simply thinking about it. In the poem "Survival," the "rough facts" became something else, not so much his death as her survival of it.

The third traumatic episode was the result of the sexual freedom she found in the Village, freedom that meant a series of casual lovers. One affair, however, was not casual and was almost disastrous for her. John Coffee possessed attractive social and political "notions" and irresistible Irish charm, which turned out to be shoplifting charm. The "notions" were perceiving himself to be a defender of the poor, calling attention to their needs by stealing furs. Louise fell for some part of this, or at least for his charm, and came close to being an accomplice to his Robin Hood criminality. Once she waited in his car while he liberated furs from a shop. Their affair lasted two months, at which point Coffee "betrayed" her sexually, plunging her into self-lacerating grief that lasted for years. Coffee was cynically dismissive of what Louise represented, insisting that he stole only to make himself more "articulate," explaining, "That is why I consorted with you litterateurs."[5] Having confessed to the police, he was placed in an insane asylum.

If she was bohemian in her disregard of sexual conventions, she was in other respects a very different sort of bohemian, less casual, more formal and disciplined, as exemplified in her non-sexual friendship with Edmund Wilson, who encouraged her to develop her talents as a critic and historian of literature. Wilson insisted that she begin to write reviews, for he quickly realized how perceptive and fair-minded she was. Louise said that she couldn't do it. He made her sit down at her desk and learn how to do it. "I remember, in the beginning, writing at that desk with tears pouring down my face trying to write a notice. Edmund…would pace behind me and exhort me to go on."[6] This would turn out to be very important to her a decade later.

These two-and-a-half years in New York were ones of hard-earned but modest achievement as a poet. She had written interesting poems, but none she regarded as remotely close to her aspirations. She had made friends and was attracting a little notice from those who read the poetry journals. All this was at the cost of being worn down by the incessant sense of guilt reawakened by the death of loved ones. As she said when she worked in the public library with Marianne Moore, she was becoming "invisible to herself." She began what would be an intense commitment to psychotherapy, going to a Freudian psychiatrist who specialized in treating writers. Occasional visits to the New England country-side, and to visit Maidie, didn't afford relief. New York, which had represented escape, was now the site of her anguish. She had never been to Europe, and in April of 1922, thanks to the generosity of an unidentified lover, she went to Vienna.

LOUISE BOGAN WAS not sentimental about her early years in New York; they were too precarious and pain-filled for that. Nevertheless, she recognized that she owed a very great deal to the city. It had, for a time, been a refuge. Even more, New York offered her "the first true test of her gifts," and nourished her soaring ambition in which she was now fixed and clear: "to become a great poet and woman of letters."[7]

PART THREE

MANHATTAN
1921–1925

1. Elinor Wylie

ELINOR WYLIE HAD "fallen in love with the idea of freedom & poetry & New York." The city offered her what
she desperately needed, to meet poets, intellectuals, and
people in the arts. She wanted "to merge quietly and unobtrusively
with other writers" and especially "to know the younger women
who are doing such beautiful work these days...and to feel I was
(more or less) one of them." She explained the separation from
Horace to her mother in Washington. "Everyone takes you seriously, over there, your work, I mean."[1]

A decade after leaving her first husband, Elinor was leaving
her second. Benét's family was hostile, which only increased his
appeal to her; opposition always emboldened her. But was marriage
to anyone the answer to anything? She had come to some harsh
conclusions about loving men. Women must understand that in
marriage as currently constituted, women were a form of coinage,
to be spent by men. Women could hope for nothing except, at best,

to be able to frustrate men by withholding themselves, sexually and emotionally. A poem written in this period but not published until after her death—was it too harsh for the general public she wished to reach?—powerfully expresses her thoughts about men and love.

From the Wall

Woman, be steel against loving, enfold and define you.
Turn from the innocent look and the arrogant tongue;
You shall be coppery dross to the purses that spend you
Lock up your years like a necklace of emeralds strung.

Lock up your heart like a jewel; be cruel and clever:
Woman, be strong against loving, be iron, be stone;
Never and never and never and never and never
Give for the tears of a lover a tear of your own.

Cover the clutch of your greed with a velvety gloving;
Take from the good if you can, from the vile if you must;
Take from the proud and alone, from the cowardly loving;
Hold out your hands for the pity; accept of the lust.

No more idle tears! No more blubbering!

She moved to 1 University Place in the Village. Like Marianne Moore, she wasn't a Village "type," and had mixed feelings about the place. She wanted to be prominent, but not as a sex symbol. "She liked to pretend that she was a Bohemian," Frank Crowninshield wrote, "but she was too delicately bred to play that role successfully."[2] Her pleasures were subdued, but it was a hard drinking time and place and she eagerly joined in. She arranged her pictures and furniture with care: eighteenth century Sheffield mirror; Wedgwood lamps, blue sofa. The room conveyed individuality but not warmth. Edmund Wilson thought it "rather grand though a little bleak;" but it was a "civilized setting, which in the Village was rather rare."[3]

She drove herself to achieve her newly found ambitions. Headaches, eye aches, and worries about her precarious financial situation—nothing stopped the flow of inspiration that had been released by her escape from personal confinement. She wrote ten poems in the last half of 1920 and continued at the same pace throughout the uncertainties of the first half of 1921, placing her work in important national magazines; six poems in *The New Republic*, four in *Poetry* and one in *The Nation*. She had virtually nothing to do with the little magazines. Occasional appearance wasn't enough, however. She wanted to publish a volume that would establish her as an important figure in the contemporary scene. She "seemed to draw together the frayed strands of her life in her poetry,"[4] collected and arranged thirty-one poems and offered them to several publishers, all of whom turned them down. Alfred Harcourt finally accepted them, and in October, 1921 *Nets to Catch the Wind* appeared. (The poet's words are nets to catch the wind of inspiration.)

THE POETRY SOCIETY awarded it the Ford Prize for the best first volume of poetry. Bill Benét arranged to find "suitable" reviewers for it, and sent it to Edna Millay who responded with the only book review she ever wrote, praising Wylie's "fine equipment of intelligence," her "full powers of sorcery." She stressed that it was an important book in itself but especially merited attention because it was the author's first and "thus marks the opening of yet another door by which beauty may enter to the world." Surprised by the appearance of work by an unknown, reviewers were uniformly impressed by the confidence manifested in the use of traditional poetic forms, and noted that the prevailing tone was a kind of "frigid ecstasy" combined with "aristocratic scorn," as in the poem William Butler Yeats called a "lovely heroic song."[5]

The Eagle and the Mole

Avoid the reeking herd,
Shun the polluted flock.
Live like that stoic bird,
The eagle of the rock.

The huddled warmth of crowds
Begets and fosters hate;
He keeps above the clouds
His cliff inviolate.

When flocks are folded warm,
And herds to shelter run,
He sails above the storm,
He stares into the sun.

If in the eagle's track
Your sinews cannot leap,
Avoid the lathered pack,
Turn from the steaming sheep.

If you would keep your soul
From spotted sight or sound,
Live like the velvet mole:
Go burrow underground.

And there hold intercourse
With roots of trees and stones,
With rivers at their source,
And disembodied bones.

Proud, aristocratic, disdainful of the common and of the sorrow of life, her women endure all with a lion's heart.

A Proud Lady

Hate in the world's hand
Can carve and set its seal
Like the strong blast of sand
Which cuts into steel.

I have seen how the finger of hate
Can mar and mould
Faces burned passionate
And frozen cold.

Sorrowful faces worn
As stone with rain,
Faces writhing with scorn
And sullen with pain.

But you have a proud face
Which the world cannot harm,
You have turned the pain to a grace
And the scorn to a charm.

You have taken the arrows and slings
Which prick and bruise
And fashioned them into wings
For the heels of your shoes.

From the world's hand which tries
To tear you apart
You have stolen the falcon's eyes
And the lion's heart.

What has it done, this world,
With hard finger-tips,
But sweetly chiseled and curled
Your inscrutable lips?

Nets to Catch the Wind did all that could reasonably have been hoped for, making the name Elinor Wylie one to be remembered and reckoned with by a small but discriminating number of readers. Most immediately helpful in establishing a reputation, in addition to Bill Benét's sedulous labors on her behalf, was the fact that Elinor attracted and charmed men who mattered in reviewing and publishing. Louis Untermeyer was the foremost anthologist of traditional poetry and composed *Who's Who* entries that were widely read. As a reviewer he had a gift for phrases that were taken up and quoted by others. On one occasion this boomeranged. He said of *Nets to Catch the Wind* that it was "too brilliant" which Elinor took exception to and caused strain between them for over a year. Eventually Elinor forgave his lapse and later dedicated a sonnet sequence to him.

The two leading members of the Wylie fan club were Carl

van Doren and Carl van Vechten. Van Doren was Elinor's closest friend and a generally positive literary editor of *The Nation*. Edmund Wilson said of him as a reviewer, "He diffuses his mild benignancy upon the excellent and the unworthy alike." Van Vechten, a flamboyant self-promoter whose fantasy novels were once much admired, saw Elinor as a kindred spirit. He thought her novels, "the beautiful essence of her character."[6] The most interesting thing about Van Vechten was that he knew and cared about African culture and played a positive role in the Harlem Renaissance.

In the meantime, hard-pressed for money, Elinor looked around for steady work. Frank Crowninshield offered her a job writing captions for *Vogue*, like Dorothy Parker. However, she turned the offer down and accepted a more suitable position at *Vanity Fair*, assisting Edmund Wilson, who at the time was the literary editor. Elinor helped choose poems for the magazine, contributed some of her own, wrote reviews and occasional articles. It was the only time in her life that she held a salaried position.

Elinor was not a success as a reviewer. She had not paid much attention to the advent of Modernism, as she was confident of her own traditional orientation. When asked, in 1922, to review T.S. Eliot's *The Wasteland*, she was uncertain what to say. Not wanting to offend but unable to offer any insight, her "review was almost unintelligible." But Eliot's poetry didn't shake her own poetic ideals. She wrote a dismissive essay in which writers listed the ten dullest poets they knew. Elinor's choices among Americans were non-traditionalists Walt Whitman and Gertrude Stein.[7]

Exhilarated by success, Elinor began planning a second collection of poems. In the summer of 1922, Benét proposed marriage. Elinor accepted but without taking steps toward getting a divorce. When she finally did file for divorce in the fall, she did not inform Horace or her family. The Benét family objected to the marriage. His mother and sister disliked her, and his father detested her. Elinor's mother was also strongly opposed since marriage would bring Benét's three children into Elinor's life, and she believed that this was the kind of responsibility Elinor would not be able to sustain.

The year 1923 was an emotional rollercoaster. In March, Elinor's divorce was granted, and she and Bill began the requisite six-month waiting period, but then, in August, Elinor heard of the suicide of her sister Constance in Bavaria, the third suicide in seven years of someone close to her, and the wedding was postponed. It was impossible for the family to find out the details about Constance's death. Elinor had not seen her for three years and their relationship had been strained. It was Constance who had been the family member most critical of Elinor's leaving Philip Hinchborn.

On October 5, 1923, Elinor and Bill were married, with no family members present. Elinor kept the name Wylie. A disconcerting flurry of lurid newspaper publicity followed, "another page of the romantic, tragic chronicle which has been Mrs. Wylie's life for the past sixteen years." Elinor was stoical about the publicity. "I hope it is over for good." Many friends were dubious about the marriage. Sinclair Lewis mordantly saw it as Bill Benét sacrificing himself, "the logical conclusion" of his affection for Henry Hoyt, who "killed himself in Bill's apartment, and Bill felt that established a claim for him to die for Elinor." Edmund Wilson said bluntly to Elinor that, from a literary point of view, their marriage was "inappropriate" since she was so superior to Bill as a poet. Instead of rebuking Wilson, Elinor responded in equally blunt terms, "Yes, it would be a pity that a first-rate poet should be turned into a second-rate poet by marrying a third-rate poet." Amy Lowell expressed the opinion of upper-class society. Meeting Elinor in Bill Benét's apartment, she combined congratulations on the "fortunate marriage" with a warning, "If you marry again I shall cut you dead—and I warn you all Society will do the same. You will be nobody."[8]

If 1923 was emotionally exhausting, it was a phenomenal year for Elinor as a writer. During this time, she produced a first novel, *Jennifer Lorn,* and a second book of poems. The novel was dedicated to her mother. It was set in eighteenth-century England and Persia. She did a great deal of reading to establish the background accurately, but the novel is escapist fantasy and the writing is elaborately descriptive. The story is about the conflict between art and human feeling. The beautiful heroine was of course modeled on Elinor, the domineering villain, Horace. The tone is icy, highly stylized, clever.

HER SECOND VOLUME of poetry was *Black Armour.* Benét acutely saw the poems as growing out of their personal situation, "putting on armor we must wear against the world," which he thought explained the darker mood. Carl Van Doren enthused about the poems' "perfect finish," and "cold fire," while Archibald Macleish discerned a masculine mind and a feminine method. Readers found a familiar theme, women sacrificing themselves for men—for what purpose?[9]

Epitaph

For this she starred her eyes with salt
And scooped her temples thin.
Until her face shone pure of fault.
From the forehead to the chin.

In coldest crucibles of pain
Her shrinking flesh was fired
And smoothed into a finer grain
To make it more desired.

Pain left her lips more clear than glass:
It colored and cooled her hand.
She lay a field of scented grass
Yielded as pasture land.

For this her loveliness was curved
And carved as silver is:
For this she was brave but she deserved
A better grave than this.

As before, reviewers noted the prevalence of something "cold" or "frozen," but one poem at least was a simple and moving plea.

Pity Me

Pity the wolves who prowl unsleeping
  Guarding the pasture from a thief;
Pity the proud leopards weeping
  Tears of subtle grief.

Pity the savage panthers sheathing
  Sharp disdain in silken gloves;
Pity the golden lions breathing
  Fire upon their loves.

Pity the prickly star that frightens.
The Christ Child with its shattered spear;
Pity the midnight when it lightens;
Pity me, my dear.

THE SUCCESS OF *Black Armour*, added to that of *Jennifer Lorn*, propelled Elinor to the next level of public reputation in which she became a recognizable personality, in her case, one of elegant haughtiness. Despite her headaches and hypertension, she ignored doctors' warning signs, saying she could "live on aspirin and scotch." A familiar party scene: George Gershwin playing the piano and singing, Theodore Dreiser sitting broodingly in a corner, Elinor Wylie "aloof and lovely." Louis Untermeyer captured her manner by likening her to the Egyptian Queen Nefertiti:

> Here were the same imperious brows; the high cheekbones and the scooped-out cheeks; the proud and narrow nose; the small taut mouth; the resolute chin; the long smooth column of the throat. The eyes were bright and a hypnotic hazel. [10]

(Though she was nearsighted, she would not mar her appearance by wearing glasses.)

She began to behave like an "outraged goddess," with public outbursts that ranged from snits to tantrums to rages. She flaunted her vanity, producing scenes and tears when she heard praise of others. "During one dinner party," Dorothy Parker reported, "a man praised Diana Manners," who had just appeared in Max Reinhardt's Broadway production of *The Miracle*, "as the most beautiful woman in the world. Elinor immediately left the party. I admire her for it." No one was spared. Someone referred to Edna Millay as America's greatest lyric woman poet. Elinor left the room in fury, telling her hostess, "I was insulted, they said Edna was our greatest woman poet. And everyone knows I am."[11] Edna and Elinor soon became good friends. Edna wasn't vain in so obvious a way.

The following year, 1924, began in hope. Elinor found that she was pregnant. "Oh. If only I had a child: You can't know, you can't imagine the sorrow of childlessness." She miscarried. Desperate for a change and for escape from their grief, the Benéts decided that they were tired of New York and bought a small house in New Canaan, Connecticut, both as a refuge from urban life and an effort to come to terms with Bill's children, ages nine, eight, and six.

Elinor wished things to go well with the children and tried hard. The situation was complicated by the fact that they were the center of familial storms. Bill's mother and sister wanted to have a say in their upbringing, and disapproved of Kathleen Norris, Bill's sister-in-law, who believed she should have custody of them. Bill and Elinor were not helped by Elinor's mother, who was madly jealous of Elinor spending time with the Benét children but never seeing her own son.

Elinor and Bill and the Benét children were crowded together in the New Canaan house: four bedrooms for Bill and Elinor, three children, a maid, and a mortgage. A mortgage was a puzzling phenomenon for Elinor, who didn't know that one had to pay interest as well as principal. Her obsession with order continually caused strain and unhappiness. She bought the children clothes they didn't want to wear. She treated them as if they were pieces of furniture, insisting that they sit at the dining table in seats assigned by her. She bought them a handsome doll's house but became furious if any of them moved its furniture without her permission and, perversely, took great pains to furnish it with fragile items—a china tea set, for instance—that had to be removed before the children could play. Elinor suffered from severe headaches, "largely brought on by trying to balance account books and by a series of fights with Bill, one of them because she bought books with the housekeeping money." The house was expensive to repair and to maintain. Elinor wrote potboiler stories for popular magazines. The *Woman's Home Companion* paid her seven hundred and fifty dollars for one of them, but she was scornful of this audience and recognized that her stories had no lasting value. She said of the *Saturday Evening Post*, "I can't bear the look or feel or the *smell* of it." No wonder "her headaches thundered and her blood pressure soared."[12]

In 1925, her second novel, *The Venetian Glass Nephew* was serialized in *The Century* magazine, and then published in book form in September. Four books in four years! Respect for the poetry, popular acclaim for the novels—all this bringing her reputation to its highest point. The *Venetian Glass Nephew* was contrived and mannered, lighthearted and charming, "a piece of Venetian glass," a fantasy or, the term Elinor preferred, a fairytale. It dealt with the questions that so absorbed her as an artist and woman: the relationship of art to nature and human feeling, of marriage and erotic love, of the relations of opposed natures and temperaments to each other. As one reviewer noted, "While appearing to be a lighthearted fairytale, it does in fact have a rather sad, cold message—perfection is possible only in art." Reviewers, as before, treated it with seriousness and were positive. Dissenters were put off by the self-conscious tone. Edmund Wilson believed that Elinor's writing had become so ornate as to impede the narrative. Elinor hoped that the story would convey the charm of a "very Light Opera," and it was, in fact, later made into a musical. Dorothy Parker, who reviewed the stage version, contrasted it favorably with the vulgarity of popular musical theater. It was a "moon-lit haven from the boop-boop-a-droops and god dams of Broadway." Elinor's own final estimate of the novel was dismissive. She wrote to a friend, "I am heartily disgusted with the... gutless Virgino now that I have him between dull commonplace blue cloth covers,"[13] and attributed the novel's limitation to the "bad conditions" in which it was written.

What "bad conditions?" Bill's three children. Responsibility for them had become intolerable for Elinor and, above all, the children cut into her writing time. Their presence "threatened to make a sandwich of me and of my darling characters, to devour us. But I am trying to find a way out."[14] Aunt Kathleen Norris actually provided the way out. Bill allowed her formally to adopt them and take them to live with her in California. The adoption infuriated the Benét family, but it freed Elinor, who did not bother to visit the children before they left for California. Thereafter, she limited herself to writing them occasional notes. Elinor was now free to concentrate on her new novel, based on the life of Percy Bysshe Shelley, who had been a favorite since, as a young girl, she had found a book of his poetry in her father's library. Late in 1925, she made up her mind that she must go to England in pursuit of Shelley and of...what else? "I have not seen England for ten years," she wrote, "& I am going alone."[15] In fact, she changed her mind and stayed in America, hoping to finish her novel before she sailed. The transformation of a fledgling poet into a writer of national prominence was achieved in the four years since Elinor had first come to Manhattan in 1921. That achievement had exacted its psychological and emotional toll. The planned trip to England was symptomatic of growing restlessness and dissatisfaction with her life, an ominous sense that she was being hemmed in by something and needed to escape somehow.

2. Marianne Moore

I N THE EARLY 1920s, Marianne Moore continued the routine she had established since moving to the Village; work and writing dominated her life. She regarded her labors at the public library as "to some extent an incubus...our time is preempted," but "on the whole...I work better here than I could in any other place." As for her writing, she said, "I have no swiftness,"[1] which was not surprising given the kind of writing she wished to do required the maximum of precision and compression.

A friend said to her, "You never go anywhere on Sunday and you say you work all week and I didn't suppose that I was ever going to see you." In fact, she and Mary had the same lively, if decorous, social life they had established for themselves. This included theater, museums, the circus (where she visited the cages to observe the animals more closely), parties, invitations to tea, and lunches with editors and writers. There was so much of this that Marianne felt they had been "a little too busy and confused," which added to

Mary's now familiar grumbling that the time Marianne spent in this way was "an affectation." Once, when she returned earlier than usual from a party, her mother was "amazed to see me home so soon and asked what had happened and if I didn't like the party."[2]

Correspondence took up a good deal of time. She wrote many long letters to Warner, who was stationed on a battleship on the West Coast. Letters were her lifelines to the larger world of contemporary poetry. She corresponded with several people with whom she would exchange letters over the next forty years or more. "It is a happiness to know," she wrote in response to a letter of T. S. Eliot's, "that I am not quite a stranger to you." Bryher wrote candidly, "I don't like what you write but I like you."[3] And Monroe Wheeler introduced her to Asian visual arts.

She and Mary took several trips to visit Warner and Constance. The first was through the Panama Canal, which gave Marianne a chance to observe the exotic bird, plant, and animal life that was "beyond expectations." The next two allowed them to experience something of Warner's daily military routine. They spent several hours on his ship, the *U.S.S. Mississippi*, which provoked a classic Marianne observation: "A thing so mechanically perfect as a battleship is always a pleasure to see."[4]

THE MOST IMPORTANT new social and intellectual relationship Marianne made in those years was with *The Dial* magazine and the people associated with it. The original *Dial*, the transcendentalist magazine of the 1840s, of Margaret Fuller and Ralph Waldo Emerson, was the advanced journal of its day. It was revived in the 1880s but languished until it was bought by Scofield Thayer and James Sibley Watson who, sensitive to the new currents in art, issued an uncompromising manifesto in defense of the modern. *The Dial* existed "to meet the challenge of the new time by reflecting and interpreting its spirit—a spirit freely experimental, skeptical of inherited values, ready to examine old dogmas; and to subject afresh its sanctions to the test of experience."[5]

This new version of *The Dial* had moved away from the magazine's previous political emphasis and toward an interest in art, psychiatry, philosophy, and literature. By 1920, it had a modest circulation of eight thousand, but "its influence and standards made it one of the most important cultural and literary journals in English."[6] Marianne met Thayer at a Village party. She had recently sent some poems to *The Dial.* They had been rejected. At the party, she was asked to read one of her poems. She did. Thayer asked her, "Will you send that to us?"

"I did send it," she said.

"Well, send it again." So began her association with the magazine. Soon after, she invited Sibley Watson to tea: "Very deep—first rate. He said nothing but what he did say was striking and the significance would creep over you as being extremely unanticipated."[7]

Soon she was offered a job at the magazine, working in the office, but she turned it down. She was then offered a position as Thayer's secretary, but turned that down also. The money was tempting. Mary and Marianne lived on the income from the Reverend Warner's inheritance, from Marianne's public library salary, and from the tiny income from poems, essays, and reviews. As well, Warner and Constance contributed twelve hundred dollars annually. But however tempting the money might have been, office work was not what Marianne wanted. She was content to write occasionally for *The Dial*, to gain the friendships of Thayer and Watson, and to be invited to a weekly tea party in its offices.

Her reviewing added to her reputation in intellectual circles.

At a time when the poet Wallace Stevens was regarded as being unreadable and trivial, she very favorably reflected on his *Harmonium*, admiring its verbal facility and carefully contrived harmonies. Another of her most important early pieces of criticism was her 1921 review of Eliot's very influential book of essays, *The Sacred Wood*. The grounds for her approval are revealing. She thought the book "thoughtful," "well-knit architecture," and believed that Eliot was correct in regarding Aristotle as the "perfect critic—perfect by reason of his having the scientific mind."[8]

JANUARY 1924 BEGAN with a surprise. *The Dial's* editors announced that Marianne Moore was the recipient of the annual Dial Award for "distinguished service to American letters." Scofield Thayer wrote the commendation, championing Marianne's verse, until then "so meagerly relished and so signally unacclaimed." *The Dial's* citation went on charmingly, "We cannot turn over the whole misinformed continent but we can light our beacon and—for a worthwhile moment—flare a name worth flaring."[9] The award came with a prize of two thousand dollars. (At the time the national per capita income was one-third of that.)

In the summer, Thayer and Watson agreed that The Dial Press should publish a volume of Marianne's poems, a fuller selection than what had appeared in *Poems*. Lincoln MacVeagh, editor of the Press, doubted the wisdom of such a book. "I by no means share your view in regard to her poetry," he wrote to Thayer. "It is interesting, perhaps, but a very long way from the 'great,' which you would apply, to it." Nevertheless, he wrote, as instructed, to Marianne, proposing publication. She wrote back refusing the offer. MacVeagh told Thayer that he would personally have to speak or write to Marianne to persuade her. Thayer did this in August, and she wrote back accepting his proposal. There was very little time to prepare a volume for publication before Christmas, the best time for such a book to appear. "A businessman as well as an aesthete, Thayer was constantly on the lookout for opportunities to shore up *The Dial's* financial situation."[10] He calculated that the Dial Press Award would be used effectively to publicize Marianne's volume and that the two combined might guarantee commercial success. Hurriedly, Marianne revised some of her poems, arranged them as she wished and added a set of notes explaining the poems, as Eliot had done for *The Waste Land*.

Observations appeared just before Christmas in 1924. It included twenty-one poems from *Poems* and thirty-two additional ones, and as a whole, it includes many of the poems for which Moore has become most famous. The title, which echoed Eliot's *Prufrock and Other Observations*, was entirely apt because many of the poems are about visual representation as well as intellectual reflection. The detached, impersonal tone is everywhere; one reviewer likened it to "a conscious bit of mathematics." If some reviewers were unimpressed, the prevailing criticism was laudatory, even if somewhat wary. Moore escaped the dismissive wrath of the anti-Modernist critics. Puzzlement rather than wrath marked most critical responses. *The Nation*, "The Literary Review" of the *New York Post*, and the *New York Times* all were positive in their assessments. Ivor Winters, in the April 1925 issue of *Poetry*, declared that it was a "privilege to be able to write of one of whose genius one feels so sure."[11]

The poems in *Observations* reveal the novel ways in which Marianne observed the world and are wide in range, with one exception. For her, alone among her peers, love was never the subject. She often reflected on what elements constituted a style of writing, and drew on the ancient Greek philosopher Democritus and the medieval philosopher Duns Scotus for their insights. Personally, she prized consciousness, or "contractility," as the "first grace of style." But who else would have found this symbolized by the humble snail?

To a Snail

> If "compression is the first grace of style,"
> you have it. Contractility is a virtue
> as modesty is a virtue.
> It is not the acquisition of any one thing
> that is able to adorn,
> or the incidental quality that occurs
> as a concomitant of something well said,
> that we value in style,
> but the principle that is hid:
> in the absence of feet, "a method of conclusions";
> "a knowledge of principles,"
> in the curious phenomenon of your occipital horn.

One personal quality Marianne greatly admired was restraint, in personal manners and in poetic style—almost to the point of silence. One haunting and forever-uncertain aspect of this poem is that the words of wisdom that make it up are put in the mouth of the speaker's father, by a poet who never knew her own father.

Silence

> My father used to say,
> "Superior people never make long visits,
> have to be shown Longfellow's grave

nor the glass flowers at Harvard.
Self reliant like the cat –
that takes its prey to privacy,
the mouse's limp tail hanging like a shoelace from its mouth –
they sometimes enjoy solitude,
and can be robbed of speech
by speech which has delighted them.
The deepest feeling always shows itself in silence:
not in silence, but restraint."
Nor was he insincere in saying, "Make my house your inn."
Inns are not residences.

Her most often-quoted poem, her song about poetry, in her most understated and detached voice, contains a quotation, "imaginary gardens with real toads in them," the source of which has never been identified. Also quoted is Leo Tolstoy, who was as uncertain as Marianne as to what was poetry and what wasn't. She revised and re-revised this poem for five decades (and not always for the better), testament to her genuine belief that the nature of this art, "all this fiddle" she devoted her life to, could never adequately be put into words.

Poetry

I, too, dislike it: there are things that are important beyond all this
          fiddle.
     Reading it, however, with a perfect contempt for it, one discovers
               that there is in
     it after all, a place for the genuine.
          Hands that can grasp, eyes
          that can dilate, hair that can rise
               if it must, these things are important not because a

high sounding interpretation can be put upon them but because
they are
useful; when they become so derivative as to become unintelligible,
the same thing may be said for all of us, that we
do not admire what
we cannot understand: the bat,
holding on upside down or in quest of something to

eat, elephants pushing, a wild horse taking a roll, a tireless wolf
under
a tree, the immovable critic twitching his skin like a horse that feels
a flea, the base-
ball fan, the statistician—
nor is it valid
to discriminate against "business documents and

school-books"; all these phenomena are important. One must make
a distinction
however: when dragged into prominence by half poets, the result
is not poetry,
nor till the poets among us can be
"literalists of
the imagination"—above
insolence and triviality and can present

for inspection, imaginary gardens with real toads in them, shall
we have
it. In the meantime, if you demand on one hand,
the raw material of poetry in
all its rawness and
that which is on the other hand
genuine, you are interested in poetry.

The first edition consisted of two hundred and fifty copies at two dollars each. The dust jacket, black lettering on bright gold foil, gave an opulent appearance. *Observations* sold remarkably well for what it was, and in March there was a second edition. Between January and the end of June 1925, four hundred and eighty-eight copies were sold, a "minor miracle." Marianne made a hundred and thirty-six dollars and thirty-five cents. *The Dial* sedulously publicized her throughout that year; in May, William Carlos Williams published a "beautifully written" review of the book.[12]

Important as *The Dial*, its Press, and Watson and Thayer had been in Marianne's life up to this point, 1925 would see a series of events that moved the magazine directly into the center of how she lived and what she did. She was offered the position of Associate Editor. She accepted. A few months later, when her friend, Alyse Gregory had to resign as Editor to look after her sick husband, Marianne became acting Editor. She gave up her half-time library job and went to work full-time, at two thousand and six hundred dollars a year at *The Dial* office, an event that would have important consequences for her poetry.

3. Edna St. Vincent Millay

Edna Millay was in Europe. "Now that I have found how easy it is to get about in the world," she wrote to her mother. "I shall probably never stay in one place long. "[1] She had predicted as much in this poem:

To the Not Impossible Him

How shall I know unless I go
To Cairo and Cathay,
Whether or not this blessed spot
Is blest in every way?

Now it may be, the flower for me
Is this beneath my nose;
How shall I tell, unless I smell
The Carthaginian rose?

The fabric of my faithful love
 No power shall dim or ravel
Whilst I stay here, – but oh, my dear,
 If I should ever travel!

She was in Rome when she was asked to review Elinor Wylie's *Nets to Catch the Wind*, staying there long enough to complete her review and then, with the much needed money, left behind the lover who had brought her to Rome and was off to Albania with a different one: "This boy who knows the place very well is all excited about giving me a wonderful time." He succeeded. She thought Albania "my most thrilling experience so far," but soon after, with a different male companion she went to Vienna, "this grey city where there is never a shred of sunlight. I smoke too many cigarettes and the German food nearly kills me. Fortunately I have to exercise, because I can't afford taxis and I loathe streetcars." She spent money recklessly wherever she was and had to borrow from friends, lovers, former lovers, and from the many other people who couldn't resist her. (Among them was the publisher Horace Liveright, who lent her five hundred dollars as an advance for a novel she never wrote.) Despite multiple lovers, Vienna found her at low ebb. "I can't leave …probably for several months yet. I am here because it is the cheapest place in the world to live in just now, & I am in one of my states of being entirely busted." Something turned up, however, or someone came through, because two months later she was in Budapest, staying at the Ritz.[2]

HER LONG-DELAYED third book, *Second April*, was published while Edna was in Europe in the summer of 1921. The poems turn conventional attitudes upside-down. "I know what I know," the poet says, insisting that even beauty, about which poets were forever carrying on, is not enough. Indeed "life in itself is not enough."

> *Spring*
>
> To what purpose, April, do you return again?
> Beauty is not enough.
> You can no longer quiet me with the redness
> Of little leaves opening stickily.
> I know what I know.
> The sun is hot on my neck as I observe
> The spikes of the crocus.
> The smell of the earth is good.
> It is apparent that there is no death.
> But what does that signify?
> Not only under ground are the brains of men
> Eaten by maggots.
> Life in itself
> Is nothing,
> An empty cup, a flight of uncarpeted stairs.
> It is not enough that yearly, down this hill,
> April
> Comes like an idiot, babbling and strewing flowers.

Twelve sonnets concluded *Second April*. Again, there is memory of love in one of them, but this time a memory no more enduring than a few puffs of smoke.

IV

Only until this cigarette is ended
A little moment at the end of all,
While on the floor the quiet ashes fall.
And in the firelight to a lance extended,
Bizarrely with jazzing music blended
The broken shadow dances on the wall.
I will permit my memory to recall
The vision of you by all my dreams attended.
And then adieu, – farewell! – the dream is done.
Yours is a face of which I can forget
The color and the features, every one,
The words not ever, and the smiles not yet:
But in your day this moment is the sun
Upon a hill, after the sun has set.

AT THE BEGINNING of her European adventure, in Paris, Edna immersed herself in French culture, dressed more smartly then ever before, and was also soon "very much allied with the Bohemians of the Left Bank." She had left New York as if she were "fleeing the scene of a crime," and what she needed most, she thought, was not to write any poetry. "When it begins to get a little easy, or one begins to write in certain forms almost from habit, it is time to stop for a while, I think, & almost forget that one is a poet...& then let it all come back to one later, fresh, & possibly in a newer form."[3]

As well as taking a break from poetry, "tired of breaking hearts and spreading havoc," she came to Europe (she said) to settle down to a new life." Whatever she might have meant by that, it obviously didn't mean giving up sex, for she had many sexual encounters, with women as well as with men. There were three that were especially intense. The first was with George Slocombe, an English journalist, young, handsome, ardent, and married. Edna agreed that if he divorced his wife, she would move to England and marry him. He expressed his undying love but finally rejected her, saying he could not leave his wife. For months after, she wrote to him, though she knew the situation was hopeless.[4]

Marriage had moved to the front of Edna's mind. Slocombe's rejection, the fact that she was approaching thirty years of age, that her younger sisters were marrying before her—these things had an effect: "Well, both my little sisters are young married women and me, I am just three months from being an old maid." This may help account for the most bizarre of Edna's affairs, a non-sexual one conducted entirely by mail, a triangular entanglement with Witter Bynner and Arthur Ficke. Since Edna's seventy-two hours with him in 1917, Ficke had divorced and remarried and was understood to be unavailable. Bynner, "Hal," was rich and available and homosexual. At Edna's instigation, Ficke served as matchmaker, with letters going back and forth from Bynner in New York to Ficke in Iowa and across the Atlantic, often crossing each other. Bynner sent a letter politely asking Edna to marry him. She responded, "Do you really want me to marry you—because if you really want me to, I will." No reply for a week. Edna cabled. "YES HAL." Still no reply. Another cable, "YES." He replied by letter. He would come to Europe to see her and they could talk things over. "Perhaps for either of us, marriage can be jolly. Perhaps not." He described himself as "half merry, half sad, half hoping, half doubting. As to what is going on inside of me, it wobbles wobbles."[5] Edna understood that this was his way of saying no.

A continuing source of guilt for Edna was feeling that she

had abandoned her mother. Edna would not write to her for lengthy periods and then try to make up for this through protestations of love, denying she had "forgotten all about my family and home and mother." She promised that Cora would come as soon as Edna found the money but, distracted by her love affairs and travel, she informed her mother that coming at a certain time would not suit her. After the Hal Bynner fiasco, Edna sent her mother the money to enable her to come to Paris.

"This old woman in a Buster Brown bob, steel-rimmed glasses," was energetic and plainspoken. "Let's go!—to the Tuileries to the Louvre! Let's bum around these back streets!" Cora's presence might have proved inhibiting, but Edna avoided difficulties by continuing to behave and to love as she had been doing. She continued to have a lesbian relationship with a woman Cora got on well with, but there were occasional awkward moments. One afternoon, they were sitting with a group in a café when "a young man, very attractive man, whom [Edna] must have just met, and with whom she had made an arrangement," kept looking over at her, as if to say, "Come, Come," and "Mrs. Millay must have noticed, for we all noticed." At last Edna said, "We'll see you later," and the two walked off. She had not seen him before and would not see him again. "A real sadness radiated from her mother."[6]

In the middle of Edna's second summer in Europe, she once more became entangled, to Cora's intense displeasure, in what proved to be an emotionally disastrous affair. He was a Frenchman whose name was Daubigny. He was tall, immaculately dressed, and a gentleman as far as breeding was concerned, who "swept Vincent off her feet." Edna's lesbian friends disliked him. Cora loathed him and kept a written record of her feelings, describing him as being a "dirty panderer," "runner-in-for-some-whorehouse," "lustful," "greedy," "full of evil," "snake-shaped head, fish eyes, carp-mouthed," and so on for pages. Cora was almost hysterical at being displaced. "Edna's devotion to mummie was easily broken, and for a very little in exchange."[7] Edna secured the documents needed for them to be able to marry, after which they would go to England. At the end of June, she found she was pregnant and did go to England with her mother. Daubigny, whatever Edna may have hoped for from him, remained in Paris and dropped out of her life.

Edna and Cora lived in Dorset, where every day they took long walks, Cora finding greens of all kinds to cook and searching through herbal guides for a particular herb. She finally found it and used it to cause her daughter's miscarriage. Edna wouldn't see any English doctors and was continually unwell. Talk of travel on the Continent came to nothing. There was one memorable moment during that time of suffering and depression, a trip to Cambridge where she glimpsed A.E. Housman in the street. In late November they returned to France, and in January 1923 they sailed for the United States.

ON THEIR RETURN, Cora went back to Maine while Edna stayed with friends in order to save money. Her reputation had grown in her absence. *Second April* had sold more than three thousand copies and was in its third printing. But she was not well. Edmund Wilson spent an evening with her and concluded that "she must have continued to live with considerable recklessness, for...she was in very bad shape again." In the spring she went to see friends at Croton-on-Hudson, where one evening she played charades with another houseguest, Eugen Boissevain. They played their parts very well "and it was apparent to us all," Floyd Dell recounted, "that it wasn't just acting. We were having the unusual privilege of seeing a man and a girl fall in love with each other violently in public." Boissevain struck one observer as having "an ability to get on with anybody. Like a cruise director." His kindness was genuine and he behaved like a male nurse to her...and of course Edna was taken with him." One of Edna's women lovers had said to her, just before she sailed from France, "You go home and you find the most marvelous man in the world, and marry him." Boissevain, for his part, said to the ever-present Arthur Ficke, who had taken a house in Croton-on-Hudson. "I don't want to have a dirty little love affair with her; I want to marry her."[8] By early May they were living together.

In May, Columbia University announced that Edna St. Vincent Millay had been awarded the Pulitzer Prize for Poetry based on *The Ballad of the Harp-Weaver*, and *A Few Figs From Thistles*, with prize money of a thousand dollars. She told a newspaper reporter that she would use the prize money to return to Maine and that she wanted to write so that readers would say "Life can be exciting and free and intense." Two weeks later, she wrote her mother with a very different kind of announcement. She was going to marry Eugen Boissevain, health permitting, for she was once again ill. "You will like him very much when you get to know him...and it is very important that you should like him." Family opinion was divided, but understanding, "He was the solution to a lot of problems for her because he was obviously the mother type."[9]

On July 18, 1923, they were married at a friend's house in the country. It was hastily organized. Her sister, Norma, made a bridal veil out of mosquito netting with roses tucked in. Eugen and Edna then drove to New York City and to a hospital where, the next day, she was operated on for appendicitis, a combination of events which excited great interest in the press.

Edna slowly regained her health in the country, but in the fall Eugen and she returned to the Village. For the extravagant sum of two hundred dollars per month, they rented a well-known landmark—the Dutch-gabled, three-story, nine-foot-wide mews house at 75½ Bedford Street. Eugen Boissevain had been born in Holland in 1880, of an affluent, intellectually distinguished family; his father was a leading newspaperman and publisher. He had moved to America when he married Inez Milholland, a Vassar graduate and champion of women's rights, a woman Millay had admired and whom she had heard speak at Vassar. Milholland died in the influenza epidemic of 1918–19, telling her husband as she died, "Go out and lead another life." The newspapers, and many people in the Village, assumed that Boissevain was very wealthy. In fact, he was an erratic businessman, as compulsive a spender as his wife; at the time of his marriage he was several thousand dollars in debt. Edna paid her mother's debts in Camden with her own money. "I wish I could have done this before I got married—because of course everybody thinks it is my rich husband who has done it, when in fact it is really myself, every cent of it, nearly a thousand dollars that I made by writing."[10]

The Harp-Weaver and Other Poems was overshadowed at the time of its publication, 1923, by the title poem of the collection. "The Ballad of the Harp-Weaver" is an allegory of Cora's self-sacrificing dedication to her children, and was a popular success as well as a prizewinner. But it now seems too consciously naïve and cloyingly sentimental, too sweetly told. By contrast, there were other poems in the book which expanded the emotional range of Edna's work, including, for instance, the following, which represents the poet as weathered, blasted by wind and storm.

Scrub

If I grow bitterly.
Like a gnarled and stunted tree,
Bearing harshly of my youth
Puckered fruit that sears the mouth:
If I make of my drawn boughs
An inhospitable house,
Out of which I never pry
Toward the water and the sky,
Under which I stand and hide
And watch the day go by outside;
It is that a wind too strong
Bent my back when I was young,
It is that I fear the rain
Lest it blister me again.

AT THE BEGINNING of 1924, Edna went on her first reading tour, two months on the road; Cedar Rapids, Evanston, Chicago, Louisville, Springfield, Pittsburgh, Minneapolis, Omaha, Cleveland, Milwaukee, St. Louis, Columbus, Buffalo, and Rochester. She was an immense success everywhere she went. This tour, and the others that followed it, made her known nationally to people who didn't buy her books or bother with reviews. She read magnificently, "expressively and enthusiastically, but with nothing of artificial rhetoricism."[11] Her voice, as always, was spellbinding, sometimes as quiet as her blue dress, sometimes as blazing as her flame-colored scarf. Some people no doubt came hoping to hear her recite erotic poems, but most people responded to all of the varied poems, not just those from *A Few Figs from Thistles*. Edna was wistful and lived up to her image as the poet-girl, a shy undergraduate more than a woman of the world. In May, at Bowdoin College, in her home state, she shared a platform with Robert Frost. The contrast was striking: Frost curmudgeonly, Edna elfin and enchanting.

The stamina she possessed was remarkable, for she seemed fresh and responsive at each appearance. It was a series of performances, of course: Edna St. Vincent Millay in her theatrical mode, and by the end of it she was depressed. "If ever I felt like a prostitute it was last night," she said after one evening. "I hope I shall never write a poem again that more than five people will like."[12] But of course, that was her frayed nerves speaking. She was deeply gratified by the adulation.

What made it all bearable, finally, was that the two thousand dollars she was paid for the tour allowed her and Eugen to plan a round-the-world trip to Hawaii, Japan, China, Java (where he had family), and the Netherlands (where he had still more family). They sailed in April and were gone until the end of 1924.

Two dominating events marked 1925, which was relatively calm. Edna agreed to write the libretto for an opera, score by the American composer Deems Taylor, whose music she had heard and admired in a concert. The opera libretto occupied her for all of that year. The other event was another change of residence. There had been trips abroad and numerous changes of address in the Village. Transience was part of the Village mystique. But as had been the case once before, she was finding city life increasingly difficult: "No, I cannot write in New York. It is awfully exciting there and I find lots of things to write about and 1 accumulate many ideas, but I have to go away where it is quiet."[13] She had often threatened to return to the sea, familiar to her since childhood. As a poem from *The Harp-Weaver* expressed it, she was "weary of words and people."

So she left the city. She and Eugen found an abandoned farmhouse with four hundred and thirty-five acres two hours north in upstate New York, near the town of Austerlitz. They named it Steepletop, after a wildflower that grew nearby. Edna's sense of place was complex. She never again lived for long in New York City, but she often returned there, and could not be away from it for very long. She longed for the sea, which she "loved beyond all words," and in a hauntingly ambiguous poem dramatized the fate of those who moved.

Inland

People that build their houses inland,
 People that buy a plot of ground
Shaped like a house and build a house there,
 Far from the seaboard, far from the sound

Of water sucking the hollow ledges,
 Tons of water striking the shore,
What do they long for, as 1 long for
 One salt smell of the sea once more?

People the waves have not awakened,
 Spanking the boats at the barber's head;
What do they long for, as I long for –
 Starting up in my inland bed,

Beating the narrow walls and finding
 Neither a window nor a door,
Screaming to God for death by drowning, –
 One salt taste of the sea once more?

In June 1925, she and Eugen moved—inland, to Steepletop.

4. Louise Bogan

Louise Bogan in Vienna. She took a room in a house seven doors from where Sigmund Freud lived. She worked out a routine: in the mornings, reading and writing; in the afternoons, walks in the splendid Viennese parks and in the countryside. There was a piano in her room and she arranged lessons with a fine teacher. As she had years before in first walking about Boston, she responded deeply to the city's magnificent buildings, statues and, of course, its music: Gustav Mahler's *Kindertotenlieder* ("children's songs of death"), which she had never heard before; and, "what became a passion for her," Mozart, "deliciously logical...like harmony rung on glass."[1]

There were complications, however, which made the time in Vienna not untroubled. The rich lover who had paid her way eventually joined her. She never referred to him in her letters and even his identity is unknown. How much his presence was responsible for disturbing her is unclear, but she wrote to a friend about the kaleidoscopic feelings that overwhelmed her at times: "grief, passion, heady joy, rage, longing." There were also disadvantages to being away from America, as she explained in a letter to Harriet Monroe. "In order to write English you must, occasionally, hear it spoken."[2] Then, one day, a copy of *The New Republic* was sent to her. In it, one of her poems was printed beside one of Elinor Wylie's.

It "thrilled" her to read Wylie's poem, for it spoke directly to her situation, the need to find relief from corrosive memories, to gain detachment from those memories by turning them into rubble, "of little worth when found." Reading this poem broke the logjam, making her daily writing stint productive. She now wrote with a heightened intensity "about men and women scorched by love and who, when it lay broken like a fragile shell, were still possessed by its memory."

These were poems in a fully mature style, dramatic but with little formal action. The "I" in the poems was often some "other," not the poet herself. Over and over she dealt with the power of memory and the need to escape it not by obliterating it but by absorbing it into one's current life, as in "A Tale." She found that she could put herself into the mind of a man (perhaps a former lover?), as she did in a poem called "The Frightened Man."

In time, she was able fully to understand the significance of her Vienna experience. Being cut off from publishers and editors made her stop "writing like magazines," and forced her to write, "hard, painfully produced poems that sounded like myself." Vienna marked the end of her first, easier period of writing: "Never again would poems simply come to her." It also marked the beginning of better work. She was finally able to regard the six months away from America as "a boon."[3]

Returning to the United States in October 1922, she went to stay with her parents for the rest of the year, with Maidie, who sensed in later years that Louise "tried very very hard to be a mother. ...She didn't instinctively want to be a mother ...but she tried to make it up to me in many ways." She was "a lovely human being," who appeared in Maidie's life from time to time. Louise read a lot of poetry in this period, e.g., Yeats and A.B. Housman's *Last Poems*. ("Are you sure it isn't too Housman?" she asked a friend about one of her poems.) [4] She returned to New York convinced that she had enough good poems to make a book.

IN THE FALL of 1923, Robert McBride & Company was perceptive enough to publish *Body of This Death*, its title taken from Romans 7:24: "0 wretched man that I am! Who shall deliver me from the body of this death!" She later made fun of her excessive solemnity in choosing that title, but it perfectly suited the tone and content of the volume. The poems are traditional in form and meter, of six and eight line stanzas, some of them rhymed couplets. Louise was a harsh critic of her own work and several fine poems in this volume were dropped from later collections, but *Body of This Death* brilliantly draws on the emotional and aesthetic legacy of her previous twenty-six years.

The reviewers agreed on one thing—that her poems were not easy. Beyond that, opinions were divided. The negative reviews were dismissive. Said one, "An inexpert craftsman striving fitfully and inchoately to express that which defies expression." And another, "An emptiness of thought that is positively painful." What had they been reading? "Inexpert." "Emptiness of thought." It was precisely the opposite things, skillful techniques and thoughtfulness, that the positive reviewers stressed: "concentrated poetry," "individual and very moving." Mark Van Doren identified thirty pages "packed as tightly with pure poetry as any thirty pages have been for a generation." Another reviewer: "Hardly a phrase could be reduced by a word." Still another declared, "It may be a classic." Robert Frost, usually sparing of praise, said, "That woman will be able to do anything."[5]

ONE EVENING, AT a fundraising party for *The Measure*, Louise met Raymond Peckham Holden. The son of a family who had been New Yorkers for generations, he grew up on the Upper West Side of Manhattan in a large house with servants and a splendid library. His father collected first editions and fine china. Raymond went to Princeton, one year ahead of Edmund Wilson, who became a friend, and thought of himself as a rebel and nonconformist. One expression of nonconformity was writing poetry, which was published in *The Measure*, *The Nation*, and *Poetry* magazine. He was married to a woman from another wealthy upper-middle-class New York family, and had two children. Holden became a follower of Robert Frost and worked on the Frost family farm. For him, it was a difficult relationship with a difficult man, but Frost did help him get his first volume of poetry, *Granite and Alabaster*, published in 1922.

By 1922-1923, when Raymond met Louise, his marriage was already collapsing and he was living alone in a Village apartment. He was twenty-nine, trim, muscular, and boyish, with curly hair and personal charm. Louise thought him "a real male beauty."[6] Their acquaintanceship quickly became sexual. It was Holden who, through a friend, used his influence to have *Body of This Death* published. (Louise did not know this.)

Louise was reluctant to talk about her past. Maidie was shuttled back and forth from Massachusetts to wherever Louise was living, and it was some time before Holden discovered that she had a daughter. A friend had sternly said to her, "Louise, stop hiding your child!"[7] Holden was very kind to Maidie, who liked him a lot. The three of them moved into an apartment on West 16th Street. Later, Maidie was a boarder at a Montessori school. Holden's wife sued for divorce and received a substantial settlement—the family property, alimony, and child support—leaving Holden virtually broke. In June 1925, Maidie was sent to live with her grandparents and Holden moved to Boston, where he found a job as a travel writer. On July 10, 1925, Louise and Raymond were married.

Publishing her poetry in *The Measure* brought Louise into contact with a group of independently minded Manhattan intellectuals, poets and social scientists, who were associated with Columbia University and were not identified with any of the prevailing orthodoxies, traditional or Modernist. The Columbia group included two anthropologists: Margaret Mead (1901-1978) and Ruth Benedict (1887-1948), who also wrote poetry. As well, their group included a poetry-writing professor of linguistics, Edward Sapir, author of an influential book, *Linguistics*. They in turn orbited around William Fielding Ogburn, a Columbia University professor of sociology, in whose office Louise worked for a time, cataloging academic papers at fifty cents an hour. Ogburn delighted in having an office filled with poets and would arrive in the mornings reciting baseball jingles. "See, I can write poetry, too."[8]

Through the Columbia group Louise became acquainted

with three people who would be important to her personally. Two were poets who would become major figures in the women's poetry movement, Léonie Adams and Genevieve Taggard. The third was Rolfe Humphries (1894-1969), a poet, classicist, perceptive critic, and a lifelong friend and candid correspondent.

The Columbians were ahead of their time in their interest in Freudian thought and in contemporary psychoanalytic theory. They spent a good deal of time together, shopping, gossiping about the emotional entanglements of their friends, and going to the movies. "Many of our poems grew out of our relationships to one another," Margaret Mead recalled, "and the intensities of the contemporary human plots were discussed and re-discussed against the background of the childhood and special temperament of each."[9]

Margaret Mead

Mead recognized that Louise was emotionally fragile, subject to bouts of jealously and, despite her beauty, lacking in self-confidence. Mead's poem about Bogan was published in *The Measure* in 1925.

For a Proud Lady

Yours is a proud and fearful heart
That snares the weather in its mood,
As once you snatched the morning mists
All veils for your one maidenhood.

The snow is but a banner white
Run up by God for your defeat;
You take cold winter days to read
Fate patterned in indifferent sleet.

And sweeter weathers have no art
To dull this prophecy of harm;
You only watch the hare-bell's tilt
To hear instead its belled alarum.

Ruth Benedict would achieve anthropological eminence with *Patterns of Culture* (1934). Margaret Mead gained fame and furious notoriety for her first book, *Coming of Age in Samoa* (1928). Mead was modest about her poetry. "I had been writing verse and continued to do so for several years, but it became an avocation—an enjoyable way of translating for myself and of communicating with friends who were poets." Poetry and anthropology were deeply connected because both were ways of identifying with "a generation of young women who felt extraordinarily free—free from the demand to marry unless we chose to do so, free to postpone marriage while we did other things, free from the need to bargain and hedge that had burdened and restricted women of earlier generations." [10] *Coming of Age in Samoa* described young women's sexuality with candor, putting it in broad perspective and linking it, for those who read it properly, with young women everywhere.

5. Léonie Adams

L ÉONIE ADAMS WAS another member of the Columbia group. Descended on both sides from old line families, by Léonie's day her immediate family was cosmopolitan. Her father, Charles Frederic Adams, was born in Cuba, where his family had business interests (his mother was Venezuelan). Like everyone else in the family, Léonie's mother, Henrietta Rozier, was dominated by her husband. If New York City was a birth right for Léonie , it was a severely restricted one. A successful lawyer, Charles Frederic so strictly supervised the Adams children—there were six—that Léonie was not allowed to travel alone on the subway until she entered Barnard College in 1917. Even then her father often accompanied her.

A shy, dutiful student in school, very short, with fine features, she exuded an ethereal quality redolent of a mixture of New England and Spain. At Barnard, she found a degree of freedom. Though her father had genuine literary interests, Léonie had felt compelled to write poetry in secret. Like Sara Teasdale, she found liberating companionship in the company of a group of young women who adopted derogatory names for themselves. "Communist Morons," the angry words of a commencement speaker, was one: another was "Ash Can Cats." On the door of their bedroom, Léonie and Margaret posted a sign, "We don't believe in private property, keep yours out," and a photograph of the currently popular Edna Millay:

> Safe upon the solid rock the ugly houses stand;
> Come and see my shining palace built upon the sand.

Léonie was appalled at the conviction of Sacco and Vanzetti in 1921, took part in a mass meeting in support of them, walked a picket line, and stuffed envelopes on their behalf. She wrote an editorial for the Barnard newspaper addressed to the Vice President, Calvin Coolidge, "Cheer Up, Mr. Coolidge," rebutting his assertion that "the 'Reds' were stalking our College Women."[1]

Léonie Adams

Edmund Wilson met her, took her up, advised her, encouraged her, and criticized her poetry. She was at this time a "delicate and articulate young woman in her mid-twenties...bird-like in gesture, brief and vivid in speech." Her lyricism and her reticence appealed to Wilson, who was sexually attracted to her. In a letter to Rolfe Humphries Louise Bogan wrote, "Léonie informs us that the Great Wilson made some hearty passes at her." More than that, Wilson and Adams began an intense sexual love affair. "She is a little shy at first," Wilson said, "but extremely intelligent and amusing."[2]

In her junior year at Barnard, Léonie published a poem in *The New Republic*. The heart is admonished to reflect on the fleeting morality of life and to recognize that art and beauty too are impermanent.

April Mortality

Rebellion shook an ancient dust,
And bones bleached dry of rottenness
Said: Heart be bitter still, nor trust
The earth, the sky in their bright dress.

Heart, heart, dost thou break to know
This anguish thou wilt bear alone?
We sang of it an age ago,
And traced it dimly upon stone.

With all the drifting race of men
Thou also art begot to mourn
That she is crucified again,
The lonely Beauty yet unborn.

And if thou dreamest to have won
Some touch of her in permanence,
'Tis the old cheating of the sun,
The intricate lovely play of sense.

Be bitter still, remember how
Four petals, when a little breath
Of wind made stir the pear-tree bough,
Blew delicately down to death.

The Columbians recognized that Léonie's poetry put her in a class by herself. "The presence of one highly gifted person whose talent is recognized," Margaret Mead wrote years later, "has an enormous effect on everyone belonging to a group." That the group's poetry talents were modest and Léonie's remarkable, meant that "we had to look at the choices we made in other fields in much stricter terms."[3] The next few years would reveal what, if anything, Léonie would make of her gift.

6. GENEVIEVE TAGGARD

G ENEVIEVE TAGGARD CAME to New York City to escape from the bigotries and narrowness of small town life and would eventually be associated with the Columbia group, but her path was a circuitous one. Born in Waitsburg, Washington, in 1894, she was taken at age three to Hawaii, where her parents, Disciples of Christ missionaries, opened a school. The subsequent emergence of Genevieve's literary interests and talents is the subject of considerable disagreement. The conventional point of view has been to emphasize the supposed restrictiveness of her family culture. Only the Bible was permitted reading at home. Therefore, when Genevieve discovered Keats and Shelley and began to write poetry, she had to do so secretly, like Leonie Adams who, in a very different urban culture, also wrote poetry secretly. The Taggard family tradition, however, presents a very different picture. It is an indisputable fact that Genevieve's parents enrolled her, at an early age, in the remarkable, progressive Punahoa School, which stressed individuality and celebrated diversity. And there Genevieve, openly, embraced literary culture, contributing to the school's literary magazine, which earned parental admiration. (Half a century later Barack Obama attended Punahou, which opened paths for achievement and leadership for him.) Genevieve's adolescence was divided between Waitsburg and Hawaii, where she began college and, after her father's death, Berkeley, California, where her mother ran a boardinghouse so that Genevieve could attend the University. She got her degree and, as well, continued to write and study poetry (with Witter Bynner), and became a Debbsian socialist.

Genevieve Taggard

Genevieve's immersion in urban culture in Berkeley culmi-
nated in her move to New York City in 1920 and was "the active
source of my convictions...what to work against and what to work
for." A job with a publisher and association with *The Measure*, propelled her into the city's intellectual life. In 1921, she met and married Robert Wolf, a novelist and critic. A daughter, Marcia, was born
that year. Her socialism was abandoned for close association with
the Communist Party, though she was not a party member. She was
also a committed feminist aspiring to infuse her poetry with the
"fire & ardency & the power & depth"[1] of contemporary women
writers.

At the same time, she wanted her feminism to encompass
the many and varied forms of love. "Indian Summer" depicts a
paradise of innocent love:

> Lovers will be
> Simple and free;
> On warm fall nights, men's sweethearts will conceive.

"Just Introduced" is more directly erotic:

> You flew, I followed, matched your stride
> And held your pause, and swung and parted wide....

Passionate, caring, the Taggard woman was also independent,
strong minded, and would have love on her own terms. She was
a woman who would not be held or hindered. And love was not
a province inhabited only by the young. In describing "everyday"
love, the love of older people worn down by incessant struggle, of
women creating peace for their men, she achieved a moment of
memorable humanity.

Everyday Alchemy

Men go to women mutely for their peace.
And they, who lack it most, create it when
They make because they must, loving their men –
A solace for sad bosom-bended heads. There
Is all that meager peace men get – no otherwhere;
No mountain space, no tree with placid leaves.
Or heavy gloom beneath a young girl's hair.
No sound of valley bell on autumn air,
Or room made home with doves along the eves,
Ever holds peace like this, poured by poor women
Out or their heart's poverty, for worn men.

She had found her voice, an authentic and unmistakable
voice; and in the decade unfolding would find her way to a range
of subjects peculiarly her own—love and politics and an exploration of traditional forms of poetry. A stream of books would
follow.

7. DOROTHY PARKER

"**A** BLEND OF Little Nell and Lady Macbeth." So Alexander Wolcott described Dorothy Parker. If Wolcott got it only half right—there was never anything of Little Nell about her—his comparison to Shakespeare's murderous lady was perceptive. Aiming at the mordantly concise in her verse, she was self-critical enough to know that she had not yet achieved what she was after. The idea of the wholly spontaneous Algonquin Dorothy was bogus. As a writer, or a punster and wisecracker, she knew she needed discipline to write and re-write and re-write some more. And she tried to do it. "I write five words and then I change seven."[1] The problem was her hectic emotional and social life, which was at odds with her intentions as a writer. Despite the distractions, she wrote prolifically between 1922 and 1924, producing forty-nine poems the first of those years, seventeen the next year, and fourteen in 1924. In her own estimation, the quality of her work went up as she slowed down. Of the forty-nine poems for example, she eventually kept only five for later publication in book form; of the seventeen, she kept five; and of the fourteen, she kept eight.

Although she insisted that she should not be called a poet, Parker was an artist who cared deeply about language, and was well aware, as the following poem demonstrates, that the language of popular culture was rich in clichés regarding idealized love:

Fantasy

Did we love each other, sweetest
      Skies would be forever blue;
Time would flutter by on fleetest
      Wings of glittering golden hue.
Joy beyond a poet's telling
      Should we learn the meaning of:
Arcady would be our dwelling --
      Did we love.

Did we love each other, darling,
      Banished ugliness and gloom;
Ever sweet would pipe the starling,
      Ever gay the rose would bloom.
Care and trouble could not find us,
      Bliss untold would be our lot.
But one scarcely need remind us,
      We do not.

Her marriage was now a miserable one. For a time, drinking seemed to bring her and Eddie together, at least for a few hours. They urged each other on; she would scold and, infuriated by her nagging, he would walk out. Some mornings she didn't know where he had been the night before. Some mornings she couldn't remember where *she* had been. Some mornings she awakened with bruises and, once, a black eye. Pathetically, she believed that drinking helped her be amusing and that she had to be amusing to interest people. As life was impossible for Eddie in New York City and since Dorothy would not move away, he told her that he wanted to end their marriage.

She moved out of their apartment. Then there were no restraints. She had an affair with Charles MacArthur, a journalist, playwright, and "a dashing mysterious fellow." There was a wildness to him. "He had to feed the daemon in him a great deal of liquor to keep it in line." It wasn't only the drinking. He got her pregnant. She had an abortion. Playing her Algonquin role, she had somehow to laugh about it, if not to laugh it off. "Serves me right for putting all my eggs in one bastard."[2]

Unfortunate Coincidence

By the time you swear you're his,
 Shivering and sighing,
And he vows his passion is
 Infinite, undying –
Lady, make a note of this:
 One of you is lying.

One evening in January, 1923, Dorothy cut both her wrists with Eddie's discarded razor blades. Her maid discovered her in time to rush her to the hospital. Many of her poems touch on suicide. None is more despairing than the four lines of "Rhyme Against Living":

If wild my breast and sore my pride,
I bask in dreams of suicide;
If cool my heart and high my head,
I think, "How lucky are the dead!"

She was often short of money, didn't pay for her room at the Algonquin, and never ate at home. She envied Edna Ferber, also an Algonquinite, whose over-stuffed novels made her a fortune and which Dorothy described as "an oil well gushing dollar bills." Dorothy derided her: "I understand she whistles at her typewriter . . . There was that poor sucker Flaubert rolling around on his floor for three days looking for the right words."[3]

She began to spend weekends at the homes of the afflu-ent. She liked their attentions and had a stream of lovers, rich, good-looking men—Roman numerals after their names also appealed strongly—who called her Mrs. Parker, and she wore "that title as grandly as if it had been inherited." At the same time, it was necessary for her to mock them as Long Island playboys, gentlemen stockbrokers, "low-brow moguls who had never heard of James Joyce."[4] She (almost) persuaded herself that she loathed them and was punishing them for sleeping with her by spending their money. Of course she knew perfectly well what she should do when encountering them.

Social Note

Lady, lady, should you meet
One whose ways are all discreet,
One who murmurs that his wife
Is the lodestar of his life,
One who keeps assuring you
That he never was untrue,

Never loved another one...
Lady, lady, better run!

When we read a good deal of Dorothy's poetry at one time it comes to seem repetitive. But the poems are brief, vigorous and, as we wait for that last twist at the end, addictive as well as amusing. We have experienced what she describes. It is all very well to say, "hide your heart and lock your door," but genuine wisdom is to recognize the irresistible power of Eros.

Wisdom

This I say, and this I know:
  Love has seen the last of me.
Love's a trodden lane to woe,
  Love's a path to misery.

This I know, and knew before,
  This I tell you, of my years:
Hide your heart, and lock your door.
  Hell's afloat in lovers' tears.

Give your heart, and toss and moan;
  What a pretty fool you look!
I am sage, who sit alone:
  Here's my wool, and here's my book.

Look! A lad's a-waiting there.
  Tall he is and bold and gay.
What the devil do I care
  What I know, and what I say?

The light-hearted tone of the following lines, among Parker's most frequently quoted, almost obscures a genuinely depressed state of mind.

Faute De Mieux

Travel, trouble, music, art,
  A kiss, a frock, a rhyme –
I never said they feed my heart,
  But still they pass my time.

SHE FREQUENTED THEATERS, beyond her duties as a reviewer, and early on fixed in her head the possibility of a dramatic success. She wrote a four-scene farce with George Kaufman, *Business Is Business*, satirizing the national obsession with money. It played as a prologue to *Beggar On Horseback*, a popular success by George S. Kaufman and Marc Connelly. The *New York Times* reviewer thought it had "scintillating ideas" and some "amusing lines," but neither of the authors kept a copy of it. She collaborated with Robert Benchley on a one-act play, *Nero*, which had a single Off-Broadway performance. She made a major effort with Elmer Rice, who had scored a great success with his play, *The Adding Machine*. Together they wrote *Close Harmony*, based on the marital difficulties of Robert Benchley and his wife and of Eddie and herself, self-laceration being one of her specialties. It got good reviews, but audiences were meager and it closed in a month. Later revived in Chicago, it was a success, running fifteen weeks and another ten in several Midwestern cities. That was little consolation to her. Manhattan's judgment was what mattered.

A perceptive contemporary described her as "a masochist whose passion for unhappiness knew no bounds."[5] There was apparently no escape from the demons of a sense of personal unworthiness, of self-destruction. She attempted suicide again and almost succeeded, swallowing a large number of barbiturates one night and not being discovered until the next afternoon, inert and barely breathing. *The New Yorker* magazine (its first issue was February 1925) gave her a sophisticated place for her work. At the same time, Dorothy published poetry in the *New York World*, in which "F.P.A."—Franklin Pierce Adams, (1881–1960)—conducted a column called The Conning Tower, made up of light verse, gossip, and clever comments sent in to him and published without payment to the authors. It was a coup to have something in the column. Some contributors used pseudonyms, others initials. Established writers, eager for publicity, happily used their own names. Dorothy had submitted poems to The Conning Tower from her first days at *Vogue*, but without success. Now, a poem by Dorothy Parker appearing there would be the talk of the town.

IN 1925, SHE came fully into her own as a writer and at moments her verse entered the public domain, for she had achieved a unique style. On July 31, the *New York World* published her poem, "Threnody."

> Lilacs blossom just as sweet
> Now my heart is shattered.
> If I bowled it down the street,
> Who's to say it mattered?
> If there's one that rode away
> What would I be missing?
> Lips that taste of tears, they say,
> Are the best for kissing.

Eyes that watch the morning star
Seem a little brighter
Arms held out to darkness are
Usually whiter.
Shall I bar the strolling guest,
Bind my brow with willow,
When, they say, the empty breast
Is the softer pillow?

That a heart falls tinkling down,
Never think it ceases.
Every likely lad in town
Gathers up the pieces.
If there's one gone whistling by
Would I let it grieve me?
Let him wonder if I lie;
Let him half believe me.

On August 16, the *World* published two poems, irresistibly quotable, which are known and repeated by people who know no other poetry. One was a bit of sociology—a simple observation in two lines:

News Item

Men seldom make passes
At girls who wear glasses.

The other poem was also easily memorized, but it probably did not fix itself in readers' minds as being autobiographical. For us, however, reading it now, in the context of a tragic life, it conveys unbearable suffering, terrifying detachment, and yet, finally, a desire to go on.

Resumé

Razors pain you;
Rivers are damp;
Acids stain you;
And drugs cause cramp.
Guns aren't lawful;
Nooses give;
Gas smells awful;
You might as well live.

So identified would she be with witty comments that when people didn't know who the author of some witticism was, they attributed it to her, a phenomenon she understood.

Oscar Wilde

If, with the literate, I am
Impelled to try an epigram,
I never seek to take the credit;
We all assume that Oscar said it.

Even today, Americans assume that Dorothy said it.

Urbane but untraveled, for the first time Dorothy now felt an intense need to leave New York City, where her life had become emotionally tangled and suffocating. At the end of 1925, she made arrangements to sail for France. Elinor Wylie and Bill Benét came down to the dock to say goodbye.

8. SARA TEASDALE

I N THE FIRST five years of the 1920s, Sara Teasdale marked
time. Though she rarely ventured into New York City's
streets, it remained her city, and she could still imaginatively
visualize it as a series of Impressionist images.

Evening (New York)

Blue dust of evening over my city,
 Over the ocean of roofs and the tall towers
Where the window lights, myriads and myriads,
 Bloom from the walls like climbing flowers.

She also described the city in very different terms. Writing to
Vachel Linday, she characterized New York City as "a bad dream,"
that "frazzles you out and breaks your heart. The emotional and
nervous strain is hellish. Subject yourself to the hot blast from this

roaring furnace ...and see what becomes of you."[1] She frequently left the furnace, but she always came back and never thought seriously of leaving. What was it the city gave her? It was an unparalleled observation post for viewing the national and international literary scene. (Like Elinor Wylie, she was wholly uninterested in contemporary politics.) Most of all, the city afforded her privacy. She could live in it almost anonymously and no one would know her personal affairs. Or would they? One of her poems suggests that this matter was not free of anxiety. When she walked in the "broken roar" of the city streets and looked into the eyes of the multitude, she believed that she could pierce their disguises and discover their sorrows. This made it likely that, when people peered into her eyes, they discerned the sorrow concealed there. What sorrow? Her marriage? Her failed love?

Faces

People that I meet and pass
  In the city's broken roar,
Faces that I lose so soon
  And have never found before.

Do you know how much you tell
  In the meeting of our eyes,
How ashamed I am, and sad
  To have pierced your poor disguise?

Secrets rushing without sound
  Crying from your hiding places –
Let me go, I cannot bear
  The sorrow of the passing faces.

– People in the restless street,
Can it be, oh can it be
In the meeting of our eyes
That you know as much of me?

Typically, she refrained from direct participation in the Modernist and anti-Modernist conflicts of the time, but though a convinced traditionalist she was nonetheless open to new work. As a member of a Poetry Society jury in 1925, she was influential in awarding first prize to Countee Cullen's *Color*, which was important recognition for an African American poet.

For her, the greatest Modernist writer was indisputably Marcel Proust, whom she read in French. "No man ever lived who understood the human spirit better." She wrote to Edmund Wilson to congratulate him on his path-breaking critical study of Proust, saying that he was "the only critic ...who fully appreciated Proust's achievement and importance." Her response to Proust was based on a profound affinity. His "curiosity for the labyrinths of human perversity, his exquisitely refined sensibility, his nocturnal insomniac imagination, his invalidism as the condition of his art, his acute sense of death and time all were mirrored in herself."[2]

At a less exalted level, she closely followed Elinor Wylie's dazzling climb to fame, noting how Wylie managed "avenues of influence" and decided: "She means to be the kingpin of the whole game. So be it! an attractive and clever person—but a great spirit? I wonder." Privately, she dashed off a jingle she kept to herself: "Elinor Wylie, Elinor Wylie what do I hear you say? I wish it were Shelley astride my belly, instead of poor Bill Benét."[3]

Wylie's astonishing fecundity contrasted with her own difficulties in writing. Poems were coming slowly now and in moments of discouragement, her previous work seemed to her to be "poor draggled baby clothes." This wasn't the view of her poetry held by her numerous readers or by her publishers, who conceived the idea of another anthology that would keep her in the public eye until a new volume of poems was ready. *Rainbow Gold*, a collection of seventy-nine poems by English and American poets, was aimed, in a special way, at children. It wasn't a book of poems by children or about children; rather, Sara thought she could select important poems that would appeal to children between the ages of ten and fourteen and, without a hint of preachy condescension, encourage their interest in good poetry. "I shall avoid poems teaching a moral lesson," she told Amy Lowell. [4] She hoped to make a good deal of money from *Rainbow Gold*. And she did. It outsold any of her previous books. When it appeared in September 1922, it was dedicated to "the beautiful memory of my father." John Teasdale had died only the month before.

Her dismissive remarks about the quality of her earlier poetry were only a passing mood. Although she was writing much less than before, she believed that the quality of her work was higher than ever. She was writing short lyrics as she had done for a decade, at a time when other poets were moving in more expansive directions and to larger forms. As always, her lyrics seemed simpler than they were. In a rare interview she explained something of what she tried to achieve in mood and rhythm if not content, something easy to overlook; "Most of my lyrics are a matter of balance and speed rather than a matter of design which can be perceived by the eyes." [5] She illustrated this by reference to one of her own poems that was a personal favorite, a seemingly simple pattern of eight brief lines.

The Unchanging

Sun-swept beaches with a light wind blowing
From the immense blue circle of the sea,
And the soft thunder where long waves whiten –
These were the same for Sappho as for me.

Two thousand years – much has gone by forever,
Change takes the gods and ships and speech of men –
But here on the beaches that time passes over
The heart aches now as then.

The picture of the seashore, she explained. "must be balanced against the mood of the maker of the poem ...which rises swiftly for the first three lines and subsides finally on the slower fourth line. It rises again for two lines and subsides finally on the slow last two lines. The short and very slow last line is an emotional echo of the 4th line."[6]

HER FATHER'S DEATH increased her sense of isolation, but her response to the external world was contradictory. She craved distance from people but also feared isolation. Often physically debilitated herself, Ernst's frantic activity annoyed and depressed her. Yet it was his all-consuming work that allowed her to live comfortably and have most everything she desired. In 1923, they spent several weeks in England, meeting writers and going to museums and theaters. Her spirits rose in observing English culture, which she found reassuringly traditional.

The success of that trip led to another, not with Ernst, but with an older cousin whom she liked. The second trip was a failure.

The weather turned cold and rainy and Sara's spirits were soon as gloomy as the weather. She increasingly felt so detached from the external world that everything seemed to come to her as dream-like and unreal. The cause of this sense of unreality was much deeper than gloomy weather. She was determined to be honest with herself in reflecting on her life and behavior and she now came to feel that the life of unchallengeable conventionality that the non-poet in her desired was a complete void. Life seemed "hideously miserable."[7] She was forty in 1924, and the almost simultaneous death of two women who had been all-important to her youth reinforced her sense of being adrift.

Sara Teasdale

After two years of painful ill health, Sara's powerful and controlling mother died. "I have been completely floored by the experience: I had thought I had realized it all before it happened. But I hadn't."[8] The death of Eleonora Duse was the second loss, though Sara insisted she no longer cared about Duse and didn't wish to be reminded of her early poetry centering on the actress as her Muse. Letters from Amy Lowell were filled with details about Duse.

As well, though she took heart from the quality of what she was writing, she began to accept the fact that her creative impulse was ebbing. For a decade poems had simply flowed through her, but by the early 1920s, she wrote no more than a poem a month, if that. At one time, she went eight months without writing any poetry. She knew that she had accumulated a considerable number of poems she thought highly of, but she insisted that it wasn't likely that she would publish another volume of verse. Some words she had written to a friend summed up her feelings. "I do nothing but dream and watch and once in a long time make a song as light and useless as a sparrow's feather. What did God do it all for anyway."[9]

9. Amy Lowell

I N THE EARLY 1920s, Amy Lowell carried on as before, lecturing, attending meetings of poetry societies, defending new verse. But there were differences. As she wrote to H.D.: "I think that the time for discussing the new poetry has gone by. I am willing to talk about it, explain it...but I will not stand up to be badgered." Most importantly, she was once again moving in a new direction as a writer, putting an enormous amount of time and energy into researching and writing a biography of John Keats, whose life and poetry had come to be as obsessively important to her as Percy Shelley's was to Elinor Wylie. As a very young girl, Amy had discovered Keats's poetry. It established "the fundamental values of life" for her. She understood him as a skeptic, "certain of nothing but the holiness of the heart's affections and the truth of imagination," which became her creed. [1]

She often worked through much of the night, getting no more than four hours of sleep, and badly straining her eyes. Sur-

rounded by piles of material as she wrote, her manuscript grew
and grew and finally became two volumes. "It looks like the Eiffel
Tower, and as though it were going to fall over and smother me."[2]
Keats undoubtedly damaged her health, but her physical problems went back to a period well before the biography. That she was
overweight was a subject not infrequently mentioned in stories
and in gossip about her, it was one of the "colorful" aspects of her
persona. It also re-enforced the picture of her as strong and overpowering. But the references to her weight also existed at a lower
and sleazier plane, one of the elements in a picture sketched by
newspaper columnists that was unrelentingly misogynist. Apparently there was no one who wished to find out and write the truth,
which was that she suffered ill health for many years and endured
agonizing pain, would never talk about it, was stoical, and did not
use it as a source of sympathy.

Amy Lowell

In the summer of 1916, Amy and Ada Russell were driving in the country when their buggy went off the road. Amy matter-of-factly lifted the rear wheels of the buggy back onto the road, and in doing so felt some internal tearing. It was eventually diagnosed as an umbilical hernia, and when she could endure no more pain, doctors operated to repair the rupture. They promised that all would be well, but it wasn't so. Over the next three years another operation followed, then another, and yet another. Amy was realistic in writing to her brother Abbot, "I do not think there is any real hope of a cure in my case ...my age and size are against me." She was vividly candid in a letter to Bryher, saying, "I do not fear the operation at all but I do terribly fear and dread the long weeks flat on my back when 1 am not myself but a hysterical maniac feeling that the ceiling is pressing itself down my throat and I cannot breathe, and all the real world and its interests seem dissolved in a nightmare of pain and discomfort."[3] Instead of cheap jibes about the "Amazon" who was a "literary hand-grenade thrower," the important and moving story should have been about Amy Lowell, courageous and heroic.

IN 1922, SHE looked back again to her own family, to cousin James Russell Lowell, whose *Fable for Critics* (1848) was a satire about contemporaries, Emerson, Whittier, Longfellow, and others. Amy did the same with *A Critical Fable*, "twenty-one modern poets popped off 'twixt a laugh and a pun,'" among them Robert Frost, Carl Sandburg, Vachel Lindsay, Sara Teasdale, and Edna Millay. ("The only omission I am sorry for is Elinor Wylie, but at the time I wrote it...she was not so prominent as she has become."[4])The purpose of the poem in couplets was to amuse, but sharp observations were mixed with affability. The form was simple. A "gentleman taking a walk," joins the narrator, listens, asks questions, and comments. Having at considerable length looked at some of the leading male poets of the time, the narrator observed:

> There's Frost with his blueberry pastures and hills
> All peopled by folk who have so many ills
> 'Tis a business to count 'em, their subtle insanities.
> One half are sheer mad, and the others inanities.

And she was very interesting in her comments about some of the women. As would have been expected, there was a good deal about H.D. and the unique qualities of the verse of her one-time Imagist colleague.

> This author's become a species of fable
> For she masks her identity under a label.
> If others have ancestors, she would forget hers
> And appear the spontaneous child of two letters,
> The printing of which is the bane of type-setters.
> They have called her a dryad just stepped from a bosk,
> But I see an ice maiden within an ice kiosk,
> With icicle stalactites hanging around her,
> And the violets frozen with which they have crowned her –

What of:

> "Our love-poet, *par excellence,* Sara Teasdale,"
> I said with a flourish. Now that was a whale
> Of a compliment, such things deserve an entail,
> 'Twas so brilliantly super even if it were true,

And I knew very well 'twas but one of a cue,
"This poet," I went on, "is a great niece of Sappho,
I know not how many 'greats' laid in a row
There should be, but her pedigree's perfectly clear;
You can read it in 'Magazine Verse' for the year."

As well:

There's Edna Millay with her 'Aria da Cap –
O'h, she dealt all society a pretty sharp rap
With that bauble of hers, be it drama or fable,
Which I certainly trust won't be laid on the table
In my time. Her 'Bean-Stalk' is a nice bit of greenery,
For one of her charms is her most charming scenery,
Few can handle more deftly this sort of machinery.

Anyone interested in the life of Amy Lowell, as well as her poetry, would find some heartfelt passages about her in *A Critical Fable*, among them her declaration of independence of the family's poetic inheritance.

"Between her and your friend. No one likes to be bound
In a sort of perpetual family pound
Tied by *espirit de corps* to the wheels of the dead.
A poet above all people must have his head.
Indeed it's been whispered the lady sees red
When the subject is broached, she will find her own latitude."
"My friend, were he here, would extol such an attitude."

And she wished readers to understand Amy Lowell as sensitive artist, easily and often wounded by fierce attacks, not as the Generalissima of the poetry wars.

And you'll guess by this time, without farther allusion,
That the lady's unique and surprising profusion
Creates in some minds an unhappy confusion.

Despite her traducers, there's always a heart
Hid away in her poems for the seeking; impassioned,
Beneath silver surfaces cunningly fashioned
To baffle coarse pryings, it waits for the touch
Of a man who takes surfaces only as such.
Her work's not, if you will, for the glib amateur,
But I wonder, would it be improved if it were?

A Critical Fable was published as a hoax, attributed to a University of California professor who had written a satire about contemporary poets. He knew nothing of the hoax and was understandably bewildered. Eventually Amy confessed to being the author. Opinions about the book varied. Conrad Aiken was not flattered to appear in its pages and thought it "damn rotten."[5]

Amy was an efficient correspondent and as it became more difficult for her to move about, she depended upon letters to maintain her wide circle of friendships, with men and women, in Boston and beyond. In the world of poetry her friendships were overwhelmingly with women, Margaret Anderson and Harriet Monroe and three other women she was especially fond of, H.D., Bryher, and Sara Teasdale.

In September 1917, Bryher sent a letter to Amy about the new poetry and asked for a reading list. In responding Amy recommended H.D.'s *Sea Garden*, among other books. Bryher then read *Tendencies in Modern American Poetry* and found out that H.D. was a woman who lived in England. Bryher wrote to H.D. and they met on July 17, 1918, a date they celebrated for the rest of their lives. Amy's writing had a great influence on Bryher, "I wanted a new world and in the Imagist writers—particularly in Miss Lowell—all I needed lay before my eyes."[6] To express her gratitude she wrote a pamphlet, *Amy Lowell: A Critical Appreciation*, in 1918. When Bryher and H.D. came to America in 1920, Amy met them and they dined together, and a steady flow of letters to Bryher and to H.D. followed.

Amy's friendship with Sara Teasdale also began with a letter, sent from St. Louis in October 1915, about *Sword Blades and Poppy Seed*. "The poems are always burning with brilliant colors, and the oftener I read them the more they flame and the more keenly they interest me." When *Men, Women and Ghosts* came out, Ernst Filsinger read it to Sara, who became "so enthusiastic that she forgot her illness and then had to rest a while."[7] That Sara was a very conventional poet in terms of form mattered not at all, as Amy respected her refusal to chase after popularity. They usually dined together when Amy descended on New York City and Sara came to Sevenels. Their lack of formal education was a bond, but the contrasts between them were also striking. Sara was thin as Amy was stout; Sara had a shy but dignified manner, while Amy's was a theatrical and public one.

Her friendship with H.D. began professionally, one poet to another, when Amy first read an H.D. poem in *Poetry* and it came over her, "Why, I, too, am an imagiste!" Personal contact in her two visits to London in 1913 and 1914 added personal affection. "The great thing which my summer has done for me," she wrote to Harriet Monroe "is bringing me the intimacy of the Aldingtons. They are a perfectly charming couple." Her affection deepened with the passage of time. She wrote to Bryher, "I get so homesick for you and Hilda sometimes that I really don't now what to do. It seems a thousand years since I have been in London." In the early 1920s, the number of letters dropped off, but Amy still felt as she had: "Although the ocean separates us, nothing else does or can and Hilda can always turn to me for anything at any time."[8]

A special and unique relationship was the respect and love she felt for Eleonora Duse. Twenty years—Amy's entire literary life—had passed since she had first seen and heard Duse in Boston, and now, in the fall of 1923, "emaciated, white-haired, frail," sixty-four, Duse had returned to New York City. Amy went to see her at the Metropolitan Opera. "The glamour of her personality and the strength of her art overwhelmed even the most captious of the youngest critics; her greatest and last triumph had begun."[9]

The day before she left for New York City, Amy had written to Duse mentioning that they had met once, long before, and offering her services if she could be of assistance. When she returned to Boston, she found a letter awaiting her from Duse, sent from England, saying that she hoped they might meet again, when, in early December, she would perform twice at the Boston Opera House. After the second performance, Duse came to Sevenels. "Her inspiration had turned the purposeless girl into a great poet." No doubt Amy conveyed these sentiments to her, but the only bit of their conversation preserved was Duse saying. "The past is dead: the future alone lives." However, she promised to come and stay at Sevenels when her tour was completed.[10]

Duse went on to Washington, D.C., and Baltimore—Amy was present in both cities—where she completed her twenty-performance tour. As she was impoverished and had little desire to return to Italy where Benito Mussolini, whom she disdained, now governed, Duse signed on for twenty additional performances (New Orleans, Havana, San Francisco, and back

East). She never made it there. She was taken ill in Pittsburgh and died on April 21st. Amy attended the funeral service in New York City on May 1. "All day long...there was a steady stream of people; I can't imagine how many there must have been in the whole three days, thousands thousands...It was all most wonderful and perfectly dignified, and not in the least a jarring tribute."[11]

After Duse's visit to Sevenels, Amy wrote a six-sonnet sequence, "Eleonora Duse," which was published in *The New Republic* at the time of Duse's death. Amy also wrote two other poems about Duse and included them all in a bundle that she sent to Sara Teasdale, who had shared her admiration for Duse and also had been influenced by her to write poetry. "I am rather anxious to know what you think of them," she wrote to Sara, adding that in her opinion the two individual poems were "better than the sonnets. I do not consider myself a star sonneteer. But I believe they all show feeling; certainly there was plenty of feeling there."[12]

The single poem which she preferred, "seems to me rather good as it is with quite a little feeling." Sara wrote back immediately. "You have praised the lady as she deserves. That is the highest praise that could be given you, I think. I know it is the highest praise you would ask." And of the single poem, "I don't know that I have ever read finer praise from one woman to another."[13]

To Eleonora Duse, In Answer to a Letter

"Regrets and memories these short December days."
How the words cut and scar themselves
Across my heart!

Dear lady of the great compassion,
All tenderness enmeshed in withes of truth,
Experience harboured for its seeking flame.
Clean burning flame of knowledge beyond thought,
Sword-blade of sheerest beauty,
As the sun sinks wanly,
Branch by branch,
Through the shaking, leafless trees,
How cruelly the twilight comes –
I watch it here,
At this long distance from you,
And rage at impotence
Which can give you no brighter present
Than the flicker of a small red candle
Lit by you long ago.
You wrong yourself dwelling upon the past;
I have it from your lips:
"The past is dead. The future alone has life."
The past is dead, save in the continuity
Of your most inaccessible loveliness.
Where touch is healing should be no regret
At that which makes it so.
You walked, and walk, incarnate soul
Of human needs and meetings.
This sight of you is the clarity of courage;
Your movements, insistent, compelling, muted trumpets in a
still air;
Your voice, ah, dear, that voice, as April rain
Dropping at evening on beds of unsprung tulips.
Where has there ever been a flesh
So rightly framing such a spirit? Tell me.
You cannot.

Words are pebbles.

A gravel path for you to tread and spurn.

Music is liker to encase your essence:

Yet you escape, for what you really are

Hangs to no swiftest flash of evocation.

But floats in rondure of its perfectness

Out of our sight as possible, impossible.

Peak of a human capability

Infinite spirit with the lightest shadowing

Of merciful and finite flesh.

Has any one ever so held the cords of life,

Of all our lives, as you?

You dare not say there has and gaze truth in the eye.

Look back, then, if you must,

But see plain fact.

Yourself the soul's wine of a generation.

The whispered bourne of blessings to a world.

ONE FRIENDSHIP, WITH Ada Dwyer Russell, became Amy's greatest love. Ada Dwyer was born in Salt Lake City in 1863. Her father, who ran a bookshop, sent his daughter to be educated in Boston. She appeared in school plays and with dramatic clubs and moved steadily into a successful career in theater, in England and the United States. Ada married Harold Russell in 1893, had a daughter by him, whom she sent to England for her education. She subsequently divorced Russell. Amy saw her perform in Boston in 1912; they soon became friends, sharing an interest in books, especially poetry. Amy read her the manuscript of A *Dome of Many Coloured Glass* and Ada frankly offered suggestions about it. For two years following, Amy urged Ada to move in with her at Sevenels and in 1914 Ada did so. "At last Amy had found the friend who understood her thoroughly and "whom she could trust utterly."[14]

Ada took over many of the responsibilities of running Sevenels and of assisting with Amy's career. She traveled to England with her in 1914; organized two secretaries to type the poems Amy wrote through the night, read proof meticulously, helped with the correspondence, chloroformed the sheep dogs that had come down with ptomaine poisoning ("but don't tell me when it is to happen")[15], made travel arrangements; and calmed and comforted her.

In return, Amy wrote for her some of the most moving and impassioned love poems in American poetry.

A Sprig of Rosemary

I cannot see your face.
When I think of you,
It is your hands which I see.
Your hands
Sewing.
Holding a book,
Resting for a moment on the sill of a window.
My eyes keep always the sight of your hands,
But my heart holds the sound of your voice,
And the soft brightness which is your soul.

Her lover was a contemporary version of the famous Botticelli painting of Venus:

Venus Transiens

Tell me,
Was Venus more beautiful
Than you are,
When she topped
The crinkled waves
Drifting shoreward
On her plaited shell?
Was Botticelli's Vision
Fairer than mine:
And were the painted rosebuds
He tossed his lady
Of better worth
Than the words I blow about you
To cover your too great loveliness
As with a gauze
Of misted silver?

For me,
You stand poised
In the blue and buoyant air.
Cinctured by bright winds,
Treading the sunlight.
And the waves which precede you
Ripple and stir
The sands at my feet

Or this febrile anticipation of erotic love:

Vernal Equinox

The scent of hyacinths, like a pale mist,
 lies between me and my book;
And the South Wind, washing through the room,
Makes the candles quiver.
My nerves sting at a spatter of rain on the shutter,
And I am uneasy with the thrusting of
 green shoots
Outside, in the night.

We can respond sympathetically to "the most fully articulated sequence of lesbian poetry between Sappho and the 1960s."[16]

Wheat-In-The-Ear

You stand between the cedars and the green spruces,
Brilliantly naked
And I think:
 What are you,
 A gem under sunlight?
 A poised spear?
 A jade cup?
You flash in front of the cedars and the tall spruces,
And I see that you are fire –
Sacrificial fire on a jade altar
Spear-tongue of white, ceremonial fire.
My eyes burn.
My hands are flames seeking you
But you are as remote from me as a bright pointed planet
Set in the distance of an evening sky

And:

A Decade

When you came, you were like red wine and honey
And the taste of you burnt my mouth with its sweetness
Now you are like morning bread.
Smooth and pleasant
I hardly taste you at all for I know your savor,
But I am completely nourished.

And:

Opal

You are ice and fire,
The touch of you burns my hands like snow.
You are cold and flame.
You are the crimson of amaryllis,
The silver of moon-touched magnolias.
When I am with you,
My heart is a frozen pond
Gleaming with agitated torches.

How was it that these love songs didn't cause a scandal in their day, that their author was not heralded as a proponent of free or perverted love? Amy never played the role of a feminist, and she certainly didn't want to be identified as a lesbian. She had the courage to stand up to public abuse but was intensely private about her personal life. Her feelings about these matters, like those of countless other people at the time (and since), were no doubt conflicted. She could write as she did and at the same time say in a letter, "That the Victorians refused to give sex its proper weight is of course true but that we are now overemphasizing it and particularly, its perversion is equally true."[17] How one dealt with explosive subjects depended on context and language. Her poems are ambiguous as to gender. They are about love and lovers and the reader may read them as she or he wishes. Shakespeare's sonnets are a famous example of such ambiguity. So successful was Amy in evading any explicit category while writing as she wished, that it wasn't until the last quarter century that critics have explored the ways in which these poems both reveal and conceal.

The biography of Keats was completed by the end of 1924. Ada had finished proofreading and Amy's publisher was organizing an advertising campaign in England, public lectures and interviews, where her poetry was not well known. She and Ada had decided to go to England in April, and all through the winter of 1925, Ada supervised packing and arrangements for taking care of Sevenels. A lavish dinner was given in Amy's honor in Boston sponsored by the city's social and intellectual elite and, as reported in a local newspaper, "Many Friends Bid Amy Lowell Adieu."[18]

Little did they know what was to come. Perhaps the preparations and the mounting excitement were too much. The day before Amy and Ada were to leave, a "terrible pain struck through Amy."[19] It was the most violent hernia attack in several years. Her doctors, initially prepared to operate at once, decided that absolute quiet would do instead. The next day telegrams and letters were sent out canceling all travel plans. Amy was constantly nauseated but was able to write a few necessary letters. She lost weight and strength. By early May she could barely whisper, "I feel like hell." Doctors scheduled an operation for May 13. On the morning of May 12,

Amy said, "Peter,'" (her pet name for Ada), "I'm done. Why can't they leave me alone? The operations never have been any good." She decided to get dressed. As she sat in front of her mirror, she noticed the right side of her face drop. "Pete, a stroke."[20] She lost consciousness and died an hour and a half later.

She was buried in the family plot in Mt. Auburn cemetery. There were no religious services. Only family members were present. The extraordinary number of people who knew of her and felt personal affection for her became clear in the next few weeks. The tributes were numerous. Marianne Moore's assessment was typically restrained but perceptive, seeing Amy as a "cosmopolitan yet isolated" person, whose "armored self-reliance sometimes obscured a generosity, a love for romance, the luster of chivalry which was essentially hers."[21]

PART FOUR

DIVERGENCE
1925–1929

1. Marianne Moore

MARIANNE MOORE'S POSITION as a detached observer of contemporary intellectual and poetic culture came to an end when she accepted the position as editor of *The Dial*. Now she was a participant, helping shape the content and tone of artistic discourse. She approached her new work with gratitude to the magazine for its previous support and determination that it maintain the highest standards, that liberality and discrimination be its watchwords, that it be receptive of the new but respectful of traditional work.

Marianne didn't think in terms of "radical" or "conservative"; for her, it was about "the entanglement of good with ill," and along the same lines she made an oblique reference to the poetry of Edna Millay by observing: "It would all but seem that figs do grow on thistles, not that I for a moment think so, but one is confused to the point of not coming to any decision respecting a good many of the thistles."[1]

Being in the middle helped define work on either side of what Louise Bogan meant when she wrote that *The Dial* made clear "the obvious division between American avant-garde and American conventional writing." But if it was in the middle, there was no question that *The Dial* was hospitable to varying forms of Modernist art. It encouraged and attracted a wide range of contributors in the next five years, many of the most celebrated European and American poets, critics, prose writers, sculptors and painters. The first issue of the *The Dial* that Marianne was responsible for as editor contained work by both Ezra Pound and the English Victorian scholar George Saintsbury. "I think that individuality was the great thing," she later reminisced. "We were not conforming to anything. We certainly didn't have a policy, except I remember hearing the word 'intensity' very often. A thing must have an 'intensity.' That seemed to be the criterion."[2]

The Dial was not open to everything. It would not publish detective stories, work that had appeared elsewhere, or unsolicited translations. There were two aspects of her editorial policy that provoked considerable criticism. She insisted that contributors accept editorial changes in their work or risk rejection, abandoning the original policy that the author had the final say. Marianne had published several of Hart Crane's poems when he was still unknown and he was grateful for that, but he resented her editorial intrusions, referring to her privately as "The Rt. Rev. Mountjoy." Maxwell Bodenheim, a radical Modernist of the day, was outraged at what he regarded as her rigid authoritarianism: "God how I hate you and your mean, unfair, half blind, apprehensively arbitrarily, literary group." She gave as good as she got, though more subtly, returning Bodenheim's "Poetic Essay" with the comment, "*The Dial* congratulates you upon lines nine to fourteen inclusive."[3]

She also gained the reputation of being priggish, unwilling

to accept work that was sexually suggestive. "My work has come to have just one quality of value in it: I will not touch or have to do with those things which I detest."[4] Mary Moore objected strenuously to a photograph of three nude sculptures by Aristide Maillol that *The Dial* was about to publish, so Marianne withdrew it. She thought well of E. E. Cummings's poetry and of him—he admired her in turn and their friendship endured through their lifetimes—but was intensely disapproving of the sexual references in some of his poems. At the same time, *The Dial* published D.H. Lawrence's poetry. One incident involving what some people assumed to be sexual censorship is ambiguous. Marianne opposed publishing an excerpt from James Joyce's work-in-progress, *Finnegan's Wake*. She said she rejected it because she disliked publishing excerpts from larger works and, with specific reference to Joyce's novel, because the excerpt was too obscure. Was the notoriously obscure poet/editor aware of the irony of this?

Marianne liked the "compacted pleasantness" of the three-story *Dial* building at 152 West 13th Street with its "carpeted stairs, fire-place and white-mantel piece rooms," and happily remembered the pleasant lunches and teas there. The prevailing feeling among the staff was one of harmonious collective activity. "Everybody liked what he was doing, and if we made grievous mistakes we were sorry but we laughed over them," she recalled thirty years later. At the time, there was a good deal of worry and anxiety and perhaps not a great deal of laughter. In one other letter, she described an especially dreadful week. "I don't know what sickness infected the office." The entire week was a "rolling up-hill of casks containing old bear's grease, & dead clams, & unpurified debris of editorial crab shells."[5]

What more than compensated for those times was the companionship of the two owners of *The Dial*, who encouraged, guided, and intellectually stimulated her. The two were a very unusual pair. James Sibley Watson, Jr., was a medical doctor, an innovator in radiology, a filmmaker, and a contributor to the magazine under a pseudonym. He was notoriously taciturn. His scientific education was of course a bond with Marianne. Scofield Thayer was a poet and businessman. Like Marianne, he had an ambivalent relationship to the Village, living on the east side of Washington Square in a very un-Village apartment with red lacquer-painted walls, bookshelves filled with first editions, and Aubrey Beardsley drawings on the walls. He subsidized his Modernist magazine, but his own poetry was conventional. He described Marianne as the most intellectual woman he had known, but confessed he didn't understand her poems, referred to the "silly cantos" of Ezra Pound, and expressed his disappointment with *The Waste Land*. Thayer also suffered from paranoia. His niece consulted Sigmund Freud about it, and Thayer withdrew from active participation in the magazine. Marianne's relationship with Watson was entirely positive but he was more and more involved with his radiology practice and with experimental filmmaking, and he spent most of his time in Rochester, New York.

When Marianne agreed to be editor she could not have anticipated the demands it would make on her time and psychic energy. "I have not read a book—outside of work—since being at *The Dial*."[6] That was said matter-of-factly; there was no complaining or whining in her letters, the number of which was reduced in these years, as she could not spare the time. However, the demands of the work and her consciousness of those demands are not the same thing. She brought to her editorship the same unsparing dedication she brought to writing poetry. "I have not one hour at my command," she explained to a friend. Family responsibilities also took their toll. Warner, wholly committed to military service and to his own family, was three thousand miles away and emotionally distant. Mary, more and more concerned with spiritual questions, continued to resent the magazine's demands on Marianne's time—including the fact that she worked on the Sabbath.

"I like the work, really delight in it," Marianne wrote, and a good deal of the pleasure came from additional aspects of her role. She contributed a "Comment" column in forty-two issues, several long essays, and numerous "Brief Mentions," paragraph-long reviews. All of these gave her a more personal public voice than the strictly editorial work and an opportunity to air her personal views. Her prose was highly individual and recognizable, Latinate in vocabulary, subtle, indirect, like her poetry, different in this respect from Louise Bogan, who felt her poetic and prose voices were very different. Marianne's reviews depended heavily on quotations from whichever book was being reviewed. In a letter to T.S. Eliot, she wrote, "To be 'excessively harsh' is not to me perhaps as it is not to you, emotionally congenial." One of her continuing differences with Ezra Pound was that she thought him unnecessarily aggressive, even belligerent, in much of his reviewing. The critic Yvor Winters said that Marianne's prose was "like a crow who picks over the ash heap and leaves the ashes behind," to which she replied, "Your metaphor of the crow is amusing the more so that it is perhaps true."[7] As editor of *The Dial,* Marianne made her mark in American intellectual history, but at great cost. In her years at the magazine she didn't write a single poem.

In 1927, Marianne Moore relinquished her editorial duties for two months and went with her mother to England, a visit that sharpened her ideas about national identity. "How could you bear to leave London?" she asked an English visitor. She read English literary journals, kept in touch with contemporary English events by means of the *Illustrated London News,* and carried on a steady correspondence with poets living there, both English and American. Yet she was proud of being Irish and fond of Ireland, though she had never visited it. "I am purely Celtic," she said.[8] Intellectually, Marianne was internationalist. She wished to establish how important national identities or stereotypes are to us while insistent that these must not become nationalistic jingoism. Her poem *England* demonstrates how her mind worked on this theme: It begins with a familiar image of England, its rivers and towns and abbeys, then jumps briefly to a list of cultural elements for Italy, Greece, and the East. It then contrasts these with America, this "wild man's land," to demonstrate that such stereotypes might produce "continents of misapprehension," since people often don't look beyond them to recognize that cultural achievements "have never been confined to one locality."

England

with its baby rivers and little towns, each with its abbey or its
cathedral;
with voices – one voice perhaps, echoing through the transept
– the
criterion of suitability and convenience; and Italy
with its equal shores – contriving an epicureanism
from which the grossness has been extracted;

and Greece with its goat and its gourds,
the nest of modified illusions: and France,
the "chrysalis of the nocturnal butterfly."
in whose products mystery of construction
diverts one from what was originally one's object –
substance at the core: and the East with its snails, its emotional

shorthand and jade cockroaches – its rock crystal and its imper-
turbability,
all of museum quality: and America where there
is the little old ramshackle victoria in the south.
where cigars are smoked on the street in the north:
where there are no proofreaders, no silk-worms, no digressions:

the wild man's land; grass-less, links-less, language-less country
in which letters
                                        are written
not in Spanish, not in Greek, not in Latin, not in shorthand,
but in plain American, which cats and dogs can read!
The letter *a* in psalm and calm when
pronounced with the sound of *a* in candle, is very noticeable,
but

why should continents of misapprehension
have to be accounted for by the fact?
Does it follow that because there are poisonous toadstools
which resemble mushrooms, both are dangerous?
Of meddlesomeness which may be mistaken for appetite,
of heat which may appear to be haste,
no conclusions may be drawn.

To have misapprehended the matter is to have confessed that
one has not looked
                                        far enough.
The sublimated wisdom of China, Egyptian discernment,
the cataclysmic torrent of emotion
compressed in the verbs of the Hebrew language,
the books of the man who is able to say,
"I envy nobody but him, and him only,

who catches more fish than
I do" – the flower and fruit of all that noted superiority
if not stumbled upon in America,
must one imagine that it is not there?
It has never been confined to one locality.

The Moores had not been to England for sixteen years, and this second visit was saturated with literary associations: in Cambridge the half-timbered plaster and brick beauty of medieval Queens College; the sculptured "hounds and dragons rampant" adorning the interior of King's College Chapel; "the item of greatest importance," a mulberry tree associated with John Milton. They went to a Blake exhibition in London and visited Stinsford, the village where Thomas Hardy had lived. In its churchyard, "the headstones with sculptured angels above members of his family, the pearl of bells and the Norman font, are component with what Mr. Hardy has told us."[9]

There were visits with contemporaries as well: Llewelyn Powys and his wife. Alysse Gregory, in Wales: and the much admired George Saintsbury, eighty, "patrician and flirtatious," old enough to be her father. He represented enduring traditional values. His Tory politics appealed to her. But one contemporary, also much admired, the Moores did not visit. In London, they stayed in a hotel a few doors from the offices of *The Criterion*, T.S. Eliot's journal. They very much wished to call on him, but did not: "Knowing that many unjustifiable calls are made by visiting Americans 1 was able to resist the impulse to add to them another."[10]

In 1929, two events altered the landscape of Marianne's life. *The Dial* discontinued publication. There had been many rumors about "mounting costs and shrinking revenues," and that the magazine was for sale. William Carlos Williams relayed these rumors to Ezra Pound in Italy. If it happened, "I am sure that it would mean the retirement of our May. She will not sell out I know but would probably go back to the library."[11] When Warner heard of this possibility and thought of the job's psychological and emotional toll on Marianne, he said it would not be a bad thing if it did shut down.

The primary reason for the closing of *The Dial* was that Watson was losing interest and Thayer's mental condition was precarious. At the beginning of the year, Watson informed Marianne that the office lease expired in May and that mid summer would be the time to end things. No new manuscripts were solicited in the early months of 1929, as there was a backlog of material. Marianne and staff planned carefully so that they wouldn't "disappoint people & end shabbily." She wrote to Warner in February: "We had better stop & suffer no selfish regrets in the matter." [12] July was the final issue. The loss of her annual salary was a significant matter, but "we lived safely and enjoyably before I quit the library," there was reviewing to do, and Warner and Constance continued their support. Marianne carried on imperturbably; perhaps what was disappearing from her life did not hit home until later. It had been just over a decade since Marianne and Mary had moved to the Village. An acquaintance had described her as living an "enclosed life" there, but it would be better described as an essentially private life, unconventionally conventional for its time and place. What could not be disputed was that New York City had been indispensable to her growth and maturity as a poet. As a biographer acutely put it, her Modernist sensibility had been "formed in the spaces of the modern city."[13]

Nevertheless, several things came together to produce the second surprise of 1929: Marianne and Mary moved to Brooklyn! Both had felt a growing unease with Village life and wanted a more orderly and quiet place, but one still within reach of the city's cultural riches. Most importantly, Warner was once again transferred, to the Brooklyn Navy Yard. Marianne and Mary would follow him as they had in 1918. More than a decade earlier, when Marianne had made her second visit to New York City, she had described it as her "sojourn in the whale." Looking back, that sojourn had been a great success. It had now come to an end. What would follow?

2. DOROTHY PARKER

DOROTHY PARKER IN Paris. At first it was very exciting. She recognized James Joyce at a distance, walking the streets of the city. But soon, Paris became boring. She had no interest in its history or monuments or art. A recent lover, Seward Collins, who had paid her way, joined her and they went to the Riviera, where Dorothy spent a "summer of a thousand parties." She met famous writers Somerset Maugham, who admired her work and years later would write about her, and George Bernard Shaw, and saw Ernest Hemingway again. She had first encountered him in New York City and been intimidated. For her, he embodied the idea of a "total artist." Even when, on subsequent occasions, Hemingway was rude and made nasty comments, she never faltered in her admiration for him as a writer. The Riviera eventually lost its charm. Dorothy and Collins went on to Spain. Hemingway arranged for them to see the running of the bulls in Pamplona and a bullfight, which she loathed. She quarreled with Collins, who returned to America, and she soon followed him.

One of the reasons for going to Europe had been to find undistracted time to collect her verse and revise it for publication as a book. The idea of a book was daunting. It heightened her awareness of the gap between what she had written and what she had dreamed of writing. Despite the parties and the inevitable drinking, she completed forty-seven poems in 1926, a third of them for *The New Yorker* and *Vanity Fair*; thirty-nine poems of that year were to be included in the book. On returning to the United States, she signed a contract and completed her selection, including some she finished writing only days before publication.

ENOUGH ROPE WAS published in December. The title was adapted from Rabelais's "you shall never want rope enough," and, in case readers didn't get it, there was a dangling noose on the dust jacket. It soon was in its third edition, at two dollars a copy. It was extraordinary that a book of poetry would sell so well, but Edna Millay had established new standards by which to measure the reading public. The reviews were enthusiastic. *Poetry* asserted that Parker had carved an individual niche for herself, a judgment everyone seconded. *The Nation* observed, "the rope is caked with salty humor" and "rough with splinters of disillusion." The *New York Times* reviewer emphasized the "simplicity of words and fine craftsmanship," insisting that there was more to her work than mere facility: "There is an outspoken manner that exploded pretense sharply and turns its sorrow into mordant wit." Edmund Wilson was restrained: "Few poems are completely successful," but the best "justified her departure from literary convention." Genevieve Taggard characterized the Parker style as "whisky straight, not champagne."[1]

As "Mistress of Manhattan," she expressed the vigor and cynicism of the Jazz Age in a New York accent, dismissing romantic notions about love.

Indian Summer

In youth, it was a way I had
 To do my best to please.
And change, with every passing lad
 To suit his theories.

But now I know the things I know.
 And do the things I do:
And if you do not like me so,
 To hell, my love, with you!

The "I" here is perkily defiant, unrepentant, a liberated woman who refuses the age-old role of the suffering and victimized woman who accepts her fate.

Observation

If I don't drive around the park,
I'm pretty sure to make my mark.
If I'm in bed each night by ten,
I may get back my looks again.
If I abstain from fun and such,
I'll probably amount to much;
But I shall stay the way I am,
Because I do not give a damn

The serious artist, determined to maintain her integrity, might find consolation for failed lovers in her art. Or could she? Might she be making a fuss about very little?

Philosophy

If I should labor through daylight and dark.
Consecrate, valorous, serious, true.
Then on the world I may blazon my mark;
And what if I don't, and what if I do?

What could be more subversive of notions of idealized love than an unabashed materialism?

One Perfect Rose

A single flow'r he sent me, since we met.
 All tenderly his messenger he chose;
Deep-hearted, pure, with scented dew still wet –
 One perfect rose.

I knew the language of the floweret:
 'My fragile leaves,' it said, 'his heart enclose.'
Love long has taken for his amulet
 One perfect rose.

Why is it no one ever sent me yet
 One perfect limousine, do you suppose?
Ah no, it's always just my luck to get
 One perfect rose.

Praise for her poetry reinforced those reiterated feelings of inadequacy. "There is poetry and there is not,"[2] she said, and she thought her work belonged in the "not" category, but her readers and the popular magazines and newspapers didn't agree. *McCalls* magazine published a Christmas article, "Christmas Poems by America's Greatest Poets," which included Parker, Wylie, and Millay. It was Bogan, Moore, and others who did not make the grade. Such an article would not have changed her mind. On one occasion, she reached for something deeper, an imaginative attempt to address a most controversial subject for a love poem, love between black and white people. Dorothy packed in a lot of sociological detail in a few lines: the rural setting, the economic and social, as well as racial, gulf between the lovers. The rhythms are jagged, the language folkish. The adjective angry refers to the attitude of society, not of the lovers.[3]

The Dark Girl's Rhyme

Who was there had seen us
  Wouldn't bid him run?
Heavy lay between us
  All our sires had done.

There he was, a-springing
  Of a pious race,
Setting hags a-swinging
  In a market-place;

Sowing turnips over
  Where the poppies lay;
Looking past the clover,
  Adding up the hay;

Shouting through the Spring song,
  Clumping down the sod;
Toadying, in sing-song,
  To a crabbed god.

There I was, that came of
  Folk of mud and flame,
I that had my name of
  Them without a name.

Up and down a mountain
  Streeled my silly stock;
Passing by a fountain,
  Wringing at a rock;

Devil-gotten sinners,
  Throwing back their heads,
Fiddling for their dinners,
  Kissing for their beds.

Not a one had seen us
  Wouldn't help him flee.
Angry ran between us
  Blood of him and me.

How shall I be mating
  Who have looked above –
Living for a hating,
  Dying of a love?

In 1927, Harold Ross asked Dorothy to write the "Recent Books" column of *The New Yorker*, under the pseudonym "Constant Reader," which fooled no one and wasn't intended to; the reviews were a way of showing off her malice, many of the reviews being essentially about Dorothy Parker, her state of mind, her moods, her prejudices, and not about the books being noticed. As with her theater reviews of the earlier years, the potboilers—*Margot Asquith: The Autobiography*, William Lyon Phelps's *Happiness*, Lew Telegen's *Women Have Been Kind*, Elinor Glyn's *It*—were setups. And also, as before, she often did not know what to make of serious work, for example, Ford Madox Ford's *The Last Post: The Journal of Katherine Mansfield*. She resorted to ponderous levity. Of Upton Sinclair she said, "He is a hell of a good writer." Scandinavians admired him and "those boys in the cold lands are not fooled about literature." Her revulsion for A.A. Milne's *The House at Pooh Corner*, celebrated among her devotees as the finest example of her pulverizing scorn—"Tonstant weader fwowed up"[4]—reveals only that she failed utterly to understand the reasons for its immense and lasting appeal.

The New Yorker also played an increasingly important role in her poetry. 1927 was exceptionally productive for her, and almost half the fifty poems written that year were published in it, a sign of her confidence in their quality. Of the twenty-one poems she completed in 1928, over half were placed there, despite—or was it because of?—continual emotional turmoil growing out of her innumerable love affairs.

Love was at the center of Dorothy Parker's poetry, and yet we don't immediately think of her as a poet of love. One reason for this is because she wasn't, like Edna Millay, a recognized symbol of sexually emancipated women. Her sexual affairs were essentially private, known to friends and acquaintances but not beyond them. However, the primary reason is that her subject was the impossibility of enduring love between men and women. And in that regard, her voice was caustic but impersonal, the voice of an observer reporting about the casualties from the field of battle.

Her own amorous entanglements fell into three types. There were the younger men, interested in her sexually and also because of her growing reputation as a writer, using her for their own purposes and careers. Persistently unfaithful, their conduct produced outbursts of rage on her part, and repeated public quarrels. As though puzzled by her own behavior, the title of one of her poems suggests that she believed it was rooted in her feminine nature.

On Being a Woman

Why is it, when I am in Rome,
I'd give an eye to be at home,
But when on native earth I be,
My soul is sick for Italy?

And why with you, my love, my lord,
Am I spectacularly bored,
Yet do you up and leave me – then
I scream to have you back again?

The second category of lovers was contemporary writers, George S. Kaufman, Robert Benchley, Henry Grantland Rice, F. Scott Fitzgerald, and Ring Lardner. The Fitzgerald fling, like most of the rest, was brief; the Lardner affair was longer lasting but understood by both as a hopeless dead-end.

There was a third, desperate category, not to be laughed at later. No one learned his name or much about him except that he was successful in business, came from a wealthy family, was (of course) tall, "highly respectable," verified by the fact that he was married with three children, and owned two Manhattan townhouses. He beat her. A friend found her one night with a black eye, cuts and bruises on her face and arms, and blood at the side of her mouth. She didn't want her friends to say anything against him. Eventually, he left her (not she him) and sometime after that committed suicide. She said, "There goes my whipping boy."[5]

THE GREAT SUCCESS of her first book led to a second, *Sunset Gun*, published in the spring of 1929. The title refers to the military tradition of firing cannon as the flag is being lowered to mark the end of day. Ten thousand copies were printed for the first edition, and it sold very well, both then and later. The reviews were enthusiastic, and reviewers expressed their delight that Parker had not tampered with her formula for guaranteed success, a prime example being the following poem:

Thought For a Sunshiny Morning

It costs me never a stab nor squirm
To tread by chance upon a worm.
"Aha, my little dear," I say,
"Your clan will pay me back one day."

And there was a splendid summing-up of the now familiar and almost reassuring certainty that "love is a permanent flop," and so are other forms of human endeavor.

Coda

There's little in taking or giving,
 There's little in water or wine;
This living, this living, this living
 Was never a project of mine.
Oh, hard is the struggle, and sparse is
 The gain of the one at the top,
For art is a form of catharsis,
 And love is a permanent flop,
And work is the province of cattle,
 And rest's for a clam in a shell,
So I'm thinking of throwing the battle –
 Would you kindly direct me to hell?

However, the poems in *Sunset Gun* also present a very different theme—that hopeless love is actually preferable to cautious prudence and Calvinist self-denial.

Partial Comfort

Whose love is given over-well
Shall look on Helen's face in hell,
Whilst those whose love is thin and wise
May view John Knox in Paradise.

She developed this theme at greater length, a thrust at the timidly conventional in the form of a delightful parable.

Parable for a Certain Virgin

Oh, ponder, friend, the porcupine;
  Refresh your recollection,
And sit a moment, to define
  His means of self-protection.

How truly fortified is he!
  Where is the beast his double
In forethought of emergency
  And readiness for trouble?

Recall his figure, and his shade –
  How deftly planned and clearly
For slithering through the dappled glade
  Unseen, or pretty nearly.

Yet should an alien eye discern
  His presence in the woodland,
How little has he left to learn
  Of self-defense! My good land!

For he can run, as swift as sound,
  To where his goose may hang high –
Or thrust his head against the ground
  And tunnel half to Shanghai;

Or he can climb the dizziest bough –
  Unhesitant, mechanic –
And, resting, dash from off his brow
  The bitter beads of panic;

Or should pursuers press him hot,
  One scarcely needs to mention
His quick and cruel barbs, that got
  Shakespearean attention;

Or driven to his final ditch,
  To his extremest thicket,
He'll fight with claws and molars (which
  Is not considered cricket).

How amply armored, he, to fend
  The fear of chase that haunts him!
How well prepared our little friend! –
  And who the devil wants him?

SUNSET GUN WAS dedicated to "John," John Wiley Garrett II, and its publication coincided with Dorothy's divorce from Eddie Parker. She alleged cruelty. He didn't contest the divorce. She hadn't seen him for years, always spoke disparagingly of him, and never saw him again after the divorce was granted. But the pain must have been deep-seated. Dorothy spent the night of the divorce with Garrett II, and for many days after was in a wretched state, sobbing uncontrollably, "half-soused" a good deal of the time. Friends worried about suicide. John Wiley Garrett II and Seward Collins were Eddie Parker's successors, a complex fate for them, had they cared about it. Garrett was tall, handsome, elegantly dressed, "his voice was intimate as the rustle of sheets." An investment banker, he enjoyed being pursued by "flotillas of women." Their relationship was soon disastrous. Heavy drinking concealed for a time that they had nothing in common intellectually, nothing to talk about.

He was faithless and treated her with casual contempt, not keeping engagements, not returning phone calls, which maddened her and increased her jealousy. "Sunk, I am," she said, "and in a big way. It is my conviction that civilization is about to collapse." There were screaming bouts in public, with Dorothy doing the screaming.[6]

The year 1929 was notable for an important recognition of her prose fiction. Early that year, she published "Big Blonde," a short story saturated with the culture of New York City in the 1920s and elements of her own family background. It is about Hazel Morse, who grew up in the garment business, was a model, a wife, an ex-wife, an available hard-drinking good sport, and an unsuccessful suicide. It won the O. Henry Award for the best short story of the year, for which Dorothy received 500 very welcome dollars. It remains her most memorable story.

The most surprising event of the year was when the ultimate Manhattanite went to Hollywood. It was directly connected with her chronic money woes. Howard Dietz, publicity agent for MGM studios, with whom Dorothy had a brief affair, arranged a contract for her as a fabulously well-paid scriptwriter. Once there, in characteristic Parker mode, and also to compensate for her heretical abandonment of her hometown, she set about with gusto biting the hand that was feeding her. Sitting in her writer's cubicle, staring out at the palm trees, "the ugliest vegetable God created," she mocked the new place and its absurd business— writing dialogue for a film she knew little about, and a song for a Cecil B. de Mille film, though it wasn't a musical. The work was as easy as it was lucrative: three hundred dollars per week. "I could do that with one hand tied behind my back and the other on Irving Thalberg's pulse."[7] After three months she had had—and had made— enough, and took the train back to Manhattan.

3. Louise Bogan

IN 1925, EDMUND Wilson sent Louise Bogan a copy of Dorothy Parker's *Enough Rope*. "I had been wanting to see it," Bogan replied. "I didn't think that the poems in the first section were so hot, rather diluted Edna Millay to my mind, but the to-hell-my-love-with-you stuff is excellent," adding, "Perhaps we gals are at our best on that note."[1]

Louise had occasionally sounded that note in her poems, but it was a minor note; and now, in the five years after her marriage to Raymond Holden, she would enjoy the happiest time of her life. Her poems achieved a deeper and richer maturity in dealing with the major themes that had always concerned her. That achievement did not come easily; for long periods of time, she found it difficult to write any poetry. She tried sitting down and forcing herself to write a certain number of lines a day. That didn't work. One could not will poetry into being. "Poems came by grace, or they did not come at all."[2]

And by the grace of whatever deity, she was able to write again. She found some escape from one of the themes that had run through *Body of This Death*, the memory of anguish in one's childhood and youth. The result was "If We Take All Gold," in which our destructive need to hoard our misery, "sorrow's gold," must be overcome by putting it away, "under ground," and then perhaps we shall "have peace."

Raymond Holden, who understood that Louise's poetry bore a complex relationship to the rage and jealousy that haunted her, wished to take care of her. This was a difficult task, as he came to find out. She was secretive. (Hiding Maidie's existence was a prime example.) She was jealous. When maddened by suspicion, she overturned tables and chairs and lamps, disappeared for nights at a time. She respected anger. Holden was neither angry nor a fighter, and his kindness seemed to Louise to be perilously close to weakness, as her father had been weak. Writing to Rolfe Humphries, she invited him to come over "any free afternoon next week...and beat me to a pulp (1 realize that that's Freudian—but 1 need a good licking and there isn't anyone around big enough to give it to me). Raymond talks when he should kick me down the stairs."[3]

Holden's divorce settlement sharply reduced their income so that nagging money problems pressed hard on them. To be able to write reviews was now financially important, and for three months she was an editor for *The Measure*. Reviewing broadened her understanding of what was being written at the time and added to her self-confidence. "My God, who said poetry was being writ in America? I've read manuscripts for hours: they're no more poetry than I'm the Piltdown man."[4] Holden got a job as editor of a travel magazine in Boston, so they moved there. "The people aren't up to much, but occasionally one hears a beautiful voice which is more than New York ever grants (with one or two exceptions)." She read Chekhov and went every Friday to Symphony Hall to hear the Boston Symphony. She fluctuated in her feelings about domesticity, writing scornfully of the "milky-breasted female, married to a he-man" who spends her time washing dishes and having babies; and then in a letter to a friend she expressed the opposite view: "I must admit domesticity thrills me to the bone. Yesterday I made peach jam!" and "Our little nest is rapidly becoming the swellest in town."[5]

Their marriage was peaceful. "There were no fights, no raised voices, no bitter scenes." That both of them were writers caused some difficulties, however. Holden admired her work but was not uncritical; she envied his facility but was dismissive of his artistic work. "A friend found her sitting with scissors in hand cutting up a poem by [him] into confetti, letting pieces float out in the air."[6] He enjoyed nature and urged her to observe the world more closely, to write about other things than psychological drama.

She was ironically amusing about her relentless struggle to write. "I have written more and worse verse than at any other time in my career," she explained to Edmund Wilson. "I think it is all wonderful, too, which makes it all the funnier." She mocked herself as an observer of nature. "Does it rain—do I look out the window and see a barn, or a cow, or a tree, or a horse and wagon, or a stray dog—does it snow, or shine, or blow? Out comes the pencil, and down go a few nature notes." She concluded mordantly, "How happy I feel! How easy art really is! Almost at once I realize that the thing is just terrible."[7]

But it wasn't all terrible by any means. She received an invitation to spend a month at Yaddo, a writer's colony/refuge in Saratoga Springs, New York. "The gardens are very lovely; roses and peonies and marble pergolas. Such grandeur!" Despite intermittent anxiety about it, she was able to write, though her time there reminded her how much she missed New York. "Really, I could live behind a billboard or on a roof, to be back among people I know." She helped support the three of them by writing short stories for *The New Yorker*, but they were not able to go back to New York. Doctors found a spot on one of Holden's lungs, so they abruptly moved to Santa Fe, New Mexico, for his health. At first, Louise was depressed by the place. "I kept saying, I knew it, I knew it—just another American town." She adopted a devil-may-care tone about her ever-present anxieties about writing. "I haven't written a line, and do not care for literature as such."[8] Then they found a pleasant house and they both cheered up.

Witter Bynner and Arthur Ficke were there. "Bynner is all right in small doses." He gave "the funniest parties in the world," with much drinking. "We all had quite a lot of liquor the other night." The sexual and social arrangements in Santa Fe were Village-like. Bynner came to their house one night at 3:30 a.m., "and invited us to a party of townspeople, who were going to take off their clothes. We refused gently but firmly. Fancy trying to live in sin in Santa Fe! As well try to live in sin in New York. There's the same lack of privacy." By spring they were preparing to leave. Holden was "as sweet as ever, and much better. What a summer in New York will do for him, I don't know." Money was as short as ever. "If you hear of a nice slave job anywhere at $100 a month," she wrote to Ruth Benedict, "do bag it for me."[9]

IN MANNER AND appearance, Louise had become a striking figure. "Half reclining on a studio couch, a martini held glittering between the fingers of her right hand...it was as if she had been dropped from the skies, as slender, as immaculate as the moon in its last quarter, her oval face in profile, clear and pale." Five feet eight inches tall, "she always had that funny aristocratic drawl in the back of her throat and upright, even portentously aristocratic posture."[10] This is a long way from the sneered-at "mick" of her youth; it reminded one of the bearing and posture of Elinor Wylie.

The person inside the haughty demeanor, however, was far from aristocratic languor, exploding in fits of jealousy and anger. She described her social life in language so exaggerated as to suggest instability. "New York can tire me with hysteria. If anyone has one word to say or has any ideas, or drive or talent, in New York he (or she) ultimately turns out to be a maniac or to have been a maniac, or about to be a maniac."[11]

It was clearly time to leave the city. They found what they were looking for upstate in Hillsdale, five acres with plum and pear trees and a pleasant view. The house needed much repair, which they mostly did themselves. Louise enjoyed the hard work. "Farewell, farewell," she wrote. "We fade into the bucolic!"[12] And somehow this was translated into the rhythms of poetry. Edmund Wilson suggested that she propose a volume of her poems to the celebrated editor, Maxwell Perkins, at Scribner's. She did. Perkins replied within two days, affirmatively. There were not enough poems she thought worth inducting, but she promised that the poems needed would be ready by midsummer of 1929.

In mid-May of that year, the house was ready and Louise and Holden moved in. The Boisevaims/Millays lived not very far away and came to visit from time to time. "The ever-blooming Millay came over one day last week with a copy of her new book, *The Buck in the Snow*, for me—that was swell of her, I thought," and Louise said, generously, that one of the poems "made the room turn round when I read it."[13] Millay's work was much on her mind.

In the summer of 1929, *Dark Summer* was published. Dedicated to Raymond Holden, and beautifully produced, it was widely reviewed and favorably judged in a few of the literary sections of national magazines; but most notices dismissed it with heartbreaking brevity and incomprehension as "high brow," "difficult," or, most often as simply "puzzling." It wasn't only traditionalist middlebrows who were put off by the poems' density and obscurity. Edward Sapir, a friend and supporter of the new verse and a highly sophisticated chap, characterized Louise as belonging to a school of "severe and lofty dictioned Parnassians," and confessed that he did not understand their verse in general and "certainly did not understand Louise."[14] The difficulty, ironically, was not at all that she was a Modernist but that it looked back to a splendid but difficult model, English metaphysical poetry. The book gave Louise unalloyed pleasure, "a great sense of elation. A female lyrist of no small ability, I said to myself."[15]

Yvor Winters, critic and poet, reviewed *Dark Summer* with great intelligence and discernment. It "bore comparison with the best songs of the sixteenth and seventeenth centuries," he wrote in a review. He went on to argue that there was an important distinction to be made in dealing with the undoubted fact that Louise's poems were not easily understood: the complexity of the ideas. Winters had no doubt that *Dark Summer* established her as, "one of the principle ornaments of contemporary American poetry." He ended his review with stirring praise: "It would take only a turn, a flicker, to transform her into a major poet;" and, "It is conceivable that the flicker may be taking place as I write."[16]

With Winter's explanation in mind, we can turn to one of her short lyrics, its subject, Cassandra of Greek myth, condemned to foreseeing the future and telling the (unwelcome) truth, for which she is thought mad.

Cassandra

To me, one silly task is like another.
I bare the shambling tricks of lust and pride.
This flesh will never give a child its mother, –
Song, like a wing, tears through my breast, my side,
And madness chooses out my voice again,
Again. I am the chosen no hand saves:
The shrieking heaven lifted over men,
Not the dumb earth, wherein they set their graves.

4. LÉONIE ADAMS

WHILE LOUISE AND Holden were living in Boston and Santa Fe, Léonie Adams came into public prominence for the first time. Holden had set things in motion by persuading the publisher of Louise's first book to publish Léonie's. The result was *Those Not Elect*, lyrics, dialogue poems, sonnets, the work of a young poet now realizing her potential. The poems are subtle reflections on the human heart, and on our place in nature. The title poem asks how unbelievers deal with the idea of a paradise denied them. And as for believers: how to reconcile human woe with the laughter of the angels? How to reconcile our dreams with the "sick heat of human flesh."

Those Not Elect

Never, being damned, see paradise.
The heart will sweeten at its look;

Nor hell was known, till paradise
Our senses shook

Never hear angels at laughter,
For how comports with grief to know
Wisdom in heaven bends to laughter, laughter,
Laughter upon woe?

Never fall dreaming on celestials,
Lest, bound in a ruinous place,
You turn to wander with celestials
Down holy space.

Never taste that fruit with the soul
Whereof the body may not eat,
Lest flesh at length lay waste the soul
In its sick heat.

Our consciousness of the human heart is ever changing and
some of the changes are surprising, reversing conventional associations. We may imagine quietness as a blessed state but unquiet,
even pain, may be preferable to the quiet of a dead heart.

Quiet

Since I took quiet to my breast
My heart lies in me heavier
Than stone sunk fast in sluggish sand.
That the sea's self may never stir.
When she sweeps hungrily to land.
Since I took quiet to my breast.

Strange quiet, when I made thee guest.
My heart had countless strings to fret
Under a least wind's fingering
How could I know I would forget
To catch breath at gull's curved wing.
Strange quiet, when I made thee guest.

Thou, quiet, hast no gift of rest.
The pain that at thy healing fled
More dear was to my heart than pride.
Now for its loss my heart is dead.
And I keep horrid watch beside.
Thou, quiet, hast no gift of rest.

Existing within nature, the heart must ultimately yield to the wind, "that rare, bright atmosphere of death, as do the leaves of the trees in this exquisite landscape."

A Wind of Fall

A wind went forth a little after dawn,
And sounded his thin horn above the trees
And there was sudden stilling of those bells
On which the treetoads rang quaint harmonies.

The languid mists upon the morning hills
Melted beneath the wind's swift icy breath;
Each tree took on a loveliness more keen
To taste the rare, bright atmosphere of death.

Each leaf was as a gallant banner flown
For that far runner the wind heralded
Would they not know the outflung delicate locks
Down all the ways the silver-limbed had fled?

Before the joy of that clear visioning
They had no sorrow, leaf and leaf, to part.
I cry the wind from out the clouds to blow
Through all the dusty summer of my heart.

In Léonie's poetry, a perceptive critic noted, "nature assumes a spiritual - one might even say a religious expression."[1]

THE LIVES AND careers of Louise Bogan and Léonie Adams were intertwined throughout the 1920s by friendship, by moving in the same social and intellectual circles, by mutual respect for each other's work and by the coincidence of publication. In writing about their poetry, critics often found similarities: but the notion of similarities was misguided and based mostly on the fact that both of them wrote intense and dense poetry that was not easily understood at first reading. The two of them understood that their work was very different.

The parallels and contrasts between them were dramatically highlighted at the end of the decade. In 1928, Léonie was awarded a Guggenheim fellowship for creative writing abroad, and she went speedily to Paris to write new poetry and to prepare a second collection. In 1929, her Guggenheim was renewed for another year and that year her second book, *High Falcon & Other Poems* was published. Among the forty lyrics making up the volume are many of her finest. And appropriately, it was dedicated to Louise and Raymond Holden.

Nature poems predominate; love poems are intermingled among them; or, more precisely, nature and love are understood as inseparable.

Song

Wind blows over the heart
But the heart is fast in the breast.
So only give a sigh after the wind.
A heart that is pinned to the wind
Turns in the side without rest.

Or if you will bear in mind
The stream and the swan gone,
Scattering from its cold plumage the drops
      of the foam,
Then liken the heart rather
To the stream sailed of a swan.

In the female figures of the marble caryatids on the Acropolis in Athens, Léonie discerned that while the "wonder" of Athenian culture had disappeared, beauty, in the "gesture of love," still remained.

Caryatid

Not at midnight, not at morning, 0 sweet city,
Shall we come in at your portal, but this girl,
Bearing on her head a broken stone,
In the body shaped to this, the throat and bosom
Poised no less for the burden now the temple is fallen,
Tells the white Athenian wonder overthrown.

There is no clasp which stays beauty forever.
Time has undone her, from porphyry, from bronze.
She is winged every way and will not rest;
But the gesture of the lover shall remain long after,
Where lovely and imponderable there leans
A weight more grave than marble on the breast.

Among the poems in *High Falcon* is one that achieved considerable recognition at the time, and since then—a song about innocents at play in nature, play which moves as all human activity must move, towards death.

Kennst du das Land

No, I have borne in mind this hill,
For once before I came its way
In hours when summer held her breath
Above her innocents at play;
Knew the leaves deepening the green ground
With their green shadows, there as still
And as perfect as leaves stand in air;
The bird who takes delight in sound
Giving his young and watery call,
That is each time as if a fall
Flashed silver and were no more there.
And knew at last, when day was through,
The sky in which the boughs were dipped
More thick with stars than fields with dew;
And in December brought to mind
The laughing child to whom they gave
Among these slopes, upon this grass,
The summer-hearted name of love.

Still can you follow with your eyes,
Where on the green and gilded ground
The dancers will not break the round,
The beechtrunks carved of moonlight rise;
Still at their roots the violets burn
Lamps whose flame is soft as breath.
But turn not so, again, again,
They clap me in their wintry chain;
I know the land whereto you turn,
And know it for a land of death.

5. Louise Bogan

For Louise Bogan, too, 1929 was a year of splendid achievement—the publication of *Dark Summer*, and as well, a period of emotional calm and of personal fulfillment: house and marriage going well, Maidie growing up. Louise was content to be away from New York City and its literary intrigues. For Christmas, Louise and Holden went to her mother's house, and when they returned, found their house in flames. The man who tended the furnace had left the damper open too wide and the wooden floor had caught fire. Almost everything was destroyed. There had been house insurance, but Holden had invested what remained of his inheritance and the life insurance in the stock market. That too had gone up in flames. They could not afford to rebuild, so they moved back to New York City, determined to overcome this setback. What they couldn't know was that Louise was about to enter a terrible downward spiral and the darkest time of her life.

Louise Bogan

6. GENEVIEVE TAGGARD

G ENEVIEVE TAGGARD SUSTAINED her friendship with
Louise Bogan and with Columbia University poets,
different as their political views were, and continued
to regard poetry as a form of revolutionary action. She and her
husband became contributing editors to the *New Masses*, the communist journal, in 1925. That same year she edited *May Days: An
Anthology of Masses-Liberator Verse, 1912-1924*. At the same time
the idiosyncratic nature of her intellect was exemplified by her
editing *Circumference: Varieties of Metaphysical Verse, 1456-1928*.
One perceptive critic grasped the point: that Genevieve Taggard
was trying to escape from the prevailing categories of contemporary poetry and desired "a move toward a new criticism," one
based on a synthesis of metaphysics, intellectuality, and the lyricism which is "the spirit's unabashed cry."[1]

In 1926, she published her major work of the decade, *Words
for a Chisel*, which was widely and positively reviewed nationally. It

included a long poem drawing on her Hawaiian childhood, short, austere poems about love and art, and a section called "Moods of Women." If the subject is almost always men, the moods are varied. Some poems are playful, others wistful. "Chanson" ends with a Parker-like dismissive twist; "Go get yourself a cozy grave!" And there is the inescapable melancholy of knowing that love, in the end, will disappear.

Man in the Wind

In the end I'll open, find
Nothing knocking but the wind.

When you come you come so lightly,
I can never know you rightly;
Vines it might be from the eaves;
You have fingers like the leaves;
You can veer upon my door
Better there, be off, before
I can even turn the lock.
It is hard to tell your knock
From the elements I love
From the tap, the knuckle of
Autumn gale or winter storm;
Always when you come, your form
Speeds upon the spinning air
And I stand and stare.

So tonight I open, find
Nothing knocking but the wind.

In 1929 came another volume, *Traveling Standing Still*, and even stern Modernists succumbed to its engaging qualities. Marianne Moore, while deprecating "an occasional limerick quality," heartily admired "a felicity of motion, a lyric contour, an ardent poring upon Nature: in short, a whorl of aesthetic contemplation that is serious and affecting."[2]

Without abandoning her interest in politics, or her commitment to political art, Genevieve at the same time felt the need to get away from New York City and her current routine, to refresh her mind and move in different directions. She began working on a biography of Emily Dickinson, and as the decade of the twenties came to an end, she did what many others had done: She went to Paris.

7. Edna St. Vincent Millay

FOR THE MILLAY/Boissevains, settling at Steepletop was exhausting. "Dearest Mummie, here we are, in one of the loveliest places in the world, I am sure, working like Trojans, dogs, slaves, etc., having chimneys put in, & plumbing put in, & a garage built, etc. We are crazy about it, & I have so many things on my mind that I hardly know if I am writing with a pen or with a screwdriver." The house needed much more work than they had anticipated. This went on for weeks, costing them thousands more than they had calculated. Then Edna became ill and was unwell for months. "What is the good of the house," Eugen wrote, "the scenery, the beauty, the apples and pears and the ripening tomatoes if Vincie is feeling rotten? What's the good of anything?"[1] A doctor in New York thought Millay on the verge of a nervous breakdown and prescribed weeks of bedrest.

She had worked sporadically on the libretto for the Metropolitan Opera she had committed herself to the year before, based on *Snow White and the Seven Dwarfs*, but she abandoned that and settled on a story set in Saxon England which would eventually be titled *The King's Henchmen*, with music by Deems Taylor. Joseph Urban agreed to do the sets. By the fall, she was correcting proofs and the singers were rehearsing the first act. By December she said the manuscript was "on the stand in the hall, all wrapped & stamped for its journey to New York," adding, "It has been a terrible job, but it's done now." She was apprehensive, and excited, writing to Taylor with giddy eagerness to inquire about rehearsals. "Listen—listen, Deems: If you hear any more news—good or bad—out with it, see?—I'm a big girl now.—Do they still like it? Did you hear the rehearsal?—Was it rotten?—How 'bout it?—Sem'me a post card."[2]

The world premiere took place at a sold-out Metropolitan Opera House on February 17, 1927. The cast was excellent, particularly Lawrence Tibbett and Edward Johnson. There were ovations, seventeen curtain calls, and applause for twenty minutes. It was performed on tour and, most astonishingly, the libretto, handsomely designed and published separately, sold more than ten thousand copies in the first few weeks. But the enthusiastic contemporary response has not held up. *The King's Henchmen* was madly overpraised, and to some extent this was attributable to admiration for Edna. The opera was never performed again at the Metropolitan and is now only a footnote in the history of opera.

THE OTHER MAJOR event in Edna's life in 1927 took her a very long way from Saxon England and translated her anti-war sentiments into the larger context of a concern for social justice. This was provoked by the most notorious political/legal event of the decade, the trial, conviction and sentencing of Nicola Sacco and Bartolomeo Vanzetti, Italian anarchist immigrants who were found guilty of a robbery and murder in South Braintree, Massachusetts, in 1920. Many doubted that the two had taken part in the robbery; no one doubted the partiality of the trial judge who spoke frankly of his hatred of anarchists. Throughout much of the world the trial was seen as yet another manifestation of American anti-radical hysteria. The conviction carried with it the death sentence. Numerous lengthy appeals covered more than half a dozen years. All failed. In early 1927, the governor of Massachusetts appointed a three-person committee to review the trial and sentence. One of its members was Abbott Lawrence Lowell, Amy's brother. The original judgment and sentence were upheld by the committee and Sacco and Vanzetti were scheduled for execution on August 23.

Several hundred people came from all over to picket the Boston State House and appeal for clemency. Among them were John Dos Passos, Dorothy Parker, and Edna Millay, who also wrote an eloquent letter to the governor to ask that he stay the execution. He did not. Sacco and Vanzetti were executed as scheduled. Appalled at what she perceived to be a cloud of injustice spreading over America, Edna wrote a poem which she would read on her later tours to hushed audiences.

Justice Denied in Massachusetts

Let us abandon then our gardens and go home
And sit in the sitting-room.
Shall the larkspur blossom or the corn grow under this cloud?
Sour to the fruitful seed
Is the cold earth under this cloud,
Fostering quack and weed, we have marched upon but cannot
    conquer;
We have bent the blades of our hoes against the stalks of them.

Let us go home, and sit in the sitting-room.

Not in our day

Shall the cloud go over and the sun rise as before,

Beneficent upon us

Out of the glittering bay,

And the warm winds be blown inward from the sea

Moving the blades of corn

With a peaceful sound.

Forlorn, forlorn,

Stands the blue hay-rack by the empty mow.

And the petals drop to the ground,

Leaving the tree unfruited.

The sun that warmed our stooping backs and withered the weed
    uprooted—

We shall not feel it again.

We shall die in darkness, and be buried in the rain.

What from the splendid dead

We have inherited—

Furrows sweet to the grain, and the weed subdued—

See now the slug and the mildew plunder.

Evil does overwhelm

The larkspur and the corn;

We have seen them go under.

Let us sit here, sit still,

Here in the sitting-room until we die;

At the step of Death on the walk, rise and go;

Leaving to our children's children this beautiful doorway,

And this elm,

And a blighted earth to till

With a broken hoe.

In September of that year of achievement and of anguish, Edna published her fifth book of poems, *The Buck in the Snow*. The themes were familiar, perhaps too familiar. Reviewers were polite but cooler than they had been. Her poems had always risen on a tide of general approval; but now, for the first time, her advocates were on the defensive. Modernist poetry, entirely alien to her aesthetic ideals, had established itself as the prevailing movement, at least among advanced readers, and Edna's partisans adopted a tone of aggressive hostility to it and in support of her traditionalism. She nurtured (but for a long time kept to herself) contempt for T. S. Eliot's poetry, which she mocked as *The Cult of the Occult* and later on wrote some satirical anti-Eliot poems, "nothing which could be considered abusive; they are merely murderous."[3]

For the first time, Edna began to feel out of step. At the time of *The King's Henchmen*, Edmund Wilson met her at dinner and thought her surprisingly "nervous, trembling, worried and dismayed." She confessed that she didn't know contemporary idioms, younger poets. Abruptly, she blurted out, "I'm not a pathetic figure—I'm not." "Whoever said you were," he replied, and in print he continued to defend her work saying that *The King's Henchmen* was one of the few events of contemporary interest. (The other was the poetry of Hart Crane, of whom Edna had never heard.) Max Eastman reviewed *The Buck in the Snow* favorably and Millay wrote to thank him. "You are quite right that it is fashionable here to be disappointed in the book. In England it isn't so; the British press has been wonderful." And then a concluding comment reveals how hurt she must have been, "You are one of the very few in our own great metropolis who has had a good word for it."[4]

The somber tone throughout the collection reflects her sense of the world as deeply threatening and hostile to her art.

To Those Without Pity

Cruel of heart, lay down my song.
Your reading eyes have done me wrong.
Not for you was the pen bitten,
And the mind wrung, and the song written.

The poet extends pity to all creatures that are the objects of the human need to kill. The title poem of the volume was based on an actual experience, observing a buck and his doe leaping elegantly over a wall only to discover the buck shot dead by a hunter.

The Buck in the Snow

White sky, over the hemlocks bowed with snow,
Saw you not at the beginning of evening the antlered buck
    and his doe
Standing in the apple-orchard? I saw them. I saw them
    suddenly go,
Tails up, with long leaps lovely and slow,
Over the stone-wall into the wood of hemlocks bowed with
    snow.

Now lies he here, his wild blood scalding the snow.

How strange a thing is death, bringing to his knees, bringing
    to his antlers
The buck in the snow.
How strange a thing,—a mile away by now, it may be,
Under the heavy hemlocks that as the moments pass,
Shift their loads a little, letting fall a feather of snow—
Life, looking out attentive from the eyes of the doe.

    The human capacity to kill had at the same time to be balanced against the human capacity to love others and to love art, which made mankind "plausible."

On Hearing a Symphony of Beethoven

Sweet sounds, oh, beautiful music, do not cease!
Reject me not into the world again.
With you alone is excellence and peace,
Mankind made plausible, his purpose plain.
Enchanted in your air benign and shrewd,
With limbs a-sprawl and empty faces pale,
The spiteful and the stinging and the rude
Sleep like scullions in the fairy-tale.
This moment is the best the world can give;
The tranquil blossom on the tortured stem
Reject me not, sweet sounds! oh, let me live,
Till doom espy my towers and scatter them.
A city spell-bound under the aging sun,
Music my rampart, and my only one.

EUGEN HAD GIVEN up his import/export business and the couple lived on the income from her poetry, which was substantial. So were their expenses. At one point Edna asked Norma to return a two-hundred-dollar loan, saying they were broke. She had to turn again to poetry reading tours. It was on such a tour, in Chicago, that a young poet was introduced to her. "I'm George Dillon,"[5] he said. Within hours, Edna became involved in a love affair that would dominate the next half dozen years of her life.

8. SARA TEASDALE

MORBID ANXIETY ABOUT illness and death continued to haunt Sara Teasdale in the second half of the decade, though there was one bright spot in her life: publishing two books of poetry. She made up her mind to collect poems of the previous five years to see if their quality justified publication and in so doing her despondent mood temporarily lifted. She was heartened by what she found, reminding herself that, irrespective of personal relations and the affairs of the world, poetic inspiration resided in herself.

On the Sussex Downs

Over the downs there were birds flying,
 Far off glittered the sea,
And toward the north the weald of Sussex
 Lay like a kingdom under me.

I was happier than the larks
  That nest on the downs and sing to the sky,
Over the downs the birds flying
  Were not so happy as I.

It was not you, though you were near,
  Though you were good to hear and see,
It was not earth, it was not heaven
  It was myself that sang in me.

She remained the poet of love but, chastened by disappointment and loss, she would turn back into herself, find new strength in the self that sang her songs. This mood infused the fifty-nine poems she arranged and published in 1926 as *Dark of the Moon*. The title made clear that her songs were somber, "unlighted by the moon of romanticism." Witter Bynner noted the "flames of sadness that have crept into your work," while another critic stressed that her poems "only gained in that austerity… which marks the really great in poetry." Readers found what they expected, and wanted, which suited the writer. "I try to say what moves me," she wrote. "I never care to surprise my reader."[1]

Previously vulnerable and easily wounded, she would now be a person "self-complete as a flower or stone."

The Solitary

My heart has grown rich with the passing of years,
  I have less need now than when I was young
To share myself with every corner
  Or shape my thoughts into words with my tongue.

It is one to me that they come or go
 If I have myself and the drive of my will,
And strength to climb on a summer night
 And watch the stars swarm over the hill.

Let them think I love them more than I do,
 Let them think I care, though I go alone;
If it lifts their pride, what is it to me
 Who am self-complete as a flower or a stone.

Sara Teasdale

Reflecting on human loss, she concluded that we cannot lose what we never had. That is what we call "wisdom."

Wisdom

It was a night of early spring,
 The winter-sleep was scarcely broken;
Around us shadows and the wind
 Listened for what was never spoken.

Though half a score of years are gone,
 Spring comes as sharply now as then –
But if we had it all to do
 It would be done the same again.

It was a spring that never came;
 But we have lived enough to know
What we have never had, remains;
 It is the things we have that go.

Another source of great satisfaction came to her in 1927 when Macmillan brought out a new and revised edition of her anthology of ten years before, *The Answering Voice*. She added another fifty poems to the original one hundred and seized the opportunity, in her new forward, to reflect on the women's poetry movement of which she was a proud member and leading representative. "In the decade since 1917 it had produced more good poetry by women than any other in the history of our language." The leading feature of this poetry, Sara believed, was that it differed radically in feeling from the poetry women wrote only twenty-five years before. Women now expressed a vastly greater range of emotion about love and could treat the subject unconventionally, were fearless in expressing their ideas and "almost cruelly analytical" in doing so. Women had freed themselves from love poetry dependent on a male beloved. Why was this? Because of the "growing economic independence women consequent to education."[2]

Among contemporary poets included in the new version of *The Answering Voice* were eight poets who appear in these pages and whose fifteen poems make up almost one-third of the additional pages: Elinor Wylie, three poems; Edna Millay, three poems; H. D., two; Louise Bogan, two; Genevieve Taggard, two; Amy Lowell, one; Léonie Adams, one. Sara modestly excluded herself, didn't include Marianne Moore because Marianne did not write love poetry, and omitted Dorothy Parker, perhaps because, as she once put it, "strident and flippant notes" marred some of her poems.

THE BOOKS WERE important, and heartening. The money was welcome. But an entirely unexpected and positive change in Sara's mental state came from a different source when, in the summer of 1926, she received a letter from Margaret Conklin, an undergraduate at Connecticut College for Women, in New London, asking for a signed photograph, not for herself but for an admired teacher who had fostered Margaret's love of poetry. Sara responded to something in the letter, "an inherent quality of delicacy, an indefinable something that touched me and made me feel I should like to know the person who wrote it." An exchange of letters and of visits followed. The first meeting together in New York City seemed "a miracle" to both of the women. From that moment on, there grew up between them deep feelings of sympathy and affection.

They spent much time together. Ernst took them to the theater and was grateful for this lightening-up of Sara's moods. Margaret was introduced to a world of letters she previously had only been able to imagine, and to a poet whose work had meant a great deal to her since she had first read it a few years before. For Sara, it was a startling return to her youth. Margaret was the embodiment of herself, of the lost youth that she had longed to recover so she "could find her way out of the maze of her adult years."[3] Sara found someone with whom she could joke and laugh and do frivolous things she had not done for years. Both also discovered that they shared other sympathies. Margaret had a deep-seeded antagonism to her mother, loved and admired her doctor father. Sara had miraculously found again another of those companions of her youth, the young women who helped her get away from home and enter the world; and of course, Margaret was also the absent daughter.

In the spring of 1927, they traveled together to England and spent the summer there. Margaret had never been abroad and was "so happy her eyes are almost dancing out of her head." She was also tactful and calmly put up with Sara's fanatical finickiness in traveling. On their return to America, while Sara went to recuperate in the country, Margaret helped move the Filsingers into a new hotel and became part of their domestic arrangements, especially helpful because Ernst was so often absent and played a diminished role in their domestic routine. He and Sara were moving apart.

BY 1928, SARA had come to the conclusion that her married life was intolerable and that the only way out of it was divorce. That prospect, if appealing, was also repellant. "For the popular poetess of love to be divorced was too much in the cynical new mode of the Twenties she had despised."[4] She desperately needed to eliminate conflict from her life, to escape from opposition and struggle, to find something like the easy, pleasurable relationship with Margaret. Nevertheless, she knew that Ernst would be astonished by what she was contemplating, would be terribly upset and opposed to what she wanted. She was determined, as well, to work out what must be a proper and orderly procedure to resolve her difficulties. Through the fall of 1928 and the winter of 1929, she perfected her plans. Margaret had graduated from college and was working close at hand, in New York City in publishing.

In the spring of 1929, Ernst's firm sent him again to Europe and South Africa. While he went abroad, Sara went to Reno, in secret, making arrangements for Margaret to take care of her mail and conceal her whereabouts from inquirers. Though it is difficult to believe, apparently Sara thought that she could obtain a divorce from her husband without having to inform him ahead of time! In Reno her lawyer explained the situation so that she had to take some initiative in informing Ernst. On June 1, she wrote him a letter announcing the end of their marriage. She explained that they both needed freedom. "I do not forget our really happy years together, nor all of the beautiful hours that I owe to you...and want to keep the remembrance of them unhurt." Therefore, the only way was divorce. Her decision, she emphasized, was irrevocable. Except "for the fact you are a man and must try to oppose, you would very likely agree with this course of action. I beg you to make this ordeal, which is for me a truly terrible one, as easy as you can. This is the last kindness you can do for me."[5]

Ernst was astounded and appalled, cabling his vehement opposition. She cabled back, urging him to accept the inevitable. She formally filed the action for divorce on August 31, charging extreme mental cruelty. She did not sue for alimony and would pay her own legal costs and lawyer's fees. As there were no children, she needed only his agreement not to contest the divorce. Ernst agreed. On September 5, the divorce was granted. Ernst was traveling and did not hear anything more until a few days later when a friend told him that the divorce had been reported in the newspapers. "Mentally and inwardly, I am in the depth of hell and despair," he said to a friend. "Life has certainly crashed and I feel horribly dazed and stunned." When Sara returned to New York City, she expressed very different feelings. "I'm a free woman. I can do anything I want."[6]

9. ELINOR WYLIE

Nᴇᴡ Yᴏʀᴋ Cɪᴛʏ had been indispensable for Elinor Wylie's writing career and had also served as the backdrop for her emergence as a public personality. In the late twenties, that personal image extended beyond Manhattan and had become nationally recognizable: expensive clothes, precisely waved and curled hair, manner and demeanor and dress representing cool, even frigid, control. Her occasional appearance in *The New Yorker* as a writer and subject helped bring this about. "I do not think I have ever known an equally beautiful woman," said Arthur Ficke, Edna Millay's great friend, "who was so little affected by what one calls one's heart."[1] It helped that, at forty, she looked a decade younger.

Like many beautiful women and men who think of their appearance as a work of art, Elinor subscribed to the idea that one should care about one's work in private and one's person in public. She extended that idea by writing a poem/profile for *The New Yorker* about herself. "Portrait in Black Paint with a Very Sparing Use of

Whitewash" combined humor and candor about her vanity, her passion for fine clothes, and the ambiguities of her personality. Only the initials E. W. identified its author, which led people to guess that E. W. stood for Edmund Wilson or Edith Wharton. When it was finally clear that this was a self-portrait by Elinor Wylie, a hubbub ensued. "All New York literary folk are excited about the rhymed description of herself that Elinor Wylie has published... The portrait is one of deadly accuracy and opinion is divided as to whether Miss Wylie should have written such a thing about herself or not."[2]

Portrait in Black Paint, With a Very Sparing Use of Whitewash

"She gives herself," there's a poetic thought;
She gives you comfort sturdy as a reed;
She gives you fifty things you might have bought,
And half a hundred that you'll never need;
She gives you friendship, but it's such a bother
You'd fancy influenza from another.

She'd give the shirt from off her back, except that
She doesn't wear a shirt, and most men do;
And often and most bitterly she's wept that
A starving tramp can't eat a silver shoe,
Or some poor beggar, slightly alcoholic,
Enjoy with Donne a metaphysical frolic.

She gives away her darling secret hope
At dinner tables between eight and nine,
And she would give St. Peter's to the Pope,
And coals to men of Newcastle-on-Tyne,
She would arrange a match for Solomon
Or give Casanova an adopted son.

She does not give advice; that I admit
Here's her sole virtue, and I'll count it double.
Forgiving her some crime because of it
But she gives tiresome and endless trouble.
If you need rest, she'll straight contrive a racket;
If gaiety, she'll fetch a padded jacket.

And she gives love of the least useful kind
At which advanced civilization mocks;
Half, a Platonic passion of the mind,
And half, a mad desire to mend the socks;
She's always wishing to turn back the page
And live with children in a golden age.

She gives a false impression that she's pretty
Because she has soft, deceptive skin
Saved from her childhood; yet it seems a pity
That she should be as vain of this as sin;
Her mind might bloom, she might reform the world
In those lost hours while her hair is curled.

She gives a vague impression that she's lazy,
But when she writes she grows intense and thorough;
Gone quietly and ecstatically crazy
Among the sea-blue hills of Peterboro;
She'll work within her cool, conventional flat
As self-sufficient as a Persian cat.

And she can live on aspirin and Scotch
Or British ginger beer and bread and butter,
And like them both, and neither very much;
And in her infancy she possessed a stutter

Which gives a strong impression that she's shy
When heard today, and this is verity.

But when she clothes herself in gold and silver
In the evening, she gives herself away;
Having remained a high, laborious delver
For all the hours of a sunny day,
At night she gives you rather the idea
Of mad Ophelia tutored by Medea.

She gives you nothing of consideration;
The effervescence of enthusiasm
Is trivial stuff; she'll give you adoration
If you belong to her particular schism;
As, that a certain English man of letters;
Need never call the Trinity his betters.

Sometimes she gives her heart; sometimes instead
Her tongue's sharp side. Her will is quick to soften,
She has no strength of purpose in her head
And she gives up entirely too often;
Her manners mingle in disastrous ways
"The Lower Depths" and the Court of Louis Seize.

Doubtless, she gives her enemies the creeps
And all her friends a vast amount of worry;
She's given oblivion only when she sleeps;
She says she loves the grave; but she'd be sorry
To die, while it is vanity to live;
"She gives herself," what has she left to give?

She'd give her eyes – but both her eyes are blind –
And her right hand – but both her hands are weak –
To be "Careless to win, unskilled to find,
And quick – and quick – to lose what all men seek."
But whether this has truly been her story
She'll never know, this side of purgatory.

Accompanying the poem was a caricature by Peter Arno who posed Elinor looking into a mirror, capturing her obsessive narcissism. Elinor's mother and her sister, Nancy, thought this the best likeness of Elinor. "Of course it is exaggerated," Nancy said, "but so was Elinor." In Peter Arno's telling recollection Elinor actually posed herself. Arno was "frightened" at having to meet Elinor, who asked him to wait a few minutes while she made herself tidy, walked over to a mirror and started primping. "In a few minutes, while she stood at the mirror," Arno had finished his sketch.[3]

The much-anticipated return to England had been postponed so that she could complete her third novel, a Shelley-inspired story. "I am working myself deaf, dumb, blind, lambagoishly lame,"[4] she complained to her mother and wrote the final page of *The Orphan Angel*, her longest and most historically detailed novel, the night before she and Bill sailed. She had decided not to go alone.

The trip was to a great extent an exercise in nostalgia, though the past she was reliving had painful memories as well. England also appealed in several contemporary ways. It was the homeland of her adored Shelley and had an immensely prestigious literary culture. As her books had been reasonably received there, Elinor was eager to be in the company of esteemed writers, to make trans-Atlantic friendships and reach an international audience. Paradoxically, given her insatiable thirst for attention, England also represented a culture of privacy that she had desperately needed in 1910, with Horace, and believed she needed now as a relief from New York's intense sociability.

The English were welcoming. There were numerous invitations to dinner and to tea. She and Bill met Edith Sitwell; Rex Whistler, the painter; Cecil Beaton, the photographer; Lord Berners, the composer; and other notables. Things went well until Aldous Huxley took them to meet Bloomsbury in the persons of Virginia and Leonard Woolf. Neither writer had read any of the other's books. Later, in her diary, Virginia's impressions were savage. "I expected a ravishing and diaphanous dragonfly, a woman who had spirited away 4 husbands…a green and sweet-voiced nymph." Instead, she found a "hatchet minded, cadaverous, acid voiced, bare boned, spavined patriotic nasal American."[5] The visit was not a success. Others were not so brutal, but began to be put off by her quickly spreading reputation for insisting that she be the center of attention. The visit was also complicated by the arrival of family. Her sister Nancy was to marry an Englishman, and with the rest of the family came Elinor's son Philip, who was at Harvard. His presence painfully revived the old scandal. A malicious story circulated that when Elinor met Philip, she did not recognize him.

They also met people of no reputation or fame in whose company Elinor could actually relax a little and make lasting friendships. Among them were George and Helen Young, whom she had met years before, in Washington, where George Young was on a diplomatic assignment. He had subsequently left the diplomatic service, taught, opened a hotel and been a Labour Party candidate in two parliamentary elections. The Youngs' company elicited from Elinor one of the few political comments she ever made, saying to Bill: "Don't you think we ought to vote Labor this year? Find out about it will you?" Another was when she complained that Edna Millay "was shouting her silly head off over Sacco & Vanzetti."[6]

Two new acquaintances were Becky and Henry de Clifford Wood-house, whose family represented for Elinor the idea of admirable English domestic life. Elinor fitted easily into the family ways. Becky and she liked each other immediately. The Woodhouses would play a vital part in her subsequent life in England.

After four months abroad, Elinor returned to the United States. Bill had been sent ahead to arrange their move to a new apartment, at 36 West Ninth Street. "I suppose all this moving and fixing houses is enough to startle an ox," she wrote her mother, "not to mention you or me." Bill had managed everything, but even so Elinor felt disoriented by the return to America and suffered excruciating headaches, often lasting two weeks. One way to rees-tablish order was to make the new apartment as she wished it, every room perfectly tidy, giving a sense of sparseness. She allowed herself one comfortable armchair in her study. "Nothing was per-mitted to stray from its place."[7] She placed a mirror prominently in the living room, sometimes making it difficult to carry on a conver-sation with her because she rose every few minutes to look into it.

Another way was to get back to work writing. She began another novel associated with Shelley; and she once again wrote poetry. Rightly, she considered herself to be primarily a poet. "As you know," she wrote, "my reputation was founded on verse. *Jennifer Lorn* would never have received too kind a hearing had not my two books of poetry preceded it."[8] It was a shrewd observation, which history has endorsed. She began planning a new volume of poems.

DURING THESE YEARS in the second half of the decade. Elinor made two friendships—with Dorothy Parker and Edna Millay—which were important to her and to them, combining personal affection and professional interests. Given the differences in cultural background and social class between Elinor and the other two, their friendship might seem surprising, especially as one would assume professional rivalry. But in addition to the imponderable things that shape personal relations, the three shared important values. Each had defied or ignored the sexual and marital conventions of the time; each had endured profound emotional turmoil in loving and living with men; each was well read in Latin and English and American poetry; and in the aesthetic conflict of the time, each was a traditionalist.

They knew each other's verse and some of their poems reveal influences of one or the other. Elinor's formidably impassive social demeanor, as well as the solemn tone of her poetry, concealed a lively wit; she wrote light verse and parodies and enjoyed foolish verbal fun, ranging in an instant from "grave to gay, from lively to severe."

Creed du Coer

I'd rather be silly and kind
Than graciously cool and refined,
The second shows poise
And a musical voice,
But the first shows a generous mind.

When, as a young woman, she had taken art classes at the Corcoran Gallery in Washington, she was teasingly asked if the models for life drawing wore clothes and she replied, "Oh yes, two blue side-combs."[9]

Elinor could enjoy and admire Parker's witticisms and repartee, and she understood the evolving Manhattan comic idiom. F. P. A. was a mutual friend; both contributed to The Conning

Tower. Their disdain for platitudes and their pleasure in puncturing pomposity was a bond. At a dinner party in the Village, one of the guests grandiosely declared that the two greatest men of history were Walt Whitman and Jesus Christ, and asked Elinor to name her most admired poet. When she named John Milton, the guest registered astonishment since Milton's influence was not apparent (to him) in Elinor's verse, which produced the following response from her: "You admire Jesus Christ but you don't behave like him, do you?" The comment charmed Parker, who "could not help liking Elinor at once."[10]

Their acquaintance dated from 1923 when both worked for *Vanity Fair*, Parker as theater critic and Elinor as an assistant editor; but while Parker's verse was saturated in the tone of a popular magazine like *Vanity Fair*, admired at the time for its sophistication, Elinor's poetry was of a different order and would have been out of place there. *The New Yorker* became the magazine they both could write for, the memorable forum for the urbanity they represented. The two sharp-tongued women were appropriately enough the subjects of a memorable *New Yorker* cartoon of 1928. Its caption is familiar, but few people would realize that Carl Rose was portraying Dorothy as the spinach-pushing mother and Elinor as the obstreperous child.

"It's broccoli dear."
"I say it's spinach, and I say the hell with it."

They shared a love of beautiful clothes, a fondness for alcohol and, as their friendship grew, discovered deeper sources of sympathy; difficult marriages, miscarriages, suicidal inclinations, an awareness that each had created a hard surface with which to meet the world. Their differences became complementary aspects. Elinor's orderly domestic arrangements must have seemed a welcome place of quiet and of refuge for Dorothy, who had virtually no domestic life. She struggled to find sufficient peace of mind to be able to select the verse to be published as *Enough Rope*, and, as Elinor's sister Nancy Hoyt described, made numerous visits to the Wylie apartment. "Vivid, sympathetic, never showing the caustic side which is in many of her poems and stories," Dorothy would "spend the afternoon in the back [room on a chaise longue] between the table and the typewriter and the bookshelves, a place where few penetrated." *Enough Rope* is dedicated to Elinor Wylie, and her personal copy bears the inscription: "With love, gratitude, and everything."[11]

It wasn't always sweetness and sympathy. There were painful moments. On the day of F. P. A.'s (second) wedding, Dorothy was invited to spend the night with the Wylies along with Edna and Eugen and the Arthur Fickes, a visit punctuated as usual with heavy drinking. Late in the evening, Elinor and Arthur Ficke asked Dorothy to recite some of her verses. She obliged and then went upstairs to bed. Sometime later Elinor and Arthur came into Dorothy's room and awakened her because Elinor wanted to show Arthur the scars left on her wrists by her attempted suicide. Not surprisingly, Dorothy burst into tears.

In one of her desperate moments, Dorothy turned to Elinor for help. Early on a Sunday morning she rang the bell at the Wylie apartment and when Elinor opened the door, Dorothy told her that "something really bad" was happening to her, if Elinor knew what she meant. The "really bad thing" was that she was again suicidal. "She spent the day with us from eleven a.m. to five p.m.," Elinor wrote to her mother, "saying she was going to kill herself & as she'd already made two attempts…it was not very soothing to the nerves." Elinor and Bill "begged, reasoned, kidded, scolded, & did all we could." Dorothy promised not to do anything, "for the present,"[12] and went away. This sympathetic solicitude contrasts with the attitude of Katherine Anne Porter in dealing with Elinor. Deeply depressed, Wylie knocked on the door of Porter's apartment. When Porter opened the door, Elinor told her that she planned to kill herself and that she had come to say goodbye. Annoyed at the interruption, which she regarded as an intrusion, Porter replied, "Well, good-bye Elinor,"[13] and shut the door.

Elinor Wylie

In a poem dedicated to Dorothy, Elinor paid tribute to her in exalted terms, representing not just the ordinary decencies but a more complex task, to be true to her greater self, "chivalric to your stronger spirit."

For a Good Girl
(For D. P.)

Two tasks confront King Honour's daughter
Whom the unlearned malign insult;
One dear and luminous as water.
The other stiff and difficult.
Pity is laid upon the noble
So plain an obligation
Its fair performance is no trouble;
The puzzle's in the other one.

To be recognizant of merit
Peculiar to yourself to be
Chivalric to your stronger spirit
Which gives the weak impunity.
This is the mental arabesque you
Must constantly contrive within
Or how shall you survive to rescue
The little wicked from their sin?

ELINOR WYLIE'S RELATIONSHIP with Edna Millay also touched deep levels of feeling. Like everyone else, Elinor had known Edna's poetry since "Renascence," but their first contact didn't come until 1921 when, as a favor to Bill Benét, Edna reviewed *Nets To Catch The Wind* favorably, and then wrote to her personally to emphasize her high regard for the volume. Some years later, Elinor reciprocated with an enthusiastic review of *The King's Henchmen* on the front page of the *New York Herald Tribune's* Sunday book section, quoting Thomas Hardy that there were "two great things" in the United States: Edna Millay and skyscrapers. Elinor's skepticism about a medieval subject had been misguided. "I had been an idiot not to trust this girl Edna Millay, even into the mists of the tenth century."[14]

The Millay move to Steepletop and the Wylie foray into country living allowed the two women to become more personally familiar, and their approval of each other's poetry grew to genuine admiration. There were a number of Wylie visits to Steepletop. Of one of them, Edna wrote: "It is too wonderful to have them here—dear Bill—my beautiful Elinor." The women spent hours discussing and arguing. "Elinor and I had a lovely row about Shelley," Edna said, "a long, gentle, jeering row."[15]

Edna's affectionate sympathy for other women induced personal confidence. One evening she told Eugen and Edna, "From the beginning to the end of the story of her strange & wonderful life up to the present moment, a most engrossing tale, full of tragedy, [Elinor] is the the most lovely creature. Gene is crazy about her. If he weren't I'd be furious." During one visit, Edna lay on a couch and Elinor read Robert Browning to her, "Things we both used to love and half know by heart... such fun." Another time, the two women shared breakfast in bed, discussing Keats. Elinor read Shelley's "Ode to the West Wind," which she considered to be "the best poem ever written," and cried when finished. Edna was tactful, humoring Elinor's penchant for personal judgments as if they were unquestionable truth. "I do not think naturally in terms of best-next-best," Edna said. In turn, she played the piano for the

Wylies. "I play badly. But not too badly, I think, to be allowed to play for them."[16]

There were moments of friction. Elinor praised *The Buck in the Snow* as Edna's best book, which gratified her greatly. But then Edna carelessly said something that hurt Elinor's feelings. "I didn't mean to hurt her, and I feel dreadful."[17] Elinor forgave her and Edna promised to write a poem to salve Elinor's distress; but for a long time she couldn't shape the poem in the way she wished and kept it to herself for a decade. When asked after Elinor's death what she was like, Millay replied with:

To Elinor Wylie: A Sonnet in Answer to a Question

Oh, she was beautiful in every part! –
The auburn hair that bound the subtle brain;
The lovely mouth cut clear by wit and pain,
Uttering oaths and nonsense, uttering art
In casual speech and curving at the smart
On startled ears of excellence too plain
For early morning! – *Obit*. Death from strain;
The soaring mind outstripped the tethered heart.
Yet here was one who had no need to die
To be remembered. Every word she said
The lively malice of hazel eye
Scanning the thumbnail close – oh, dazzling dead.
How like a comet through the darkening sky
You raced!...would your return were heralded.

In the spring of 1927, Elinor was invited to be an honored guest, along with Edna and others, at the Author's Breakfast of the League of American Pen Women, in Washington. Elinor was pleased since this was a sign that her scandalous past was no longer held against her in that city. Within days, however, the invitation was withdrawn. Washington still objected to her presence. Dismayed and furious, she remained silent, but Edna did not. She wrote a fierce letter to the Pen Women, cancelling her acceptance of their invitation, chastising them for seemingly honoring writers for the "circumspection" of personal lives and not for their literary accomplishments. "It is not in the power of an organization which has insulted Elinor Wylie, to honor me."[18]

ELINOR RETURNED TO poetry as the center of her creative life with the publication of *Trivial Breath* in 1928, which consisted of twenty-eight poems. The title came from one of her earlier sonnets, "Self-Portrait":

> This soul, this vanity, blown hither and thither
> By trivial breath, over the whole world's length.

The collection was more affirmative about the possibility of love, an attitude that makes what happened to her subsequently in England more understandable. Even a pervasive sense of sorrow could be lifted by the power of love, "gone like a cloud," no longer a gravestone over one's heart. The title comes from Shelley's *Prometheus Unbound*.

Desolation is a Delicate Thing

> Sorrow lay upon my breast more heavily than winter day
> Lying ponderable upon the unmoving bosom of the dead;
> Yet it was dissolved like a thin snowfall; it was softly withered away;
> Presently like a single drop of dew it had trembled and fled.

This sorrow, which seemed heavier than a shovel of loam,
Was gone like water, like a web of delicate frost:
It was silent and vanishing like smoke, it was scattered like
foam;
Thought my mind should desire to preserve it, nevertheless it
is lost.

This sorrow was not like sorrow; it was shining and brief;
Even as I walked and was aware of its going, it was past and
gone;
It was not earth; it was no more than a light leaf,
Or a snow flake in spring, which perishes upon stone.

This sorrow was small and vulnerable and short-lived;
It was neither earth nor stone; it was silver snow
Fallen from heaven, perhaps; it has not survived
An hour of the sun; it is sad it should be so.

This sorrow, which I believe a gravestone over my heart,
Is gone like a cloud; it eluded me as I woke;
Its crystal dust is suddenly broken and blown apart;
It was not my heart; it was this poor sorrow alone which broke.

IN APRIL 1927, Elinor sailed alone for England where she
rented a house and began a round of social visits. She said that she
intended to live in England permanently. Whatever one makes of
such a declaration from someone as chronically restless and unset-
tled, the English visit was an effort—as was the poetry she had
just written—to come to terms with her past life and her current
situation. England had meant Horace and once settled there she
wrote to him, describing her letter as a "strange" thing, perhaps

even a "devilish" one but something that was necessary to write, expressing sentiments which might give both of them pain but were founded on "deep principles of truth and affection."[19]

> "I love you Horace, with an unchanged love which is far more than friendship & which will certainly persist until my death… In England…you are constantly in my thoughts, & remembered with an affection which is undoubtedly the strongest I shall ever feel."[20]

She was not about to divorce Bill—yet. "He is the best boy imaginable." But, "if you ever want me, I will come back openly. I have never cheated anyone. But I don't suppose you do want it & I think it is better as it is," an assertion undercut by her adding: "I loved you first, I loved you more…I love you best." Horace replied with exemplary restraint, saying that he did not blame her for leaving him. "The situation was too much for your flesh and blood, though the fault of neither of us."[21] But she *had* left him, and there was no going back. Her letter was helpful because it allowed him to accept her offer to be friends.

If coming to England meant coming to terms with Horace and her second marriage, it equally marked the beginning of her reconsideration of her third marriage and of her relationship to Bill. England represented escape and what was now suffocating her and driving her to find a way of escape was marriage to Bill. The process of separation produced an extraordinary turmoil in terms of her personal behavior. The next months were marked by bursts of furious anger, rows with friends or former friends, conversations that somehow became explosions. People came to be dismayed at the perilous prospect of entertaining her. "Being in England brought out the worst in her, while she steadily professed to prefer it to New York." Perhaps turmoil was necessary to her, for at the time she was writing "reams and reams of poetry. I write a poem every morning before I get up. Honest Injun."[22]

After a few months, back she came to America, now settled in her determination to live in England, returning only in order to make necessary financial arrangements. That was not easy since their means were modest and she managed her financial affairs terribly. "The expense of living in New York is appalling beyond words," she said, but she was extravagant and never resisted the luxuries she craved. Bill worried about money but found it difficult to deny her anything. She was counting on a good return from the novel soon to be published. What made her trans-Atlantic expeditions possible anyway was a monthly allowance from her mother who at this point agreed to add it to three months rent for a London house, commenting without irony: "I do approve of the rest & recreation you enjoy there."[23] Such dependence was also a source of irritation compounded by Elinor's belief that her mother favored Nancy and Morton.

In April 1928, Elinor returned to England alone. Her father-in-law had died just before she sailed and she found it simplest to be away from the Benét family at that time. Bill, for his part, found himself turning back to his brother and sister and mother. Elinor decided to give up London and live in the country. She was entertained by the Woodhouse family, who lived near Henley. "Becky Woodhouse… is one of my great friends," Elinor wrote Bill. "She has a nice husband & two dear children."[24] She pressed herself upon the family, eager for their attention and almost demanding their affection. The consequences of this intimacy were entirely unexpected.

Within days Elinor fell madly, obsessively, in love with Henry Woodhouse, swept away by the power of her feelings, delighted to be swept away, rhapsodizing about love. A friend reported that "in all spare moments we talk of her affairs and she ended the day sobbing in my bedroom at 11 o'clock and being revived by a hot whiskey." Elinor immediately wrote three sonnets about her love, "this best poetry of my life, strange but true."[25] She took walks with Woodhouse and they read and discussed John Donne's poetry. It is obvious that she was transferring to Woodhouse the affection she felt once for Horace. However, neither Woodhouse nor his wife discerned what was going on. How could they? It was largely in Elinor's mind, where she was creating another of her fantasy novels.

One afternoon she fell down a flight of stairs and cracked a vertebra in her back, was taken to London by train in agonizing pain and put to bed for a month. She did not write Bill about this, nor about her feelings for Woodhouse. Bill was now irrelevant to what most concerned her. Eventually her "fall" received a good deal of unwelcome publicity in American newspapers, reviving notions about the Curse of the Hoyts. Elinor was reported to have plunged down four flights of stairs, was near death, had attempted suicide, etc. There was also publicity about one of her brother Morton's hijinks. Infuriated by such trashy journalism, Elinor lashed out in all directions. "The bad boy Morton is petted, while I who try to be brave get plain kicks for it." Her mother had ignored her. "Mama has been a brute to me. Two lines on a bit of notepaper & my allowance *tout simple*." Her friends in New York had also let her down, in unspecified ways. "I wish to heaven I never see New York again."[26] Adding to her misery, she suffered an episode of Bell's Palsy, which distorted one side of her face, making it asymmetrical.

In August, Bill came to England. By this time, Elinor was on her feet again and they did pleasant things together: picnics; canoe paddling; and walks in the countryside, which included an uneventful visit with the Woodhouses. At some point, Elinor told Bill of her love for Woodhouse. He apparently accepted as fact that their marriage had entered a different phase and was grateful for her frankness. But when, in September, Bill returned to America, he was less accepting. He referred to the "Woodlice," and thought their friendship was "essentially false," adding, "They are an experience I do not desire to repeat."[27]

In September, after Bill's departure, Elinor's passion for Woodhouse came to a climax: she thought she was pregnant. The question as to how this could have come about was not susceptible to a rational answer. However much Woodhouse may finally have come to understand the depth of Elinor's love, they had never been intimate. She was obviously suffering a breakdown in which her imagined pregnancy might be seen as a case of extreme wish fulfillment. In any case, within a few days she regained a degree of mental control and said that her hopes were over. Perhaps it was when Woodhouse made clear that there would be no sexual affair between them. Perhaps the fantasy was not about him primarily but about having a child, with Henry/Horace as the fantasy father. Henry Woodhouse's much later comments suggest that he was largely unaware of the extent of Elinor's imaginings about him. "I know that she attributed to me qualities which I don't possess and only wish I had." He said, with superb English understatement, "Her imagination, I think, ran away from her."[28] Subsequently, the Woodhouse family made concerted efforts to efface any connection between them and Elinor. Bill Benét also destroyed a number of letters. It was not until forty years later that a scholar unearthed the facts.

Is it certain that Elinor had finally come to understand that her dream of a supreme love affair with Henry Woodhouse was unrealizable? Some comments that she made to Carl Van Doren, a supporter and confidante who was in London at this time, lead one to wonder. Elinor spoke to Van Doren as if there might yet be some future time when she and Woodhouse would be together. "I don't want much, I don't expect it. I could be satisfied if I could know that sometime, maybe when we are very old, we could spend the same night under one roof. It would not have to be together. Only under the same roof, peacefully. Is that too much to expect? Don't you think I could dare hope for that?"[29]

What remained of all this, with a reality of its own, was the poetry Elinor wrote about it, a group of sonnets, which she entitled *One Person*. Rather than wait to include them in her next volume of verse which she was preparing and would call *Angels and Earthly Creatures*, she had the sonnets published privately in a small paper version in Henley, England. Bill understood the significance of her determination to publish them in this way—she sent a copy to the Woodhouses—and her doing so shows how pulverizingly dismissive she had become of Bill, writing to her mother, "I really like Bill, if only he were not such a weak-minded idiot. I have no intention of being otherwise than married to him for the rest of our lives, but I won't be married" to Mrs. Benét and Laura. At this time *Poetry* magazine awarded her its Levinson Prize, which pleased her and led her to reflect "for the thousandth time on the beauty and strangeness of life."[30]

AT THE END of November she sailed back to the United States, though Elinor made it clear to Bill that she would be returning to England in January. She avoided all but a very few friends. She had lunch with Nancy, spent most of one afternoon at the hairdresser. At the apartment of a friend, after dinner, she recited the *One Person* sonnets entirely from memory. Her headaches were terrible and she was taking massive doses of aspirin and bromo seltzer. On Sunday, December 16—surely Elinor remembered that it marked eighteen years to the day when she ran away with Horace—she was busy at home answering letters, among them one from Horace. She then looked through the typescript of *Angels and Earthly Creatures*, which was to go to her publisher the following week. She picked up a volume of John Donne's sermons, and asked Bill for a glass of water. As he brought it to her from the kitchen, the book slipped out of her hands and she murmured quietly, "Is that all it is?"[31] and fell to the floor, dead of a stroke. She was forty-three.

IN HOLLYWOOD, THE following day, Dorothy Parker was so shattered by the news of Elinor's death that she was unable to speak even to Robert Benchley about it. In New York City, Edna Millay was about to go onstage at the Brooklyn Academy of Music to recite her poetry when someone casually mentioned that Elinor Wylie had died the day before. Dazed by the news, Edna walked on the stage and, in a low but steady voice, said, "A greater poet than I has died, and with your permission I'd like to read her poems to you."[32]

A funeral service took place on December 18 at the Benét/Wylie apartment, with only a few close family friends present. Edna leaned down over Elinor's body, dressed in a splendid silver dress, looking "like a marble effigy, peaceful and serene," placed a laurel wreath around her immaculately groomed hair, and quietly recited a poem Elinor had written about her:

On a Singing Girl

Musa of the sea-blue eyes,
Silver nightingale, alone
In a little coffin lies:
A stone beneath a stone.

She, whose song we loved the best,
Is voiceless in a sudden night;
On your light limbs, O loveliest,
May the dust be light!

Seated next to his grandmother Hoyt, Philip Hichborn sat silently through the service, which gave him a rare look at his mother.

PART FIVE

AFTER:
1935

1. Overview:
The End of the Roaring Twenties

THE STOCK MARKET crash in October 1929 and the turn of the calendar combined to bring the Roaring Twenties to an end. Cycles of boom and bust were a familiar aspect of American economic and literary history. The momentary deflation of the 1930s was paralleled by the collapse of some literary reputations, but in time others would rise dramatically. National attention now focused much more on the District of Columbia than on Manhattan. The New Deal eclipsed the new poetry. The decline of the women's poetry movement was not surprising; it was diminished by death, by the dispersal of its members, and by its achievements. Many more women could assume the possibility of personal independence than had been true in 1912. And while political awareness became more prominent in the prose and poetry of the Depression decade, women poets still sang their songs of love.

What follows are some snapshots and a few more extended scenes from the lives of these women as they move through time.

2. DOROTHY PARKER

AFTER HER FLING in Hollywood, Dorothy Parker went back to New York City, where she thought she belonged. But was it clear any longer where she belonged? In search of an answer to that question she went to Europe, spending most of her time with wealthy acquaintances on the Riviera and in Switzerland. She tried (again) to write a novel—"daily she prayed, 'Dear God, please make me stop writing like a woman'"[1]—convinced that only a novel revealed a writer's true stature. Nothing came of her prayers.

Europe was an interlude, not a financial destination. When she returned to New York City, in January 1930, one glance at the lines of unemployed in the streets was enough to bring vividly to mind the new cultural and political reality. Previously, except for her involvement with Sacco and Vanzetti, Dorothy had no political views to speak of. She had never voted in an election. She began to recognize that it was not enough simply to feel sympathetic for the unemployed and dispossessed, and that there should be a positive political alternative, which, eventually, for her was the Communist Party.

Dorothy Parker

She lived on the royalties from her books and from the "Constant Reader" reviews for *The New Yorker*. In that year, Viking Press published *Laments for the Living*, a collection of her stories and sketches. The book sold remarkably well; there were ten printings between 1930 and 1936. What had not changed was her personal and social situation: the endless round of parties, drunkenness, perpetual hangovers, and random sexual encounters with men who meant nothing to her. Revealingly, she praised Ernest Hemingway for avoiding New York. "He has the most valuable asset an artist can possess, the fear of what he knows is bad for him."[2] She too knew what was bad for her, but seemed powerless to do anything about it. In the meantime, she looked back and drew on the work of the previous three years.

Requiescat

Tonight my love is sleeping cold
Where none may see and none shall pass.
The daisies quicken in the mold,
And richer fares the meadow grass.

The warding cypress pleads the skies.
The mound goes level in the rain.
My love all cold and silent lies –
Pray God it will not rise again!

SHE WAS ALMOST forty, very conscious of age and of aging, which made it all the more poignant when she fell for one of the younger-type men. Such a one, in 1930-1931, was John McClain, a college football player, well built, good looking, a "male Ruebens," ten years younger than she. Persistently and flauntingly unfaithful, he also lied to her, which produced outbursts of rage on her part and repeated public quarrels. And yet, when he finally left her for another woman, she was devastated. In 1933, there was a second collection of stories, *After Such Pleasures*, and in 1934, a farewell to the rapidly disappearing memory of the Algonquinites, a profile of Alexander Woollcott for *Vanity Fair*, and then suddenly everything turned upside down. Love came back into her life.

ALAN CAMPBELL WAS a writer—he had published stories in *The New Yorker*—and an aspiring actor, with "golden good looks," "fine bone structure," the well-bred manner of Eddie Parker, but without Eddie's "habits or inhibitions." His well-bred manner was misleading since his background was much the same as Parker's; his father was Scottish, his mother Alsatian Jewish. He graduated from Virginia Military Institute, but his artistic ambitions brought him to New York. Determined to break into Broadway theater, he had some modest success, appearing in a dozen shows.

When they met in 1933, Dorothy was forty, Campbell twenty-nine, and she was very self-conscious about it. They shared likes and dislikes as well as background. She made him laugh, and he took care of her, running the household. They moved in together soon after meeting. When she had drunk too much, she was venomously derisive about him, and there were frequent scenes. Alcohol unleashed her self-pity, her rage, and unappeasable sense of guilt. So this pairing must have seemed to Dorothy's friends to be certain to turn out disastrously.

In the summer of 1934, Campbell was offered an acting role in Denver. Dorothy was enchanted by the West—all that space she had avoided between the two coasts. Impulsively, they went to New Mexico and were married on June 18. Both were eager to continue this new life. When they were offered a contract with Paramount Pictures as a husband-and-wife writing team, they accepted. Their honeymoon would be in Hollywood. Within weeks, they were settled in Beverly Hills. For a while, Dorothy stopped being snooty about the movie industry. Being Campbell's wife was "lovelier than I ever knew anything could be," she wrote Alex Woollcott. They were living in a "coma of happiness,"[3] and when they came out of the coma, moved into a Colonial mansion, with white pillars, manicured lawns, and magnolias. She stopped talking about killing herself.

Autumn Valentine

In May my heart was breaking –
Oh, wide the wound, and deep!
And bitter it beat at waking,
And sore it split in sleep.

And when it came November,
I sought my heart, and sighed,
"Poor thing, do you remember?"
"What heart was that?" it cried.

Was she on the verge of becoming sentimental?

3. Sara Teasdale

S ARA TEASDALE WAS liberated by her divorce and was now
free to do—what? Not poetry. "I am almost completely out
of the writing game,"[1] she wrote to Genevieve Taggard. She
thought that prose might be a way to break the writing block.
Her publisher encouraged her to write a biography of Christina
Rosetti, whose poetry had been important to her; but when she
realized how much time and energy would be required, she was
reluctant to attempt it. Instead, Sara signed a contract to edit a
volume of Rosetti's love poems to be ready the next year. This also
reassured her financially. She had been very slow to take in the
extent of the Depression and was suddenly overcome with anxiety
about her financial future. (Actually, she had over eighty thousand
dollars in the bank and was financially secure, but this was just
one instance of the way she was attacked by fierce anxiety about
things.)

Nothing diminished her loneliness and her sense of the futility of life. Margaret Conklin remained loyal. Although she had a busy life of her own, and very little money, she walked miles, as an economy measure, to reach Sara's uptown apartment only to be greeted frequently with Sara in a cross and critical mood. Sara continued to take for granted that her life would be conducted on her own terms. If acquaintances came to visit, she often made a fuss if they were even moments late in arriving.

Erratic behavior and mental instability were symptoms of acute depression, which she recognized. Struggling to find a way out of the maze, in March 1931, she took a step that allowed her to be able to write poetry again. This was, once and for all, to resign herself to the acceptance of death. She could leave the world with her pride intact and if one accepted that the battle with the world was over, one might be granted "unassailed repose." Amazingly, this mood of acceptance unlocked her poetic resources and she began to write again. The first step was to free herself of worldly possessions that had served their purpose and now could be put away.

In a Darkening Garden

Gather together, against the coming of night,
  All that we played with here.
Toys and fruits, the quill from the sea bird's flight,
  The small flute, hollow and clear;
The apple that was not eaten, the grapes untasted –
  Let them be put away.
They served for us, I would not have them wasted,
  They lasted out our day.

FAR FROM RESIGNATION and acceptance of death, what came next was one of Sara's most dizzying mood swings—exhilaration. She now felt that she could get away, and in June 1931 she sailed to England accompanied by a nurse. She had been reading Virginia Woolf's *A Room of One's Own*, thought very highly of it, and hoped to be able to meet its author, but was too proud to arrange a meeting. Sara's respect wasn't solely literary. "Virginia Woolf is a lady, and God knows the race is vanishing. I rather pride myself on being one, but I may not be one after all," concluding these ruminations with a poignant understatement: "I suppose one never knows oneself."[2]

For a few weeks, London was merciful liberation from those feelings of futility. "I adore being out of New York. I have become a bit stale in that city." She went to museums and to the theater, looked up places where Christina Rosetti had lived, and (how this was arranged is unknown) met Virginia Woolf and was "charmed by her noble bearing and generosity."[3] And then this upward manic cycle came to an end, her spirits collapsed, and she returned to New York City and the dark fog of despair, terrified by the certainty of her coming death.

Two meetings in November dominated the fall. The first was with Ernst. Sara was finally able to face meeting him and was genuinely pleased to find that their divorce had not crushed him as she had feared. "He had survived perhaps better than she had," and this observation was followed by one more perverse. She found Ernst "more appealing than ever...because they were not living together." The next meeting was with Vachel Lindsay. The two old friends, "worn out by the battle of life,"[4] comforted each other. And then, three weeks later, came the devastating news that Lindsay had killed himself, swallowing the contents of a bottle of Lysol. Sara was hysterical for a few hours, but regained control of herself by the next day and wrote at one sitting a marvelous tribute.

In Memory of Vachel Lindsay

"Deep in the ages," you said, "deep in the ages,"
  And, "To live in mankind is far more than to live in a
    name."
You are deep in the ages, now, deep in the ages,
  You whom the world could not break, nor the years tame.

Fly out, fly on, eagle that is not forgotten,
  Fly straight to the innermost light, you who loved sun in
    your eyes,
Free of the fret, free of the weight of living,
  Bravest among the brave, gayest among the wise.

BELIEVING THAT ANOTHER trip to England might revive her interest in the Rosetti biography, she traveled there in July, 1932, the first time she'd made the journey alone, without nurse or companion. She called on A. E. Housman, but after that, the English visit became a disaster. She fell ill with bronchitis, which turned into pneumonia and forced her to cancel the rest of her plans and return to America. Once home, she seemed calm, almost cheerful at times but in reality was submerged in emotional darkness, morbidly fearful of dying, but also possessed by an overpowering sense that she must be the one who would determine how and when her life must end. Yet, terrified by physical illness, such as pneumonia, she was at the same time aggrieved that it had not done "what she was reluctant to do herself."[5]

A trip to Florida at the end of December, to visit her friend Jessie Rittenhouse, was futile. Sara lay in bed in a darkened room for two weeks, wishing to be alone, but also needing to hear the voices of visitors in other rooms. When she returned to New York City, a broken blood vessel in her hand convinced her that a massive stroke was about to kill her. She spent the evening of January 28 with Margaret Conklin, peacefully listening to Beethoven's Fifth Symphony. As Margaret left, Sara said: "Beethoven knew all the answers."[6]

In the early hours of January 29, she ran a bath, took a heavy dose of sleeping pills, and lay down in the warm water. Her nurse didn't look in on her until nine the next morning. Sara had died a few hours earlier. Medical examination revealed that drugs, not drowning, were the cause of death.

WHEN ERNST HEARD the news, in South Africa, he gallantly remembered what "a glorious thing it was to have had so many years,"[7] with Sara; later, he confessed that since her death his life had been an unhappy one. He moved his business to China and died in Shanghai of a heart attack in May 1937, age fifty-seven. Margaret Conklin, as literary executor, edited *Strange Victory*, the poems Sara had left in her notebook. It appeared in 1933; and with John Wheelock's assistance, *Collected Poems* appeared in 1937. Harriet Monroe reminded readers of Sara's historical importance, two decades earlier, as a lyrical voice for women. John Wheelock believed that in her last poems, Sara had achieved a "real Beethoven cry."

Perhaps. But one of last poems testified rather to her firm belief that nothing she left behind would survive for more than an instant, "a brief alighting."

All That Was Mortal

All that was mortal shall be burned away,
  All that was mind shall have been put to sleep.
Only the spirit shall awake to say
  What the deep says to the deep;
But for an instant, for it too is fleeting –
  As on a field with new snow everywhere.
Footprints of birds record a brief alighting
  In flight begun and ended in the air.

Although she had left instructions that her ashes should be scattered at sea, so that "there may be neither trace nor remembrance," her wishes were ignored and her last "alighting" was in the family burial plot, in the city she had longed to leave, St. Louis.

4. LOUISE BOGAN

NOTHING COULD REPLACE what Louise Bogan and Raymond Holden had lost in the fire that destroyed their hillside house, but they found the determination to carry on. This meant abandoning their idea of country living. They would start again in New York City. Holden became managing editor of *The New Yorker*, Louise worked at home and also found regular employment at the magazine. Instead of publishing only light satirical verse, *The New Yorker* began featuring serious poetry, and editor Harold Ross asked Louise to become the regular poetry reviewer, as well as contribute an occasional poem.

Around *The New Yorker* there also grew up a social and intellectual group, lively, witty, urbane: Rolfe Humphries, Léonie Adams, Edmund Wilson, Wolcott Gibbs, Peter Arno. At the end of 1930, *Poetry* awarded Louise its John Reed memorial prize and Louise wrote to Harriet Monroe, "I cannot think of any recognition that has ever touched me so deeply."[1]

However, things were falling apart at home. Louise became subject to paranoid suspicions: that people were gossiping about her in a hurtful way, that Holden was being unfaithful. This he denied and protested his love. She was unappeased. There were now bitter recurrent arguments. She described herself as suffering from a "fever in the brain," and lived and worked in "angry solitude." [2] Desperate for help, Louise entered the Neurological Institute on the Upper West Side of Manhattan, and after a time moved to a sanitarium in Connecticut where, in the midst of her suffering and her delusions, a complete poem came to her. It was ostensibly about Jonathan Swift, incorporating phrases from his *A Journal to Stella*, but was essentially a poem about mental breakdown. Theodore Roethke wrote of this poem, "For one terrifying instant we were within Swift's mind…sharing the glitter, the horror and the glory of his madness." [3] At the heart of his anguish was Swift's incapacity to love. And Louise's?

Louise Bogan

Hypocrite Swift

Hypocrite Swift now takes an eldest daughter.
He lifts Vanessa's hand. Cudsho, my dove!
Drink Wexford ale and quaff down Wexford water
But never love.

He buys new caps; he and Lord Stanley ban
Hedge-fellows who have neither wit nor swords.
He turns his coat; Tories are in; Queen Anne
Makes twelve new lords.

The town mows hay in hell; he swims in the river;
His giddiness returns; his head is hot.
Berries are clean, while peaches damn the giver
(Though grapes do not).

Mrs. Vanhomrigh keeps him safe from the weather.
Preferment pulls his periwig askew.
Pox takes belittlers; do the willows feather?
God keep you.

Stella spells ill; Lords Peterborough and Fountain
Talk politics; the Florence wine went sour.
Midnight: two different clocks, here and in Dublin,
Give out the hour.

On walls at court, long gilded mirrors gaze.
The parquet shines; outside the snow falls deep.
Venus, the muses stare above the maze.
Now asleep.

Dream the mixed, fearsome dream. The satiric word
Dies in its horror. Wake, and live by stealth.
The bitter quatrain forms, is here, is heard,
Is wealth.

What care I; what cares saucy Presto? Stir
The bed-clothes; hearten up the perishing fire.
Hypocrite Swift sent Stella a green apron
And dead desire.

She left the sanitarium in the summer of 1931, returning to Holden and to their apartment. She managed to maintain a precarious emotional equilibrium and wrote at a feverish pace—five short stories for *The New Yorker* and a profile of Willa Cather. Her marriage alternately attracted and appalled her; she admired and wanted to possess fine things, but she also felt at times an upsurge of the "little Irish girl" who yearned for, but also derided, things associated with upper-class refinement. In "continuous turmoil," she probed memories of her childhood and youth and wrote chapters of a psychological autobiography coming back again and again to the trauma she suffered because of her mother's adultery. She longed to get away and applied for a Guggenheim Fellowship for study abroad, which she was granted. Holden had lost his job at *The New Yorker* and was out of work. Her decision to get away was a decision to leave him, for they both knew he could not go with her. In the spring of 1933, Louise sailed for Italy.

She spent time in Florence, Venice, Salzburg, and in each of those places fluctuated between feeling that she might never write poetry again and sensing that "the nameless going on that means poetry beats out rhythms in my head from morning to night, so that something of the sort will happen." She analyzed what had been the sources of her inspiration, "I can write only when in a rage (of anger or hatred), or in a state which I can only describe as malicious pity." Such no doubt had been the source of "Hypocrite Swift," but now, stimulated by the gorgeous Italian and Austrian countryside and by the superb Baroque architecture that she adored, she created a charming visual picture of a fountain, created in bronze by the sculptor's arm and hammer and in words by the poet beating out an image. "The opening lines," wrote Theodore Roethke, "are one of the greatest felicities of our time: the thing put down with ultimate exactness."[4]

Roman Fountain

Up from the bronze, I saw
Water without a flaw
Rush to its rest in air,
Reach to its rest, and fall.

Bronze of the blackest shade,
An element man-made,
Shaping upright the bare
Clear gouts of water in air.

O, as with arm and hammer,
Still it is good to strive
To beat out the image whole,
To echo the shout and stammer
When full-gushed waters, alive,
Strike on the fountain's bowl
After the air of summer.

Louise taught herself Italian and realized that the word that most frequently recurred in her mind was "destino." Her return to the United States revealed what that destiny would be. When Holden met her at the boat, almost the first thing he told her was that he had been having an affair with another woman and had been living with her for some time. Never mind that she had been planning to leave Holden. She now felt betrayed by him and, with the tenuous equanimity she had achieved in Europe in ruins, Louise committed herself in November to a hospital in White Plains, New York, in "an earnest effort to clear the whole thing finally. Month or years, I really do not care, as long as I can, after whatever period it is, feel and live humanly again."[5] Mysteriously, through all this, she was able to leave the hospital. In July, she obtained a legal separation from Holden.

In the months after, Louise spent time in Boston, not yet quite able to face the complex demands of New York City. There she had a sexual affair with a man whom we know only as European, a librarian, kind, amusing, interesting. She wrote what she described with amused self-deprecation as "a lot of subliminal mewlings, roarings and retchings, on odd scraps of paper." The anonymous librarian in Boston was not Louise's only lover. "A frank, though never a vulgar sensualist, she considered physical love one of the great gifts of being alive."[6] And so it was with amused delight that she could write to Edmund Wilson, who was in the Soviet Union, that she had "been made to blossom like a Persian rose-bush, by the enormous love making of...one Theodore Roethke by name. He is very, very large...and he writes very, very small lyrics. We have poured rivers of liquor down our throats."[7]

They had met at a party given by Rolfe Humphries. Shy, awkward, obsessively self-doubting—"like a country boy at his first party—such an oaf, such a boob, such a blockhead," Humphries had said of himself. He was abashed to be in the presence of a poet whose work he had read enthusiastically for years. Roethke ranked Louise, Elinor Wylie, and Léonie Adams as the finest of contemporary poets. He wanted to write poetry that might someday "gain Louise's respect." About Roethke, she managed to keep her head. "He is a ripple on time's stream," she wrote to Edmund Wilson, "because he is soon going to Michigan."[8] A steady friendship eventually evolved out of their erotic attraction. They sent each other their poetry, and criticized it candidly but respectfully. In time, Roethke wrote one of the finest critical essays about her work. The calmer, disillusioned understanding of herself was directed at explaining what it was men sought in sexual love, "that passionate look, the laughter." And when that "long rage" was over, she wondered, would men and women be anything but strangers to each other?

Looking back at the first half of the decade, Louise described it as "a sick and terrible four years. A broken time." To begin her recovered life, she returned to the Village, 82 Washington Place, with Maidie, determined to be the kind of mother she never had. Beyond family, she accepted the fact that she would never have many readers. "*Dark Summer* fell into a dark deep well. It is never stocked in bookstores and is known to a small group only."[9] So she would work again at poetry and reviewing and focus her energies in the service of her art.

5. ELINOR WYLIE

THE MANUSCRIPT ELINOR Wylie held in her hands
as she died was published the year after her death as
Angels and Earthly Creatures. It provoked a complex
response. The voice was unmistakably hers and it seemed as if
she were still present. At the same time, critics began to estimate the nature and extent of the now completed poetic achievement. The nineteen sonnets dedicated to "One Person" made up
the first section of the book and monopolized critics' attention.
"I thought them the best things that she had done,"[1] Louise
Bogan wrote to Ruth Benedict. They are love sonnets, a narrative
sequence about the love of a woman poet for an Englishman. The
varied aspects of love are developed in the first two thirds of the
narrative, which concludes with the woman's realization that love
between them is impossible except in spiritual terms. A prefatory sonnet is about the difficulty of understanding love through

language, developing the paradox that art, while often untrue to love, can also convey truths of a different sort.

> Although these words are false, none shall prevail
> To prove them in translation less than true
> Or overthrow their dignity, or undo
> The faith implicit in a fabulous tale;
> The ashes of this error shall exhale
> Essential verity, and two by two
> Lovers devout and loyal shall renew
> The legend, and refuse to let it fail.
> Even the betrayer and the fond deceived,
> Having put off the body of this death,
> Shall testify with one remaining breath,
> From sepulchers demand to be believed;
> These words are true, although at intervals
> The unfaithful clay contrive to make them false.

The sonnet "VI" emphasizes the erotic aspects of love, even as it is clear that this particular love is unconsummated. The poet recognizes the miracle of body and soul, far from the "sharp ecstasies" of the body.

> VI
>
> I have believed that I prefer to live
> Preoccupied by a Platonic mind;
> I have believed me obdurate and blind
> To those sharp ecstasies the pulses give;
> The clever body five times sensitive
> I never have discovered to be kind.
> As the poor soul, deceived and half-divined,
> Whose hopes are water in a witch's sieve.

O now both soul and body are unfit
To apprehend this miracle, my lord!
Not all my senses, striving in accord
With my pure essence, are aware of it
Save as a power remote and exquisite,
Not seen or known, but fervently adored.

The second section of the book, "Elements and Angels,"
includes "Felo De Se," ("Suicide"), which explores renunciation as
an ultimate expression of love.

Felo De Se

My heart's delight, I must for love forget you;
I must put you from my heart, the better to please you;
I must make the power of the spirit set you
Beyond the power of the mind to seize you.

My dearest heart, in this last act of homage,
I must reject you; I must unlearn to love you;
I must make my eyes give up your adorable image
And from the inner chamber of my soul remove you.

Heart of my heart, the heart alone has courage
Thus to relinquish; it is yourself that stills you
In all my pulses, and dissolves the marriage
Of soul and soul, and at the heart's core kills you.

IN 1932, BILL Benét edited and wrote an effusive introduction to
Elinor's *Collected Poems*, which included poems previously uncol-

lected. It was published by Knopf, who kept it in print throughout the 1940s and '50s. A twelfth printing appeared in 1960. In 1933, came the *Collected Prose of Elinor Wylie*, all four novels in one hefty volume, two of which had separate introductions by her faithful critic friends, Van Vechten and Van Doren, and a further printing of that also appeared as late as 1960.

For those readers who had known and admired Elinor's art, and for new readers as well, both poetry and prose were available. Nevertheless, changes in circumstances and taste would be very unfavorable to her reputation, especially for her novels—the Thirties were not a time when prose fantasy had much appeal. But the poetry, too, if read, was not discussed. Few of the anthologies of American or of contemporary Anglo-American verse found any place for her poems. A re-appraisal finally began in the 1970s and after—a much needed biography and two excellent studies of her work. But among general readers today, her name remains unknown or only faintly recalled.

If Elinor's name faded in the Thirties, members of the Hoyt Hichborn families continued to attract the sort of publicity that had haunted her. Nancy's several marriages and love affairs—there was an English Earl, an heir to the Reynolds Tobacco fortune, and a taxi driver with whom she attempted elopement after knowing him for ten days—kept gossip columnists on their toes, hoping for more. In between escapades, she wrote three novels, and in 1935, in an effort to retrieve her sister's reputation, a biography, *Elinor Wylie: The Portrait of an Unknown Lady*. Nancy outlived her mother by five years, Morton outlived his sister by fifteen days. Nancy's daughter, upholding the tradition of scandalous behavior, testified against her mother in a custody trial. It was she who inherited most of her grandmother's fortune (Mrs. Hoyt left Nancy and Morton only a thousand dollars each), but she quickly squandered it, bringing "Hoytmania" to an end.

Philip Hichborn, brought up by his father's family to hate his mother, insisted that he did not do so. When he saw her, once, before her death, he thought her very beautiful but, poignantly, "had not known what to say or how to say it."[2] In many respects, he emulated his father. At Harvard, he wrote for the *Lampoon*, as his father had done, and like him became a lawyer. His society wedding in 1933 received some notice...as did his divorce, which followed soon after. Philip then moved to California where, after an "alcoholic episode," he died of a fall in his hotel. At his death, Philip was the same age as his father was when he had died: twenty-nine.

6. MARIANNE MOORE

MARIANNE MOORE SETTLED in Brooklyn, in the quiet and respectable Clinton Hill district, living the life of "tame excitement on which I thrive."[1] She had worried about losing the congenial social and intellectual atmosphere of *The Dial* but found that her fears were unfounded. The Wall Street crash that followed soon after the move and the ensuing Depression added to her sense of anxiety. Hard times meant that there was no other suitable magazine where Marianne might find work as an editor. She was unemployed and she was not writing.

The move to Brooklyn also coincided with a profound sense of estrangement on her part from the political and cultural spirit of the 1930s. An uncompromising individualist now living in a more collectivist era, Marianne defiantly proclaimed her faith in the Republican Party and in Herbert Hoover. "America is pestered at present by a man named Franklin D. Roosevelt, as Germany has been with Hitler," she wrote in October 1932, "but I think

Mr. Hoover will 'win' as our neo-Hitler would put it." Hoover had "worked for the good of the country to the point of martyrdom,"[2] so she wrote a poem about Hoover, comparing him to Jesus Christ and his opponents to Judas. No newspaper or magazine was interested in publishing it.

As Marianne began to take advantage of Brooklyn's cultural resources, her sense of isolation gradually diminished. The Pratt Free Library and the Brooklyn Institute of Arts and Sciences provided a steady array of readings and lectures on a wide range of subjects by distinguished visitors, among them, poets: Harriet Monroe, William Butler Yeats (to whom she was introduced), and Edna Millay. In time she read her own work there. She also traveled to Bryn Mawr College to read poetry and to talk with students; it was the first of many visits. Her interest in contemporary art remained wide-ranging and highly individual. Of the much discussed Gertrude Stein/Virgil Thompson Modernist opera, *Four Saints in Three Acts*, she said, "A blasphemous but talented thing, well worth hearing."[3]

Residence in Brooklyn didn't curtail her varied and extensive correspondence. There were few letters to Warner, who was close at hand until 1932 when he was (again) transferred, this time to Pago Pago, Samoa. She became interested in the poetry of the young Elizabeth Bishop, encouraged her and took her to the circus. She continued reviewing, for T. S. Eliot's *Criterion* and for *Poetry*, whose assistant editor, Morton Zabel, exchanged many letters and ideas about poetry with her. She kept her voluminous correspondence with Bryher, which meant she was in touch with H. D., even if the two of them rarely wrote each other. She wrote regularly to Ezra Pound, whom she had not yet met in person; and, as always, her most extensive correspondence was with Warner.

Marianne Moore

IN 1931, SHE had told William Carlos Williams that though she was not writing poetry, "I am as strong for it as ever and have various things in mind. Perhaps, like snails' eggs…they will hatch in time."[4] They did. She composed eleven poems between 1932 and 1934, among her most complex and ambitious. The upward arc of regained activity was marked by being awarded the Levinson Prize from *Poetry*. Then Marianne received a letter from T. S. Eliot, who proposed a new collection of her poems for which he would write an introduction. She was initially hesitant about this, but wrote to express her gratitude for his offer. "If something by me were to come out, I should like to have your hand in it."[5] Eliot

did more than have a hand in it, he made many of the major decisions about the book. He realized that it had been eleven years
since *Observations* and Marianne had written little poetry since
then. So Eliot chose the word "selected" for the title precisely because it would convey the sense that the poems had been chosen
from a considerable body of work. He also determined the order of
the poems, putting a new one, "The Steeple-Jack," first. Ever after,
Marianne would begin her collections with that poem.

Selected Poems, published simultaneously in England and the
United States, appeared in 1935. When she read his introduction,
she wrote Eliot a moving letter of gratitude—"You do it with
such sobriety and fine dignity," and thanked him for his restraint.
"The summit of pervasiveness is in making a claim that seems
not to be claiming more than could be claimed."[6] By this time,
Eliot had gained that position of unrivalled influence as a critic,
his judgments delivered with pontifical certitude. He explained
to readers puzzled by Marianne's poetry what it was that merited
this collection; his praise was measured but emphatic. Her poetry
was not like anyone else's. He could not "fill up my pages with
the usual account of influences and development." Marianne's prevailing quality, Eliot went on, was "genuineness," a quality so rare
that "only a small number of contemporaries" could lay claim to
it. Her genuineness eluded the conventional categories. While not
hostile to new forms, she avoided the impulse to fashionable novelty, "stale goods in new packages." Descriptive rather than lyrical
or dramatic, her verse was anything but "free," presenting formal
patterns and irregular rhymes. He admired her skill at detailed
observation, "the exact words for some experience of the eye." The
majority, he believed, would characterize her work as frigid but the
majority, as so often, would be wrong. Her greatest achievement
was one attained only by the finest writers, in an age of clamorous

and shabby expression, "her original sensibility and alert intelligence and deep feeling have been engaged in maintaining the life of the English language."[7] (What H. D. had written twenty years earlier.)

T. S. Eliot's words foretold and shaped the future estimate of Moore's poetry. It was unique. It was difficult. It was for the discriminating few. Although she understood her situation, she wrote ruefully to Eliot, "One could scarcely be human and wish your introduction might have the effect of a tidal wave on the public that it has had on me." She consoled herself by remembering that "an array of appreciators is unessential if one is valued by five or even by two."[8]

OBSERVING AND DESCRIBING various creatures became a feature of her poetry known even to those who barely knew her other poems. She read a great deal of natural history, regularly visited museums and took copious notes. She believed that aspects of animal behavior were like that of humans, but she didn't compose fables about them, didn't imagine them as semi-human. Her creatures do not participate in a story. They are often exotic, which makes it more difficult to humanize them. The animals she especially admired were the self-reliant ones who richly adorn *Selected Poems*—in such poems as "The Buffalo," "The Pangolin," "The Jerboa," and "Frigate Pelican."

One poem combines description, heroism, and a sense of place. "The Steeple-Jack" seems on the surface a depiction of a small New England coastal town. Among the local sights are a student, with his books; and a steeple-jack climbing to gild a church steeple. The picture is one of Yankee orderliness, but it is also something else, something in addition, for we become aware that there is disorder in this, as in all human environments. The first word of the poem is "Dürer"—Albrecht Dürer, the sixteenth-century German painter. "Dürer would have seen a reason for living in a town like this," the poet tells us. Why? Because Dürer in his work placed "apocalyptic visions in everyday settings." The student and the steeple-jack are members of an ordinary human community that accepts the precariousness of life as well as possibilities. This, too, is a form of heroism.

The Steeple-Jack

Dürer would have seen a reason for living
   in a town like this, with eight stranded whales
to look at; with the sweet sea air coming into your house
on a fine day, from water etched
   with waves as formal as the scales
on a fish.

One by one, in two's, in three's, the seagulls keep
   flying back and forth over the town clock,
or sailing around the lighthouse without moving the wings –
rising steadily with a slight
   quiver of the body – or flock
mewing where

a sea the purple of the peacock's neck is
   paled to greenish azure as Dürer changed
the pine green of the Tyrol to peacock blue and guinea
grey. You can see a twenty-five
   pound lobster; and fishnets arranged
to dry. The

whirlwind fifeanddrum of the storm bends the salt
   marsh grass, disturbs stars in the sky and the
star on the steeple; it is a privilege to see so
much confusion. Disguised by what
   might seem the opposite, the sea-
side flowers and

trees are favored by the fog so that you have
   the tropics at first hand: the trumpet-vine,
fox-glove, giant snap-dragon, a salpiglossis that has
spots and stripes; morning-glories, gourds,
   or moon-vines trained on fishing-twine
at the back

door; cat-tails, flags, blueberries and spiderwort,
   striped grass, lichens, sunflowers, asters, daisies –
the yellow and crab-claw blue ones with green bracts –
                   toad-plant,
petunias, ferns; pink lilies, blue
   ones, tigers; poppies; black sweet-peas.
The climate

is not right for the banyan, frangipani, the
   jack-fruit tree; nor for exotic serpent
life. Ring lizard and snake-skin for the foot if you see fit,
but here they've cats not cobras to
   keep down the rats. The diffident
little newt

with white pin-dots on black horizontal spaced
   out bands lives here; yet there is nothing that
ambition can buy or take away. The college student

named Ambrose sits on the hill-side
   with his not-native books and hat
and sees boats

at sea progress white and rigid as if in
   a groove. Like an elegance of which
the source is not bravado, he knows by heart the antique
sugar-bowl shaped summer-house of
   interlacing slats, and the pitch
of the church

spire, not true, from which a man in scarlet lets
   down a rope as a spider spins a thread;
he might be a part of a novel, but on the sidewalk a
sign says C. J. Poole, Steeple-jack,
   in black and white; and one in red
and white says

Danger. The church portico has four fluted
   columns, each a single piece of stone, made
modester by white-wash. This would be a fit haven for
waifs, children, animals, prisoners,
   and presidents who have repaid
sin-driven

senators by not thinking about them. There
   are a school-house, a post-office in a
store, fish-houses, hen-houses, a three-masted schooner on
the stocks. The hero, the student,
   the steeple-jack, each in his way,
is at home.

It could not be dangerous to be living
   in a town like this, of simple people,
who have a steeple-jack placing danger signs by the church
while he is gilding the solid-
   pointed star, which on a steeple
stands for hope.

One of Marianne's best loved poems is also about "a variety of hero," the last stanza rising to a level of magnificent, subdued eloquence which makes one proud to be identified with it.

The Student

"In America," began
the lecturer, "everyone must have a
degree. The French do not think that
all can have it, they don't say everyone
   must go to college." We
incline to feel, here,
   that although it may be unnecessary

to know fifteen languages,
one degree is not too much. With us, a
school – like the singing tree of which
the leaves were mouths that sang in concert –
   is both a tree of knowledge
and of liberty, –
   seen in the unanimity of college

mottoes, *lux et veritas,*
Christo et ecclesiae sapiet`
felici. It may be that we

have not knowledge, just opinion, that we
  are undergraduates,
not students; we know
  we have been told with smiles; by expatriates

of whom we had asked, "When will
your experiment be finished?" "Science
is never finished." Secluded
from domestic strife, Jack Bookworm led a
  college life, says Goldsmith;
and here also as
  in France or Oxford, study is beset with

dangers – with bookworms, mildews,
and complaisancies. But someone in New
England has known enough to say
that the student is patience personified
  is a variety
of hero, "patient
  of neglect and of reproach," – who can "hold by

himself." You can't beat hens to
make them lay. Wolf's wool is the best of wool,
but it cannot be sheared, because
the wolf will not comply. With knowledge as
  with wolf's surliness,
the student studies
  voluntarily, refusing to be less

than individual. He
"gives his opinion and then rests upon it;"

he renders service when there is

no reward, and is too reclusive for

  some things to seem to touch

him, not because he

  has no feeling but because he has so much.

WARNER'S OWN RESPONSE was heartfelt. Though a conventional person, he had always thought his sister's unconventional art admirable. It was for him a reaffirmation of the family's indissoluble unity. "It is like the intimate fire of a diamond," he wrote to Marianne, in unusually heightened language. "It lights the present moment with divine fire, and at the same time, speaks of our entire history, of our life hid in each other. In there is the witness to our origin, to our period of growth, to what we shall ever be."[9]

7. Léonie Adams

WHEN, AT THE end of the Twenties, Léonie Adams returned to New York City after her two years in France, she began the new decade by embarking on a career as a college teacher. She taught at New York University where, in 1932, she met and married the critic William Troy. Thereafter she taught at Sarah Lawrence College and in 1935 she took a position, as did her husband, at Bennington College, Vermont. Teaching became the center of her intellectual life. Well liked by students and colleagues, she was exceptionally reserved and didn't argue about poetry. A colleague said: "She was above pedagogic doctrine. She had no need of it. The purity of her spirit was the doctrine she followed."[1] On one occasion, she invited Louise Bogan to give a poetry reading, which was a great success, and the two poets at dinner talked to and with each other about French Symbolist poetry while the others present listened. She wrote a little if any poetry, only once offering an explanation to an interviewer. She felt that poetry was entering an entirely new phase, one in which she did not feel at ease. "I have been silent a long time because I am now grappling with the limitation of the lyric."[2]

8. GENEVIEVE TAGGARD

I N 1930, GENEVIEVE Taggard returned to America after her
year in France. She began a decade marked by varied achievements in poetry and in literary scholarship and by changes in
her personal life and career. In 1931, her marriage to Robert Wolf
ended when he had to be institutionalized. In 1935, she married
Kenneth Durant, a journalist who ran the New York office of the
Soviet News Agency TASS. She taught for a while at Bennington
College, Vermont, and then returned to New York City and taught
at Sarah Lawrence.

She completed the biography she had worked on for many
years, *The Life and Mind of Emily Dickinson* (1930), which found
eager readers; three printings in two months. It opens with a
charming "Dedication" from one poet to another:

Emily!
The book is bound
Index says Emily.
Where are you found?

Deity will see to it
That you never do it.

Deity did.

You are vexed.
You vanish, with a text.

Still you have been
Some months my shy companion. While I wrote
The slow prose,
You watched, alert, amused. Your words
Fell on the page, consenting with my words.   .

Index offended you,
The binding, and the print,
The sold book, possession, *the review.*
Emily, where are you?

Go to her verse, reader,
To the great verse.
Here is nothing of hers.

She will elude us all,
Run from any but her own call.
Read her own page, reader.
Wait…read the great verse. Do not look up if you think you

Do not for a moment stir.
She will come near, confidently nearer,
Even as I write this, she is here.

Two books of poems appeared in the middle of the decade: *Not Mine to Finish: Poems 1928-1934* (1934), and *Calling Western Union* (1936), both mixing reflective lyrics and strident ideology. *Not Mine to Finish* contains subtle reflections on various states of mind, as in this wryly resigned consideration of that inescapable human illness, love:

Try Tropic for Your Balm
(On the Properties of Nature for Healing an Illness)

Try tropic for your balm,
Try storm,
And after storm, calm.
Try snow of heaven, heavy, soft and slow,
Brilliant and warm.
Nothing will help, and nothing do much harm.

Drink iron from rare springs; follow the sun;
Go far
To get the beam of some medicinal star;
Or in your anguish run
The gauntlet of all zones to an ultimate one.
Fever and chill
Punish you still,
Earth has no zone to work against your ill.

Burn in the jeweled desert with the toad.
Catch lace
Of evening mist across your haunted face;
Or walk in upper air, the slanted road.
It will not lift that load;
Nor will large seas undo your subtle ill.

Nothing can cure and nothing kill
What ails your eyes, what cuts your pulse in two
And not kill you.

How to move beyond love as madness? One of her finest poems continues this theme and adds to it political madness, "the outrageous wrongs men do," which we must also transcend, to achieve a state where joy is moderate, toil is steady, its harvest somber work passed on from generation to generation.

Return of the Native

Now, after years serving demonic excess.
Exalting those whose god-passions send them mad,
I am stranded on a simpler shore, much less
Sumptuous, – a land permanently sad,

Bearing a somber harvest – an old island,
With cactus and asphodel and olive on
The rock itself. This oddly, is my land.
Here a moderate joy yellows the sky each dawn.

We toil – here toil has lost its hectic haste.
The outrageous wrongs men do lessen, diminish.
We are frugal, we share, we despise waste.
The work I have is good. It is not mine to finish.

Calling Western Union was philosophically materialistic; the mind and human behavior are shaped by the material work. Ideas are superficial and external to these material laws of being.

The book was widely dismissed as propaganda, the poems like "labels on a can."[1] The reformist thrust of the New Deal had undercut more radical political positions and there was increased concern with, and bitter disagreement about, international affairs, less with domestic ones. Taggard's reputation underwent an eclipse.

9. Edna St. Vincent Millay

I N THE HALF dozen years after the Crash, and despite worsening economic conditions, Edna Millay extended her national reputation, taking part in widely publicized poetry reading tours to all areas of the nation. She also published two volumes of poetry which sold very well, especially in towns and cities she visited on tour. This wasn't by chance. Her tours were often timed to precede and then coincide with the publication of her books. A new technology broadened her audience. She read her poems on a national radio network, eight Sunday evening broadcasts to rapturous listener response. Hearing a recording of her voice for the first tine, she was, like everyone else, charmed. "Is that really my voice? Quite lovely, isn't it?"[1]

She crossed and re-crossed the country, traveling by train, interviewed everywhere for local newspapers, everywhere described in flattering terms. Eugen sent cryptic reports of her triumphs—"sold-out," "standees," "overflow." It was relentless and exhausting. "We arrived here [in Oklahoma City] at 7 am. She gave a reading at 11 am…and at 5:20 she leaves for Waco, Texas, where she reads tomorrow."[2] Her person, her dress, her manner, her voice all received careful attention, often more than her poetry. She was forty and yet surprisingly youthful, elfin, fragile, with bronze hair and gray-green eyes. For people who had never seen or heard or met a poet, she personified poetry.

Edna St. Vincent Millay

In the audiences were students who had invited her to read at their various colleges, young people still eager to identify with her as a symbol of rebellion against conventional values. Yet she talked about how ordinary she was. People liked her poetry, she believed, "because it is mostly about things everybody has experienced. Most of it is fairly simple for a person to understand." She was a small town girl. "I never went to a big city, you know, until I was twenty years old." She identified her primary subjects—love, death, nature. "You can just sit in your farmhouse, or your home anywhere, and read it and know you've felt the same thing yourself."[3]

The tours reassured her that poetry still mattered, and they brought her a great deal of money. (Louise Bogan couldn't help being envious. "Edna Millay has a lovely new Cadillac car. She is off reading now, at six hundred a throw.") The money she was making apparently shielded her from an immediate sense of what the Depression was doing to the lives of those ordinary people. She said guilelessly: "I never knew money so sticky as it is this year." She needed the tours and at the same resented needing them, the same feelings she had when she first began touring. One afternoon, having just tired herself autographing three hundred and sixty copies of expensive limited editions of her poems, she exploded in anger: "That's the trouble with being a celebrity. One gets sucked into the whirlpool. One does things that one shouldn't be doing and says things one shouldn't be saying and life grows horribly cheap and perfunctory and vulgar. I should never have consented to read my poems in public. It makes them sound so blatant. I feel like a prostitute."[4]

ADULATION, MONEY, FAME, the tours brought all these; but more immediate consequences flowed in November of 1928 from meeting George Dillon in Chicago. He was then twenty-two and a poet. Born in Florida, his parents moved throughout the South, finally settling in Chicago, where he was an undergraduate at the University of Chicago. In his senior year, his first book of poems, *Boy in the Wind*, was published. When he met Edna he was working as the associate editor of *Poetry*. He was tall and Edna took his hand "as if she were falling into him."[5] She was. The next day she presented him with a sonnet she had written overnight, and declared her feelings for him. They became lovers.

Her love for him was the overmastering center of her emotional life for the next decade. She deluged him with letters: "I shall love you always and I shall never let you go out of my life again." Nonetheless, her work, her tours, and geography kept them apart. After their first rapturous meeting she did not see him for almost a year; more was involved than distance and work; they both wanted sexual intimacy, but she wanted more, and he always drew back. She was demanding. "Do you ever want to see me? Does it ever bother you at all, not seeing me? What does one do about it?"[6] She was famous, he was unknown, which complicated things. He was often angry and sulky. None of this put her off. She wanted him—desperately, but on her own terms. She told Eugen everything. True to the "open" nature of their marriage, he was more than understanding; he approved of a passion which would help her fulfill her destiny as a poet. Edna invited Dillon to visit them at Steepletop, and Eugen wrote to him as well. "[Eugen] loves you already,"[7] she wrote. Eugen was actually less unperturbed than he seemed, but believed that time and patience were on his side. He was less honest with Edna than she was with him; he was having an affair with a younger woman of which Edna was unaware. Dillon, who told friends he did not feel at ease at Steepletop, rarely visited there.

Edna's love for Dillon stimulated her to write love poems again. Distance only added to her inspiration. In one letter to him she enclosed five sonnets, in another twenty-six! "I've done acres of them. I have never worked so hard. Some of them were written when I hadn't heard from you for a long time, and thought maybe you didn't love me anymore." She occasionally struck a plaintive note, rebuking him for his elusiveness. "If I don't see you soon. I shall lie on the floor and kick and howl till something is done about it."[8]

THIS WAS INTERTWINED with personal sadness, the breakup of the Millay family. Edna saw less and less of her mother. She was often away from Steepletop when Cora might have visited. She rarely made it to Camden; but one time when she did, Edna gave her mother three mountain laurels. "Next year they will blossom like anything." Edna's letters were increasingly dotted with apologies for not writing, mixed with protestations of her affection: "terribly busy...please forgive."[9] Even the apologies were infrequent. Cora seemed indomitable as ever, published a book of her poems, *Little Otis*, and gave poetry readings. There were annoyances and rivalries and upsets among the sisters; both Norma and Kathleen felt that Edna was ignoring them. Cora continually attempted to keep the peace, exasperating Edna. "I wrote Kathleen ages ago about her book. I told you I would, & I did. And that's that."[10]

After the stock market collapse, Eugen sent Cora one thousand dollars. "Things all around look dark and sad, and what is worse," he wrote, "it does not look as if times are going to be much better in the near future."[11] In 1930, Cora had recurring bouts of illness but concealed these from her daughters. By late January 1931, she admitted that she had been ill but insisted she was now better. The last two days of that month, Cora and Edna exchanged poems by mail, and Edna burst into tears when she read the second stanza of Cora's "My Little Mountain-Laurel-Trees," thinking it a premonition of death.

> My little Mountain-Laurel trees
> If you should ever grow
> Where I was very sound asleep,
> I think that I should know.
> Then I needn't dream of Cypresses
> Where cold their shadow fall,
> But of Mountain-Laurel trees I loved
> When I was small.

On the evening of February 4, Edna and Eugen received a telegram from Cora's brother, Bert, in Camden: "COME MOTHER VERY SICK ANSWER IMMEDIATELY TO ME." As no train could get them to Camden quickly, Edna and Eugen drove through a stormy night. When they arrived at the door of Cora's house, they saw a wreath on the door. "From the moment we got there everything was done for her as if she were a queen which of course she was." Cora was to be buried at Steepletop in a grove of mountain laurels. The site was granite and it took several days to blast out a grave. After a week it was ready. The family went into the woods, the coffin was put into the grave, the sisters sang together over it. Eugen fired a volley with his shotgun. "It seems strange to think of leaving her here," Edna wrote later, "but she never minded being alone." In April, she wrote to a friend: "It's a changed world. The presence of that absence is everywhere."[12]

Two months later Edna published *Fatal Interview*, a fifty-two-sonnet, four-season love story, based on her love for George Dillon that began with their fateful meeting in Chicago three years before. Told in a woman's voice, the sonnets are independent but also linked together in describing a first encounter, passionate intimacy and painful separation, very like Elinor Wylie's sonnets about her love for Clifford Woodhouse. With eerie appropriateness *Fatal Interview* was dedicated to Elinor Wylie:

> When I think of you,
> I die too.
> In my throat, bereft
> Like yours of air,
> No sound is left,
> Nothing is there
> To make a word of grief.

Asked frequently about the personal element, if any, in the sonnets. Edna characterized them as "very intense, very passionate...Personal? Of course, everything is personal. But if it were actual reporting of my own experience, I certainly wouldn't admit it."[13] She didn't admit it, she *proclaimed* it publicly, publishing some of the sonnets in *Poetry* and in popular magazines. In the first part of the cycle, she rejected the traditional attitude that a woman must withhold herself, virginity protected by lock and key.

XI

Not in the silver casket cool with pearls
Or rich with red corundum or with blue,
Locked, and key withheld, as other girls
Have given their loves, I give my love to you;
Not in a lovers'-knot, not in a ring
Worked in such fashion, and the legend plain—
Semper fidelis, where a secret spring
Kennels a drop of mischief for the brain:
Love in the open hand, no thing but that,
Ungemmed, unhidden, wishing not to hurt,
As one should bring you cowslips in a hat
Swung from the hand, or apples in her skirt,
I bring to you, calling out as children do:
"Look what I have!—And these are all for you."

Sonnet "XXX" is a catalogue of the many things love is not and yet the sonneteer concludes that she will not give up her love for anything imaginable.

XXX

Love is not all: it is not meat nor drink
Nor slumber nor a roof against the rain;
Nor yet a floating spar to men that sink
And rise and sink and rise and sink again;
Love can not fill the thickened lung with breath,
Nor clean the blood, nor set the fractured bone;
Yet many a man is making friends with death
Even as I speak, for lack of love alone.
It well may be that in a difficult hour,

Pinned down by pain and moaning for release,
Or nagged by want past resolution's power,
I might be driven to sell your love for peace,
Or trade the memory of this night for food.
It may well be. I do not think I would.

At the time—and since—critics have given *Fatal Interview* a mixed reception, but its supporters have been unstinting in its praise. "It is doubtful if all of Miss Millay's previous work put together," wrote Allen Tate, "is worth the thin volume of these fifty-two sonnets. At no previous time has she given us so sustained a performance…From first to last every sonnet had its special rhythm and sharply defined imagery; they move like a smooth machine, but not machine-like under the hand of a masterly technician." Genevieve Taggard believed that Millay "is really the first woman poet to take herself seriously as an artist" and that "if you love the truth of exaggeration, [Millay] is a new thing under the sun."[14] The general public had no doubts. Within eight weeks, *Fatal Interview* was on the bestseller list, and after seven months had sold sixty-five thousand copies. This, for a book of sonnets.

IF EDNA MILLAY declared her love publicly, Dillon declared his love indirectly. In 1932, he received the Pulitzer Prize for his second book of poems, *The Flowering Stone*, dedicated to Harriet Monroe, but much of it was inspired (though not explicitly acknowledged) by his love for Edna.

As before, Edna continued her pursuit. Brazenly, she visited Dillon at his parents' home. He was an only child, and his mother was fiercely possessive and "grim" in Edna's presence. In any event, the decisive scenes in the affair took place in France, where Edna and Eugen planned to spend most of 1932. Dillon had received a Guggenheim Fellowship, and joined them. Soon after, Eugen sailed back to America, bombarding Edna with letters in which he not very subtly reminded her of how pleasant life (with him) was at Steepletop. A man who had a brief affair with Edna in France believed that she was driving Dillon away with jealousy and that her sexual demands were wearing him out. "She wanted George," he wrote. "Whether it was to dance with him or to sleep with him she wanted him on her own terms. And when he would not or could not accept these terms, she retaliated." It is not clear that Edna ever made up her mind as to what her terms were. There were quarrels, reconciliations, more quarrels. "George and I are bad for each other, & we both know it,"[15] she wrote to Eugen. In Paris, after two days together, Dillon took a ship back to America without saying goodbye. Eugen was recalled to France. It was not the final act, but it foreshadowed what that act would be. Dillon and Edna would see each other again and collaborate on a translation of Charles Baudelaire's *The Flowers` of Evil*, working together on it at Steepletop. But once again, Eugen's patience had prevailed.

NOT SURPRISINGLY, EDNA had written no poetry; but now poems came. She was convinced that her love for Dillon was responsible for this creative surge. *Wine from These Grapes* was published in November 1934. It sold over thirty-five thousand copies. It was somber, autumnal in tone, and death was a presiding subject. Louise Bogan thought the work a step forward. "Millay at last gives evidence that she recognizes and is prepared to meet the task of becoming a mature and self-sufficing woman and artist…a task she never completely faced before…She has crossed the line, passed into regions of colder and larger air." [16] Many critics were rather dismissive. Edna sensed, rightly, that *Wine from These Grapes* marked the beginning of the slow decline of her popularity, that the thrust of contemporary poetry, as one critic put it, was toward "the more intense, more sensitive verse of Léonie Adams and Louise Bogan" (which would have come as a surprise to them). Publicly, Edna was proudly stoical. "You say 'loved,'" she said, responding to a compliment about her past work. "It's all over then? Never mind. It's rather a blow but there are worse things that can happen, even to the best of us." [17] The response of the reading public to *Wine from These Grapes* was subdued; this might have been due to the volume's preoccupation with death. One of these poems is among her best known, a memorable example of the association of childhood and grief.

Childhood is the Kingdom Where Nobody Dies

Childhood is not from birth to a certain age and at a certain
    age
The child is grown, and puts away childish things.
Childhood is the kingdom where nobody dies.

Nobody that matters, that is. Distance relatives of course
Die, whom one never has seen or has seen for an hour,
And they gave one candy in the pink-and-green stripéd bag,
    or a jack-knife,
And went away, and cannot really be said to have lived at
    all.

And cats die. They lie on the floor and lash their tails,
And their reticent fur is suddenly all in motion

With fleas that one never knew were there,
Polished and brown, knowing all there is to know,
Trekking off into the living world.
You fetch a shoe-box, but it's much too small, because she
    won't curl up now:
So you find a bigger box, and bury her in the yard, and   weep.

But you do not wake up a month from then, two months,
A year from then, two years, in the middle of the night
And weep, with your knuckles in your mouth, and say Oh,
    God! Oh, God!
Childhood is the kingdom where nobody dies that matters,
    – mothers and fathers don't die.

And if you have said, "For heaven's sake, must you always
    be kissing a person?"
Or, "I do wish to gracious you'd stop tapping on the window
    with your thimble!"
Tomorrow, or even the day after tomorrow if you're busy
    having fun,
Is plenty of time to say, "I'm sorry, mother."

To be grown up is to sit at the table with people who have
    died, who neither listen nor speak;
Who do not drink their tea, though they always said
Tea was such comfort.

Run down into the cellar and bring up the last jar of rasp-
    berries; they are not tempted.
Flatter them, ask them what was it they said exactly
That time, to the bishop, or to the overseer, or to Mrs.
    Mason;

They are not taken in.
Shout at them, get red in the face, rise,
Drag them up out of their chairs by their stiff shoulders
    and shake them and yell at them;
They are not startled, they are not even embarrassed; they
    slide back into their chairs.

Your tea is cold now.
You drink it standing up,
And leave the house.

In another poem even a positive image—"the spiny poppy that no winter kills"—is suffused in melancholy since the poem is about Cora Millay.

Spring in the Garden

Ah, cannot the curled shoots of the larkspur that you love so,
Cannot the spiny poppy that no winter kills
Instruct you how to return through the thawing ground and the
thin snow
Into this April sun that is driving the mist between the hills?

A good friend to the monkshood in a time of need
You were, in the lupine's friend as well;
But I see the lupine lift the ground like a tough weed
And the earth over the monkshood swell
And I fear that not a root and all this heaving sea
Of land, has nudged you where you lie, has found
Patience and time to direct you, numb and stupid as you still
must be
From your first winter underground.

IN SEPTEMBER OF 1935, Edna received a letter from her father. She hadn't heard from him for several years. He told her that he had lost everything, had nothing left to live on, and asked for a few dollars a week. Edna sent him what he asked for and he wrote again to thank her. He died in December. Eugen went to Maine for the funeral. None of Henry Millay's three daughters bothered to go.

PART SIX

After:
1950

1. Louise Bogan

HOW TO BEGIN again after the anguish, the breakdowns, the time in mental institutions, the end of her marriage, and the indifference of the reading public? Louise Bogan found inspiration and reassurance in the life and music of Mozart—"the purest and loveliest in the world…so exquisite, so amusing, so amorous and melancholy. So mathematically constructed that he could stand beside Euclid unashamed." The great lesson of Mozart's life was his response to the obtuse audience of his day, which paralleled her own situation. Audiences wanted easy entertainment, "Tunes written for a play was what the old boys wanted." But Mozart fooled them by "introducing his heart, mind and highly organized nervous system into his art."[1] So would she organize her heart and mind.

The immediate problem she faced wasn't heart and mind, however. It was money. She was poor; the income for her reviews for *The New Yorker* barely sustained her. "Poets have never been able to make a living by writing poetry and it has never entered my mind that I could do so," she wrote in 1939. The serious and honest writer's place in American culture is both "small and cold." At the lowest point in her struggles, she was evicted from her apartment for nonpayment of rent and her furniture was put out on the street. Her legal separation from Holden had become a formal divorce, but he did not always pay the monthly money promised by their settlement. Their legal affairs were finally settled, and after a chance meeting in August 1937, Louise never saw him again. In private life, she still went by the name Louise Bogan Holden and "those close to [her] believed she never stopped loving him."[2]

There was a different sadness in her life as well. Her mother and father had moved to Manhattan where Daniel worked as a clerk. Mary returned to her Catholic faith and became pious. She had never gotten over the death of her son, and in 1930 went to France to visit his grave. The day after Christmas, 1936, Mary Bogan died. A torrent of emotions and images engulfed Louise: her mother screaming and crying, her mother and her male "familiars," her mother "tender as well as terrifying." She had worked through her sense of Mary as betrayer of her innocence and childhood and achieved forgiveness. Her mother's faults were "always big faults. Big faults you can forgive."[3]

Louise moved about nomadically until finally settling in an apartment on West 169th Street, where she would remain for the rest of her life. She had a number of love affairs. One was an eight-year liaison with a mystery man; her friends never met him, didn't even know his name. He was an electrician, not married, who lived in the Bronx. His love and companionship gave her great pleasure.

Contemporary politics, domestic and international, depressed and angered her. Like Marianne Moore, she was deeply estranged from the prevailing political values and shared Marianne's disdain for Franklin Roosevelt, who represented "a disguised State Socialism that is being put over on people without their full knowledge or consent." She disliked socialism and hated communism. "To hell with the crowd,"[4] was her motto. She gave up reviewing for *The New Republic* and switched to the more conservative *The Nation*. Unlike Marianne Moore, who was a detached nonparticipant, Louise was an outspoken dissenter, writing essays and letters on current affairs. Her dislike of collectivist politics was a reflection of her overriding need for independence and her disdain for authority. "The only way to get away is to get away," she said. "Pack up and go. Anywhere." She had a child by age twenty "but I got up and went just the same. God help us." She was a woman, she recalled with pride, living those first few years in the Village on eighteen bucks a week. Her marriage, her breakdowns were involved with her need for freedom, which she achieved at great cost. "I went to the mad-house for six months...Under my own steam, mind you, for no one sent me there, and I got free." Work and art were the best weapons against one's childish need for the approval of others. "When one isn't free, one is a *thing* of others."[5]

As she came out of her depression and began writing poetry again, she started planning a new volume and had known for some-time what its title would be. In a museum in Rome, she had seen a Hellenistic relief sculpture, *L'Erinni Addormentata* (*The Sleeping Fury*), a very beautiful woman's head, eyes closed, lips half open, a face that perhaps represented what she had gone through as well as the peace she had sought. *The Sleeping Fury* was published in the spring of 1937, and was dedicated to Edmund Wilson. Many of its poems speak to Louise's struggle to accept things beyond the power of reason, to learn to turn the heart away from the sensual natural world.

Life wasn't bleak. There were rewards, precious rewards; speech, memories, images, the powerful exaltations of the life of the mind, as expressed in "Henceforth, from the Mind."

"Richly modulated, grave and slow, Miss Bogan is not repeating herself," Theodore Roethke wrote of these poems, "but moving into another world."[6] Other critics were also enthusiastic and admiring. But whatever else, it wasn't a popular world. Bogan remained a poet for the few. *The Sleeping Fury* sold two hundred and eight copies.

FOR THE NEXT four years, as a reviewer and a poet, Louise Bogan worked steadily. Her supportive editor, delighted by her continuing creativity, urged her to prepare another volume. She rose above the disheartening commercial failure of *The Sleeping Fury* and agreed that she would try; but the poems did not come easily, were not "given" to her. She determined that she would broaden the range of her subjects and lighten the tone in the next volume. "Why shouldn't I be allowed to break my tone occasionally?"[7]

Poems and New Poems appeared in 1941. W.H. Auden admired "the steady growth of wisdom and technical mastery," and was struck by a new aspect of her work, the observation of natural objects. Louise said that she had always wished to write about things "naturally elegant, like pineapples and shells and feathers," but had been inhibited by Marianne Moore's poems of this sort. "M. Moore has rather a lien on objects characterized by natural elegance, hasn't she? I'd have to be very very lyrical about them, in order to get out of her class."[8] The volume included satirical poems and there was also a "deceptively simple quatrain, so just in style, so mature and witty in sensibility, that a long life can be predicted for it." (This had begun extemporaneously in conversation with Edmund Wilson.) Sixteen lines were whittled down and shaped over the next half dozen years.

To an Artist, To Take Heart

Slipping in blood, by his own hand, through pride,
Hamlet, Othello, Coriolanus fall.
Upon his bed, however, Shakespeare died,
Having endured them all.

A poem of a more familiar kind, "the deep night swarming with images of reproach and desire," was regarded by the poet Stanley Kunitz as one her three greatest. [9] It is directly autobiographical. "I really did have this dream." And she explained further what it meant to her. "It is the actual transcript of 'a nightmare' but there is reconciliation involved with the fright and horror. It is through the possibility of such reconciliations that we, I believe, manage to live." The horse, she explained, was "fear kept for thirty-five years," but it was also an allegory of the unconscious on a final and mutually triumphant struggle with the self." [10] The other woman is Louise's new self, the cured woman: The glove represents the poet's whole self, triumphant over the submissive beast.

The Dream

O God, in the dream the terrible horse began
To paw at the air, and make for me with his blows.
Fear kept for thirty-five years poured through his mane,
And retribution equally old, or nearly, breathed through his nose.

Coward complete, I lay and wept on the ground
When some strong creature appeared, and leapt for the rein.
Another woman, as I lay half in a swound,
Leapt in the air, and clutched at the leather and chain.

Give him, she said, something of yours as a charm.
Throw him, she said, some poor thing you alone claim.
No, no, I cried, he hates me; he's out for harm,
And whether I yield or not, it is all the same.

But, like a lion in a legend, when I flung the glove
Pulled from sweating, my cold right hand,
The terrible beast, that no one may understand,
Came to my side, and put down his head in love.

By 1948, *Poems and New Poems* had sold four hundred copies.

LOUISE FELT THAT the publication of *Poems and New Poems* marked the end of the turmoil of the previous decade-and-a-half. *The New Yorker* increased her salary by forty dollars a month. Her social isolation diminished: she felt less embattled politically; strained friendships were restored; the affair with her mystery lover came to an amicable end without "regret or sadness." Her father, who had been ill, went back to Maine, where friends looked out for him. And the result of all this? She was able to write no poetry for the next seven years. The ways of poetic inspiration are mysterious. Prose came, but not poetry.

Over the years, her work as a reviewer of poetry for *The New Yorker* not only solidified her reputation as a fair-minded, readable critic, but it also introduced her name to a much wider circle of readers. She wrote much-applauded essays for the *The Nation* and *The Partisan Review.* In her journal in the mid-forties she asked herself if she was "out? Freer? Firmer?" And the answer she recorded was "Yes. Not very far out," but "out." [11] And yet she couldn't write poetry.

She began to receive more attention and accolades. She was made a Consultant in Poetry for the Library of Congress and lived in Washington, D.C., in 1945-1946, but she found she was dreadfully bored away from New York and went home every other weekend. She was invited to serve on the jury for the Harriet Monroe Poetry Award and to give a Distinguished Lecture at the University of Michigan. This led to a good deal of lecturing and teaching at many universities. Former students sent her appreciative letters, aspiring poets sent their poems for her criticism and advice. She received the Harriet Monroe Award for achievement in poetry. W.H. Auden and she admired each other's work and reviewed it discerningly. Auden introduced her to Elizabeth Mayer, a German refugee. They became good friends and embarked on a series of translations of works by Goethe, a collaboration that extended over many years.

She had been almost reclusive for many years but now she was determined "to come off it, or come out of it and accept all invitations to speak, read, teach or turn handsprings in public." Louise did all those things—except the handsprings—and did them very well, as she did everything she put her hand to. There were some notable poetry readings. One evening at the Young Men's Hebrew Association, she appeared with Dorothy Parker. What a pair they made! Dorothy was dressed in a magenta turban and mink-lined coat, Louise in a tweed suit and small hat. Dorothy "took it all quite nicely, too, and I rapidly worked out my dismay at facing a totally Parker audience, (Maidie sat there sweating with sheer terror, after seeing what I had gotten into)." There were also encounters with Marianne Moore, whom Louise had not seen since her earliest days in the Village and whose poetry Louise knew intimately and admired greatly. Like her, Moore's reputation was created by a small number of discerning critics and readers. In Louise's view, Moore was eminent in the way Wallace Stevens was eminent: "THEY ARE FIXED AND FINISHED. They will never *surprise* anyone again." A meeting with Fellows in American Letters of the Library of Congress "went beautifully. She had drinks, went to dinners, and, to her surprise, discovered that she enjoyed every minute of it."[12]

When *Poems and New Poems* came out, Marianne Moore reviewed it admiringly. She was impressed by Louise's restraint, "an unusual courtesy in this day of bombast," and went on: "She refused to be deceived or self-deceived. Emotion, with her…is itself form, the kernel which builds outward form from inward intensity. Women are not noted for terseness," she concluded, "but Louise Bogan's art is compactness compacted."[13] At their next meeting, Marianne greeted her with "great pleasantness." Another time, after a poetry conference at Sarah Lawrence College, the two rode in a train together. "I must see Marianne in the spring," Louise wrote, but she was puzzled by what Marianne said to her. "She keeps making rather awe-struck remarks about my nature, the sources of which I can't make out. She thinks I live in some sort of danger…I don't understand where she got that idea." The next meeting was not puzzling but deeply flattering. Marianne attended one of Louise's classes at the YMHA, "took notes constantly, asked many questions, and entered into discussions with enthusiasm."[14] The students were rather intimidated by Marianne's presence—and so was Louise.

A memorable moment: In 1948, T.S. Eliot, everywhere recognized as a master poet, came to America before he was about to go to Stockholm to receive the Nobel Prize in Literature. Louise met him for the first time and found him enchanting. They talked easily about many things. "How beautiful is the combination of physical beauty (even in a slow decay)," she wrote. (Eliot was sixty.) He communicated to her "high qualities of mind and heart, and perfect humility," and Louise reflected on Eliot, on the passage of time, and on the infinite forms of love, "Well, it is all too late and too sad, but I must love him in a mild, distant, sisterly way."[15]

2. DOROTHY PARKER

FOR DOROTHY PARKER, the years from 1935 to 1950 were Hollywood years. She abandoned poetry and fiction and devoted most of her time, energy, and talent to film writing and to Hollywood social life. She never blotted New York from her mind, but moved back and forth from one coast to the other, first by train and then by plane (which had the advantage, she said, that she needn't look at the country in between). Far from being sentimental, she railed at the stupidity of the film industry and of the people who ran it. Her sentiments were genuine and many others shared them, but they were, like so many other aspects of her character and attitudes, rooted in self-contempt. She and Campbell made a great deal of money from what she derided.

At the heart of the wastefulness and capriciousness of Hollywood film culture was contempt for writers and writing, and its effect on Dorothy's career was destructive. For no apparent reason, her scripts were so altered that the originals were unrecognizable.

In fifteen years, she successfully completed written work on only two occasions. In 1937, the screenplay by her and Campbell for *A Star Is Born* was nominated for an Academy Award. In 1947, she and a collaborator were nominated for an Academy Award for *Smash Up: The Story of a Woman.* In neither case did she win an Oscar. Her career as a film writer was at best disappointing however one assigns the blame—her limitations, the system.[1]

The tragedy is that Hollywood stymied her as a writer of any sort. The years there were a wasteland. Much as she mocked Hollywood culture among her friends, it never became a subject she could write about in any manner, let alone in the corrosive Parker fashion. The only poem she wrote about Hollywood, one of the last three she ever wrote, while touched with ironic thrusts, is playful.

The Passionate Screen Writer To His Love

Oh come, my love, and join with me
The oldest infant industry.
Come seek the bourne of palm and pearl,
The lovely land of Boy-Meets-Girl,
Come grace this lotus-laden shore,
This Isle of Do-What's-Done-Before.
Come, curb the new, and watch the old win.
Out where the streets are paved with Goldwyn.

Film writing was also a source of friction between her and Campbell. She promoted the idea, widely accepted by outsiders, that he found work only because he was married to a famous writer. Actually, Campbell was proficient and disciplined and deserves credit for driving her to do whatever she was able to do.

His reward? To be persistently derided. To try to keep their marriage intact, and as Hollywood was unlivable and New York irrelevant, they bought an old farmhouse in Bucks County, Pennsylvania, and poured money into renovating it, an enterprise doomed to failure. Dorothy was totally bored by country life, never tried to feel at home there, and tolerated it only because she was not too far from New York City.

The void in her life was now filled by politics. The Civil War in Spain was the immediate catalyst for her emerging political consciousness, a deeper commitment than with Sacco and Vanzetti. Dorothy and Campbell were in Valencia, Spain, during air raids by German planes. The Spanish War brought out her generous side and she joined numerous groups in support of the Loyalists and helped raise over a million dollars for the cause. The Spanish War also engaged her intellectually to some extent though she was never really interested in political ideas. She identified herself with communism as the wave of the future that would raise the dispossessed. Some people dismissed her views as fashionable radicalism, but she was trying for the first (and only) time in her life to make sense of her historical situation. This led her to be active in supporting Communist front groups, though it is doubtful that she was a Communist Party member. She also became very active as a proponent of labor, in this instance, the Hollywood Screen Writers' Guild: "The bravest, proudest word in all dictionaries was 'organize,'" she said, though her activity stored up enmity for her later on. Impulsive, reckless in regard to money, she gave generously to groups and individuals. Dawn Powell, the New York novelist of the Thirties who knew her well, said that she got "too much credit for witty bitchery and not enough for completely reckless philanthropy—saving many people, really, without a thought."[2]

This frantic activity was alcohol-sodden. She joked and quipped and drank and drank, said clever things and all-too-often cruel things and then was quoted for her quips and her cruelties, and drank and drank. She was pregnant twice. The first pregnancy, at forty-three, excited her. "She wanted to have babies," talked incessantly about the possibility of a family, began to knit baby clothes, and allowed studio publicity to photograph her and report that she was "expecting a stork." Her friends were predictably caustic about it, describing her as "knitting for the camera."[3] She miscarried at three months. She was forty-six at the time of her second pregnancy and was fatalistically sure she would not bear a child however careful she might be. Again, she miscarried. Biographies have assumed that Campbell and Dorothy would not have been suitable parents and that both of them were, to some extent, relieved not have the responsibility of children. But who knows?

The second miscarriage marked the beginning of the disintegration of their marriage. Campbell represented sexual rejuvenation and was a man who wished to care for Dorothy, but she found it impossible to accept simple kindness and began deriding him in public as she had Eddie Parker, pushing to see how far she could go in rejecting him even as age was closing in on her. She gained weight and looked worn. As the Wall Street Crash had brought the roaring, drinking Twenties to an end, for Dorothy, the drinking Thirties and Forties sufficed. Encroaching mortality appeared with the death of Alexander Woollcott in 1943 and Robert Benchley in 1945. She lost her much-maligned family: her sister Helen, whom she saw often, and her brother Bert died within three months of each other in 1944. Death had been a familiar subject in her verse, so it wasn't surprising that it would appear, ambiguously, both threatening and beguiling, in her second-to-last poem.

Threat to a Fickle Lady

Sweet Lady Sleep, befriend me;
    In pretty mercy, hark.
Your charming manners, tend me--
    Let down your lovely dark.

Sweet Lady, take me to you,
    Becalm mine eyes, my breath....
Remember, I that woo you
    Have but to smile at Death....

Her publisher assured her that there was a demand for her stories. Dorothy didn't doubt it. The problem was writing them. "I've got to write a lot of stories—if of course I can."[4] She managed three new stories. In April 1939, the collection *Here Lies* appeared. It included those three stories but all the rest of the twenty-one came from previous collections. It sold well. The critics liked it. What Dorothy most liked about it was its title. In 1947, she made another effort at writing for the theater, collaborating on a play, *The Coast of Ilyria,* about Charles Lamb, the early nineteenth-century English essayist and his sister Mary, beneath whose respectable public manner there was a maelstrom of drink and drugs and psychotic behavior, a version also, of course, of her life with Campbell. It was performed for three weeks in Dallas, Texas, and was well attended, but never made it to Broadway.

The year 1944 marked a major event in her writing career: the appearance of Viking's *The Portable Dorothy Parker,* with a perceptive introduction by Somerset Maugham, bringing together poems, stories, and theater reviews. Widely acclaimed, it remains in print, and is the form in which countless readers have been introduced to her work. Nevertheless, we can see that its importance was also retrospective; it represented a writer whose writing career was over.

WHEN AMERICA ENTERED World War II, Dorothy mocked Campbell as effeminate and cowardly because he had not volunteered to fight Fascism. He escaped her contempt by enlisting in the army and spent the next five years away from her. Nevertheless, it apparently came as a shock to her when Campbell wrote to say that he had fallen in love with another woman. In 1947, the Pennsylvania farmhouse was sold and they divorced. An entanglement soon followed with a man twenty-five years younger than she. He was a former athlete, then a radio announcer, attractive, muscular, and "she was constantly pawing him and couldn't keep her hands off him." [5] He was also divorced and an alcoholic. This pathetic affair lasted three years. In 1950, at his insistence, they drove to Cuernavaca, Mexico. She hated it there and after a month left him and returned to New York City where, to the amazement of all, she once again took up with Alan Campbell, who had not found any permanent alliance either. They were remarried in August. "Who in life gets a second chance?" the delighted bride asked, and then answered that question with another: "What are you going to do when you love the son of a bitch?"[6]

3. MARIANNE MOORE

SELECTED POEMS FIXED Marianne Moore's eminence as
a poet and confirmed the narrowness of her audience. It
sold five hundred copies when Edna Millay's books sold
tens of thousands. She retained her international circle of friends
and correspondents. Brooklyn respected her privacy; but she was
disheartened by Franklin Roosevelt's overwhelming re-election in
1936, convinced that the New Deal was damaging national morals, a view relentlessly reinforced by her mother. "All of political or
civic nature is disturbing," Marianne explained to Bryher in 1937,
and though she insisted that she refused to be "darkened or embit-
tered," she was oppressed by a feeling of futility, describing herself
as no more than a "candy-box that plays when you pick it up." The
passing of time—she was fifty in 1937—added to her sadness: "It
is hard work trying to keep from being disappointed in people."[1]

Valued contemporaries were disappearing. Harriet Monroe
died in 1936, and Marianne's obituary tribute to her in *Poetry* sin-

gled out certain qualities that gained resonance by contrast with the contemporary scene. "I think of her valor, her goodness to us all, her imperviousness to plebian behavior... her air of aloneness."[2] Marianne wrote reviews of the works of contemporaries whose poetry mattered to her and, whatever her discontents, continued to write poems, slowly, laboriously, establishing a pattern that would become familiar for the next fifteen years. Every four or five years she would publish a very slim volume.

The first of these was *The Pangolin* (1936), made up of the title poem and four others that form a sequence she called "The Old Dominion." They are about a place, Virginia, and about creatures—the pangolin, a scaly anteater, birds and butterflies. She was especially proud of "Bird-Witted," based on her observation of birds from the windows of the Brooklyn apartment and in the composition of which Mary participated. The poem is both a love song of a very different order, a paean to maternal love, and a realistic recognition that the parent, "nerved by what chills the blood," must do whatever is necessary for the family's security. The threatening, hostile world of the late thirties is everywhere in this poem.

Bird-Witted

With innocent wide penguin eyes, three
     large fledging mocking-birds below
the pussy willow tree,
     stand in a row,
wings touching, feebly solemn,
till they see
     Their no longer larger
     mother bringing
something which will partially
feed one of them

Toward the high keyed intermittent squeak
     of broken carriage-springs, made by
the three similar, meek—
     coated bird's-eye
freckled forms she comes; and when
from the beak
     of one, the still living
     beetle has dropped
out, she picks it up and puts
it in again.

Standing in the shade till they have dressed
     their thickly filamented, pale
pussy-willow-surfaced
     coats, they spread tail
and wings, showing one by one,
the modest
     white stripe lengthwise on the
     tail and crosswise
underneath the wing, and the
accordion
is closed again. What delightful note
  with rapid unepected flute –
sounds leaping from the throat
     of the astute
the remote
     unenergetic sun-
     lit air before
the brood was here? How harsh
the bird's voice has become.

A piebald cat observing them,
      is slowly creeping toward the trim
trio on the tree-stem.
      Unused to him
the three make room – uneasy
new problem.
      A dangling foot that missed
      its grasp is raised
and finds the twig on which it
planned to perch. The

parent darting down, nerved by what chills
      the blood, and by hope rewarded –
      of toil – since nothing fills
      squeaking unfed
mouths, wages deadly combat,
and half kills
      with bayonet beak and
      cruel wings, the
intellectual cautious-
ly creeping cat.

In 1941 appeared *What Are Years,* dedicated to Warner, a collection that emphasized moral and ethical concerns, most of the poems dotted with quotations from obscure sources that she identified in explanatory notes: "Since in anything I have written, there have been lines in which the chief interest is borrowed, and I have not yet been able to outgrow this hybrid method of composition, acknowledgements seem only honest."[3] The title poem—she specified that it should not have a question mark—finds guilt and innocence mixed in everyone. All are naked, none is safe. Satisfaction is a "lowly thing" compared to joy. Courage stirs the soul to be strong.

What Are Years

What is our innocence,
what is our guilt? All are
    naked, none is safe. And whence
is courage: the unanswered question,
the resolute doubt,—
dumbly calling, deafly listening—that
in misfortune, even death,
    encourage others
    and in its defeat, stirs

    the soul to be strong? He
sees deep and is glad, who
    accedes to mortality
and his imprisonment, rises
upon himself as
the sea in a chasm, struggling to be
free and unable to be,
    in its surrendering
    finds its continuing.

    So he who strongly feels,
behaves. The very bird,
    grown taller as he sings, steels
his form straight up. Though he is captive,
his mighty singing
says, satisfaction is a lowly
thing, how pure a thing is joy.
    This is mortality,
    this is eternity.

Nevertheless, six poems, was published in 1944. She described it as "a neat and businesslike book," and added that she was more interested in it than in her previous volumes. A visit to the Brooklyn Museum of Art resulted in one of her finest poems of careful observation united with continuing interest in questions of national culture. Her mother, regressing to her old ways, strongly disapproved of the poem. Why? Because there is no moral lesson to be derived from it? Because it is playful?

A Carriage from Sweden

They say there is a sweeter air
    where it was made, than we have here;
    a Hamlet's castle atmosphere.
At all events there is in Brooklyn
something that makes me feel at home

No one may see this put-away
    museum-piece, this country cart
    that inner happiness made art;
and yet, in this city of freckled
integrity it is a vein

of resined straightness from north-wind
    hardened Sweden's once-opposed-to-
    compromise archipelago
of rocks. Washington and Gustavus
Adolphus, forgive our decay.

Seats, dashboard and sides of smooth gourd-
    rind texture, a flowered step, swan-
    dart brake, and swirling crustacean-
tailed equine amphibious creatures
that garnish the axle-tree! What

a fine thing! What unannoying
    romance! And how beautiful, she
    with natural stoop of the
snowy egret, gray-eyed and straight-haired,
for whom it should come to the door,—

of whom it reminds me. The split
    pine fair hair, steady gannet-clear
    eyes and the pine-needled-path deer-
swift step; that is Sweden, land of the
free and the soil for a spruce-tree—

vertical though a seedling—all
    needles; from a green trunk, green shelf
    on shelf fanning out by itself
The deft white-stockinged dance in thick-soled
shoes! Denmark's sanctuaried Jews!

The puzzle-jugs and hand-spun rugs,
    the root-legged kracken shaped like dogs,
    the hanging buttons and the frogs
that edge the Sunday jackets! Sweden,
you have a runner called the Deer, who

when he's won a race, likes to run
    more; you have the sun-right gable-
    ends due east and west, the table
spread as for a banquet; and the put-
in twin vest-pleats with a fish-fin

effect when you need none. Sweden,
    what makes the people dress that way
    and those who see you wish to stay?
The runner, not too tired to run more
at the end of the race? And that

cart, dolphin-graceful? A Dalén
    light-house, self-lit?—responsive and
    responsible. I understand;
it's not pine-needle-paths that give spring
when they're run on, it's a Sweden

of moated white castles,—the bed
    of densely grown flowers in an S
    meaning Sweden and stalwartness,
skill, and a surface that says
Made in Sweden: carts are my trade.

The great long distance runner called "The Deer" was Gun-
der Haag.

WITH THE END of the war, Marianne's spirits rose: "I think I
shall be writing again." T.S. Eliot offered to publish a volume of
her collected poems and she began to contemplate a translation

of *The Fables of La Fontaine*. Given her passion for animals, it seemed ideally suited to her. She gave occasional talks and readings with considerable success. A professor who attended one of them delighted Moore with her praise. "All your statements are new & fresh and at the same time grains of common sense…It's a gift & that means you must use it."[4] And she did, making an exceptionally rewarding poetry-reading visit to Bryn Mawr, along with W.H. Auden, whom she was coming to like very much for his gallantry, as well as for his poetry.

However, all that faded into insignificance because of the decline in her mother's health. In 1944, Mary Moore fell and hurt her head. "Vigilance & prompt antidotes for swelling and inflammation, delivered us from what threatened to be desperation." Her mother recovered. Marianne's immense relief led her, at the same time, to reflect on, and to give fuller expression to, the religious faith which had been the center of her mother's life and of her own childhood and youth. "I cannot feel that we are alone in our battles," she wrote to a friend. "A stronger presence endows us with a power that we would declare impossible to us."[5]

By 1945, her mother's gradual decline absorbed Marianne's time and attention. "Not a soul have I seen or been to see—all these months." As Mary Moore required a lot of medication, domestic help was needed. Marianne and her mother spent much of their time reading from the family Bible and praying together. Struggling to accept the inevitable, Marianne wrote, "Patience, reverence, gratitude, faith; it seems as if we cannot have them easily." Bryher visited the Moores in early 1947 and was "frightened" by Marianne's state of mind. "As her mother could neither eat nor speak," she thought that Marianne had "determined that she also would not eat" and as a result was ill.[6] As late as May of that year Mary Moore was intermittently capable of writing notes to friends but in early July was admitted to the hospital. Warner came to be with them. Mary Moore died on July 9. The funeral was austere—no flowers or singing, organ only. She was buried beside her parents in Gettysburg.

Marianne was fifty-nine. Except for four years at Bryn Mawr, she had lived all her life with her mother, who had not only been the major influence on Marianne's character and values but also, both inhibiting and supportive, on her work, "untold help with words and errors." What consolation was there for such a loss? "'Consolation,' a word, just a word I have always felt, but now?" Sternly she resisted pity, quoting her brother. "If you hadn't pitied me, I'd have been all right."[7] For the next three years she moved restlessly about, often away from New York, staying with friends. But when she was back in Brooklyn, there were memorable moments that relieved the prevailing sadness. One of them brought together her Modernist transatlantic past with her current preoccupation with her mother's memory. At a party one evening, she sat next to Stephen Spender, "who is quite a treat," and who talked knowledgably about W.B. Yeats, whom he had known, and about W.H. Auden and T.S. Eliot. Then Louise Bogan came in. "She has reviewed me *twice* you know very boldly and ardently." Louise brought up the subject of religion. "I'm not religious or wouldn't call myself so," she said, "but certain sayings that are part of religion indeed are true," and she continued: "We prove them true and one that doesn't mean much to some is a real statement to me: 'He that loseth his life shall find it.'" This brought great relief for Marianne. Her mother was no longer "stumbling and struggling" as she had done in those last months but was now "safe," and with that realization, wrote Marianne, "joy fills my heart."[8]

She always returned to Brooklyn. "I have an affection for 260," and felt "an obligation to do certain work there."[9] And so by 1950, Marianne was again writing poetry and her career would take a surprising turn.

4. Léonie Adams

TEACHING SUSTAINED LÉONIE Adams throughout the Thirties and into the Forties, at which time she secured a position in New York City and returned home. There was a homecoming of another sort when, in 1947, she became a lecturer at Columbia University, where twenty-five years before she had come into her own as a poet. The passing of so many years since *High Falcon*'s publication in 1929 had dimmed her reputation as a poet with the general public, but not with a modest group of discerning poets, critics, and readers. Some national attention began to come her way. She was elected to the Chair of Poetry at the Library of Congress in 1948 and as a member of the National Institute of Arts and Letters in 1949. She wasn't certain that she had found the basis for lyric poetry that she talked about earlier, but she was writing a poem or two a year. While at the Library of Congress, Léonie began to consider the possibility of a new volume of her poems.[1]

5. GENEVIEVE TAGGARD

G ENEVIEVE TAGGARD'S FADING reputation in the late
Thirties was due to the persistent labeling of her as only
a political and social protest poet. The dismissal of the
wide range of her work meant, not surprisingly, that the publication in 1938 of her *Collected Poems* received less serious attention
than it deserved. As well, a fair-minded evaluation of two decades
of poetry was made less likely because the poems selected for the
collection were predominantly political ones. In defiance of contemporary views, she rejected her own earlier non-political verse.
Long View (1942) was a book of poems of social dissent with an
emphasis on popular songs and lyrics. "Song is collective. (Poetry
should be.)" She wrote no more biography, and continued writing
poetry through the war years.

In 1946 came *Slow Music*, lyrics subdued in tone, quietly
reflective, no militant political statements. "There is light, if not
heat, in her lyrics," wrote one reviewer.[1] Many of these poems

are about love, about the love of women for women, about women's "priceless" feminine nature, as represented in the person of the Greek goddess of fecundity.

Demeter

In your dream you met Demeter
Splendid and severe, who said: Endure.
Study the art of seeds,
The nativity of caves
Dance your gay body to the poise of waves;
Die out of the world to bring forth the obscure
Into blisses, into needs.
In all resources
Belong to love. Bless,
Join, fashion the deep forces,
Asserting your nature priceless and feminine.
Peace, daughter. Find your true kin.
              –then you felt her kiss.

The rise and decline of artistic reputations is a familiar phenomenon. Even so, the persistent neglect of Genevieve Taggard's work has been the result of a succession of historical circumstances. The wide range of her nineteen books should have dissolved the notion that she was "only" a political poet and writer, but when her writing that emphasized social consciousness went out of fashion, the academic New Criticism which followed it also resolutely ignored her work.

Neither did she attract attention because of her personal life, which remained private. She didn't symbolize anything. Her persistent concern, in her last years, was with the teaching of poetry in American public schools. She was interested in the use of radio and film to increase the public's familiarity with it. Nor did she lapse into cynicism or pessimism. Quite the reverse. She wrote in 1940: "I am a radical—that is. I believe in the future of American life: I hope to live to see it achieve an economic democracy and by this means to lay a foundation for a great culture."[2] In declining health after the publication of *Slow Music*, she remained a New Yorker and it was in that city that she died on November 8, 1948.

Genevieve Taggard

6. Edna St. Vincent Millay

I N THE LATE 1930s, Edna Millay's name was so frequently in the public mind that she was voted one of the ten most famous women in the country. Early in 1936, she and George Dillon published their translation of Charles Baudelaire's *The Flowers of Evil.* Critics were divided about its merits, but it stayed in print for three decades, which Dillon generously attributed to Edna's lively readable style. (He never published another book of his own poems.)

By 1937, she had been awarded honorary degrees by five universities and colleges. The degree from New York University produced anger. When offered it, Edna accepted and was told there would be a dinner in her honor, but she soon discovered that the male degree recipients were to be given a separate dinner. It was by then too late to change the arrangements and she expressed her views about such blatant gender discrimination in a dignified letter to the University Chancellor:

On an occasion then on which I shall be present solely for reasons of scholarship. I am, solely for reasons of sex, to be excluded from the company and the conversation of my fellow doctors. Had I known this in time. I should have declined not only the invitation to the dinner, but also… the honour of receiving the degree as well.

And she concluded, "I beg of you…that I may be the last woman so honoured, to be required to swallow…the gall of this humiliation."[1]

In 1937 came *Conversation at Midnight*, a play in verse—sonnets and lyrics interspersed with declamation—in which seven men come together in a Village house to talk about art, horses, hunting, women and, especially, contemporary American political and economic ideas. It was a wonder that the play was ever completed. The original manuscript was destroyed in a fire in a Florida hotel where she and Eugen were staying and Edna had to reconstruct it, "digging piece by piece out of my memory."[2] In its printed form it enjoyed popular success and was a Book-of-the-Month Club selection. It is yet another anti-war play, but is more than that—her most wide-ranging inquiry into the nature of human violence. Those who disliked it said it was boring and it is rarely, if ever, performed today, but it is a play ripe for rediscovery in the twenty-first century.

As before, Edna's reading tours were the chief means to public recognition and applause. In 1939, she managed a monstrous tour, from Boston to Los Angeles, from Buffalo to Fort Worth, thirty-five cities and towns. Her reading of her poems was the finest "we have heard voiced by a poet, and we have heard several of the world's greats," one observer wrote. She read some of her early poems, which audiences clamored for, and she dramatized passages from *Conversation at Midnight*. "She put one hand on her hip and glared. She squared her shoulders and stuck her chest out. She tossed her head. She peeked out from under her curls. She stamped her foot. She grinned. But whatever she did she pleased her audience. She conveyed, as always, courage in demanding, as a woman, the freedoms allowed men. Women in the audience were heard to catch their breath."[3] It was the reading of poetry, but it was also an act of will, an assertion of self.

In 1939, she published *Huntsman, What Quarry?*, which was her first book of poetry in five years. It was a success, selling twenty-nine thousand copies in the first month, not exceptional for her, but astonishing for any other poet. It is a large collection, thirty-five poems, miscellaneous in its range of subjects: depictions of the relentless struggle for survival in nature, one creature preying on another, rueful love poems, resigned to the loss of love, political poems about Spain and Czechoslovakia.

The title poem considers what it is that hunters seek, and concludes that not even erotic love can deter the hunter from the chase.

Huntsman, What Quarry?

"Huntsman, what quarry
On the dry hill
Do your hounds harry?

When the red oak is bare
And the white oak still
Rattles its leaves
In the cold air:
What fox runs there?"

"Girl gathering acorns
In the cold autumn,
I hunt the hot pads
That ever run before,
I hunt the pointed mask
That makes no reply,
I hunt the red blush
Of remembered joy."

"To tame or to destroy?"

"To destroy."

"Huntsman, hard by
In a wood of grey beeches
Whose leaves are on the ground,
Is a house with fire;
You can see the smoke from here.
There's supper and a soft bed
And not a soul around.
Come with me there;
Bide there with me;
And let the fox run free."

The horse that he rode on
Reached down its neck,
Blew upon the acorns,
Nuzzled them aside;
The sun was near setting;
He thought, "Shall I heed her"
He thought, "Shall I take her

For a one-night's bride?"
He smelled the sweet smoke,
He looked the lady over;
Her hand was on his knee;
But like a flame from cover
The red fox broke –
And "Hoick! Hoick!"cried he.

THE POETRY TOURS, the books, the political pronouncements, signs of a flourishing career of great public esteem throughout the 1930s, concealed a very different private life of psychological crisis, of physical decline, of emotional instability, which had in common that Edna was living a secret life in an attempt to conceal the reality of her behavior and the sources of her anguish. One of her secrets involved George Dillon. After their collaboration on translating Baudelaire, after it was obvious that, living with his parents in Virginia, he was not available to her for any long-term relationship, she still needed him to sustain the illusion (she was approaching fifty) of her erotic appeal. She asked him to come to her in New York, which he did. She left Eugen behind at Steeplechase and spent much of the winter and spring of 1937 in a dismal rented room in the Village, a room she tried to brighten with flowers. And when that too was finally and completely over, she converted it into poetry that appeared later in *Huntsman, What Quarry?*, and concluded with a statement of devastating realism.

Rendezvous

Not for these lovely blooms that prank your chambers did I
    come. Indeed,
I could have loved you better in the dark;
That is to say, in rooms less bright with roses, rooms more
    casual, less aware
Of History in the wings about to enter with benevolent air
On ponderous tiptoe, at the cue "Proceed."
Not that I like the ash-trays over-crowded and the place in
    mess,
Or the monastic cubicle too unctuously austere and stark,
But partly that these formal garlands for our Eighth Street
    Aphrodite are a bit too Greek,
And partly that to make the poor walls rich with our unaided
    loveliness
Would have been more *chic*.

Yet here I am, having told you of my quarrel with the taxi-
    driver over a line of Milton, and you laugh; and you
    are you, none other.
Your laughter pelts my skin with small delicious blows.
But I am perverse: I wish you had not scrubbed – with pum-
    ice, I suppose –
The tobacco stains from your beautiful fingers. And I wish
    I did not feel like your mother.

A second secret, sustained throughout the Thirties, seems
trivial, but Edna took pains to conceal it. Early in the decade she
became interested in thoroughbred horses and horse racing. Bill
Brann, who owned a stable of thoroughbreds in Maryland, lived
near Steepletop, was a friend of Eugen's and of Edna's, and enjoyed

driving them to the races at Saratoga in his Roll Royce. She read a great deal about horses and the history of horse racing and carried on a voluminous correspondence with Brann about training and racing horses. She invested a good deal of money in his stable and began betting heavily, increasingly obsessive about all details of the stable's operations. "If I wasn't so busy finding out what horses won the races in Maryland, today, I might have time to write,"[4] she said. She probably was not joking.

Why keep this secret? Edna's father had gambled. Cora, who tolerated many things, vehemently disapproved of gambling and Edna had begun to be involved in horse racing while her mother was still alive. Why remain secretive about it for a decade after her mother's death? Most likely it was that horse racing culture and the betting that is so much a part of it seemed inappropriate for a poet whose public image was far removed from anything as mundane as the turf. Whatever the explanation, it seems curiously timid behavior for a person who had not hesitated to defy propriety and convention in more important respects. What is clear about this is that Eugen and she spent a great deal of money on their horses and lost a great deal betting, which helps explain the fact that though she was earning an estimated twenty thousand dollars a year from 1935 to 1939—the equivalent of at least ten times that in contemporary currency—she was continually broke and, month after month, had to ask her publisher for advances on forthcoming books. But horses were not her only great expense.

In 1939, Edna stopped her reading tours because of the exhausting emotional demands they made on her. (Her last public poetry reading was in 1941.) The explanation for this reveals another secret and another obsession, this one profoundly destructive, which goes to the heart of the downward plunge in her life in the 1940s.

A trivial moment opens things up for us. During one of her tours, a friend came to hear her and was invited back to the Millay hotel suite after the performance. The friend recalled that Edna was nervous, "very edgy, pacing. That sort of thing." She was suffering from post-performance exhaustion. Then: "We were sitting there. And then she did it. I don't think she even knew that I noticed. Then she went into her bedroom and fell asleep." Eugen told the friend, "This happens sometimes, you must not be troubled by it."[5] Millay had always been a drinker; during her Vassar and Village days, and on through the Roaring Twenties. She drank even more in the Thirties; morning, afternoon, evening, until friends became concerned for her and a doctor warned that she would kill herself if she continued it at that rate. But this "it" was something else. She had injected herself with morphine. Whatever the causes of her chronic pain, whatever her depression about aging, about George Dillon, about losing her sexual appeal and her beauty, the answer, from the early Thirties onward was increasingly morphine, in staggeringly large doses.

Eugen and her doctors and a few close friends knew, and went along with it. In the first few years, Eugen injected her; later, as a sign of support, he injected himself as well. Soon she was doing it herself. The doctor who supervised her health in the late Thirties was accommodating. "I did not wish to have any discussion by the [hospital staff] of the amount of morphine [Millay] was taking. To avoid this I signed for it daily and personally ordered the drug."[6] Two pharmacies were also accommodating. By this time Eugen was buying huge quantities of Dilaudid, paregoric, Nembutal tablets, codeine, Progynon, Phenobarbital, Benzedrine, hypodermic syringes, needles, and one hundred, sometimes two hundred, quarter-grain tablets of morphine at a time, as well as cases of gin, scotch, rum, and vermouth. Edna was so enfeebled that she found it difficult to change her nightgown or get out of bed. St. Vincent's Hospital came ironically into her life again when her sister Kathleen died there of acute alcoholism, in November, 1943. She was unable to go to the funeral.

In 1944, Edna had a complete breakdown and entered Doctor's Hospital. She told Edmund Wilson that it was because of years of writing war poetry. "I can tell you from my own experience there is nothing on this earth which can so much get on the nerves of a good poet, as the writing of bad poetry. Anyway, I finally cracked up under it."[7] It wasn't war poetry that did it, of course, but her agreeing to enter the hospital was an indication that she recognized the extent of her problems. Witter Bynner and Arthur Ficke (who was dying of edema) encouraged her to get professional help. "What you are going through is the most excruciating misery for a human consciousness to experience."[8]

She refused treatment because she thought medical interventions prevented poetic inspiration. Even without that, however, she was no longer writing any poetry. Arthur Ficke's death in November 1945 was a terrible blow. She could not bear the sound of a telephone ringing so the lines were taken out at Steepletop, making her life now almost entirely reclusive. Finally, admitting her inability to help herself, she again entered a hospital in February 1946, for detoxification treatments. There she answered the doctor's question as to whether she really wished to live, with a ringing affirmation. She was released in March and spent two months in a psychiatric clinic and was able to leave, convinced that she could swear off drink for good. A year later she said, "I am clear of drugs now and clear of alcohol, eight months without drink, six months without even a drop of wine."[9]

Very few friends were invited to visit. Vincent Sheean, memoirist and music critic, came and was shocked at how worn and on edge she was. Edmund Wilson, with his new wife, came to visit. He had not seen Edna for nineteen years. Steepletop seemed to him very much the same as in 1929, only now very faded, like its occupants. Edna "was terribly nervous: her hands shook; there was a look of fright in her bright green eyes," he later wrote. The scene was too pathetic to bear. The Wilsons stayed only long enough to hear Millay recite some of her poems. In August 1949, Eugen was suddenly very ill. At a Boston hospital he was found to have lung cancer, was operated on and seemed to be recovering when, on August 29, he died of a stroke. Edna collapsed and was in the hospital for a month.

The adoring audiences on her tours were long gone, the rapt radio audiences had faded away, there was no Eugen to protect her. Drawing on the strength and determination that were part of her flinty upbringing, she went back to Steepletop and to what remained for her there: translating Latin and writing poetry. First, however, she had to struggle through a very harsh winter. And then came a more intractable problem. "You wonder how I am going to stand the spring. I'm wondering myself, I can tell you," she wrote to a neighbor. "And I'm plenty scared. Not scared that I shan't muddle through in some way or other. Just scared." Spring without Eugen turned out to be "more terrible than anything I could possibly have imagined." Finally, summer came and she could proudly say, "I have done it."[10]

She began thinking of a future collection of poems. On the night of October 18, 1950, probably in the early hours of the 19th after working all day, she placed a glass of white wine (she had begun to drink moderately again) and the wine bottle on the staircase and went upstairs, then apparently returned to the head of the stairs, stumbled, fell down them to the bottom, and broke her neck. Her body was discovered by the caretaker later that morning and along with it what proved to be a farewell note to her editor. "It is so wonderful to be writing again."[11]

Her body was cremated and her ashes interred with Eugen's near her mother's grave, in the grove of mountain laurel.

PART SEVEN

AFTER:
1972

1. Léonie Adams

IN 1954 AFTER her long period of silence, Léonie Adams published *Poems: A Selection*, a summing-up of her entire career. It is made up of twenty-four poems written in the previous twenty-five years, along with sixty-two poems from *High Falcon* and *Those Not Elect*. Dedicated to William Troy, it is remarkably consistent in tone and point of view, poetry which moves from the consideration of the natural world to a spiritual one.

Alas, Kind Element

Then I was sealed, and like the wintering tree
I stood me locked upon a summer core;
Living, had died a death, and asked no more.
And I lived then, but as enduringly,
And my heart beat, but only as to be.
Ill weathers well, hail, gust and cold I bore,

I held my life as hid, at root, in store:
Thus I lived then, till this air breathed on me.
Till this kind air breathed kindness everywhere,
There where my times had left me I would stay.
Then I was staunch, I knew nor yes nor no;
But now the wishful leaves have thronged the air.
My every leaf leans forth upon the day;
Alas, kind element! which comes to go.

The Reminder

All night there had sought in vain
To coax a sullen eye,
(And pressed to the black pane
The brilliance of their sky)
The winter moon blown high,
And the starred and the clouded train.

They have passed me glittering,
And I heard tone on tone
Of the cold nightchime ring,
With will that churned alone
And sight pinned bleak as stone
To what the heart could bring.

Till now the night wears thin,
A roof leans out awry,
And cocks and wheels begin;
And from past morning-cry
A lone, a steadfast eye
Silently looks in.

Léonie had no doubt anticipated a muted response to *Poems*, but demonstrating their admiration for a book which represented her work, her contemporaries awarded her the Bollingen Prize (which she shared with Louise Bogan).

The Walk

A walk above the waters' side,
None else to hearken there was come,
Where through haunt green and wellaway
I watched the low brook waters glide.
The heart rose stifling where it lay:
A voice dwelt there and was dumb.

The waters glided wellaway,
Hoarfast-hasting, jewel-swung;
And still that sound went breathing by
Of what they all at last would say;
An ear could overcatch the cry,
Though yet not all its tone was wrung.

The will shall learn itself alone,
For walking by the waters' side,
At every step my ear I bowed,
And heard from rift and runnelstone:
Away, they told delight aloud,
Away, it was the heart replied.

She had avoided publicity and lived quietly and privately, teaching and writing, a life seemingly tranquil. However, she wrote many tormented letters to Edmund Wilson about her situation. William Troy was difficult, abusive, and alcoholic. Eventually, she underwent a religious conversion and became a fervent Catholic. As her poems had never been popular, she was relatively untouched by the "revolution in literary taste, theory and practice."[1] Serious readers would always find her poetry absorbing. A New Yorker all her life, she outlived her husband, all of her poetic contemporaries, several poetical movements, and her own reputation, and died on June 27, 1988, at the age of eighty-eight.

2. DOROTHY PARKER

THE PARKER/CAMPBELL remarriage, graced by a mordant wisecrack—many of the guests, Dorothy observed, hadn't spoken to each other for years, "including the bride and groom"—was lavishly celebrated, with much drink, party games, and high spirits. But it was all downhill after that. The 1950s proved a dismal decade. One of Dorothy's biographers characterized her life as tragic. If anyone had said the same thing about her career as a poet, she would have thought it pretentious since it implied a fall from (potential) greatness she did not think she deserved, describing herself as "a person who had slogged along in Millay's footsteps, unhappily in my own horrible sneakers."[1] In fact, whatever its ultimate value, she had failed to take her talent seriously and had betrayed her gifts as a poet. She reproached herself bitterly for this. She rued the day she had written "News Item" and wished she had the power to destroy it. As for the Algonquin set, "The Round Table was wildly over-rated," she said. "These were no giants."[2]

By the 1950s, Dorothy's reputation as a popular poet had diminished, and academic Modernism, which commanded the field, failed to notice her, even as a minor writer of light verse. But her books still sold and she was widely quoted and misquoted. Many discerning observers blamed Hollywood for damaging Dorothy the poet, but the film industry, ironically, was now closed to her. The anti-communist red scare of the time destroyed the careers of several hundred film workers. Dorothy's support of numerous Communist front organizations resulted in her being blacklisted for years though, eventually, the FBI solemnly concluded that she did not constitute a risk to national security. She remained defiant and did not apologize or attempt to disguise what she had done. McCarthyism poisoned Hollywood social life and undermined her spirits. She and Campbell were cut off from their source of income and had to move into a dingy apartment, living on unemployment checks, quarreling and drinking incessantly. In the summer of 1951, after only one year together, they separated.

She returned to New York City, but soon found that she had lost her ear for the contemporary vernacular. So desperate was she about her inability to write that for the first and only time she apparently experimented with the form of what she was writing, emphasizing narrative and not dialogue. "I'm not going to do those he-said and she-said things anymore. They're over honey, they're over."[3] Visiting her, Edmund Wilson was heartened to see her typewriter on her desk, surrounded by a stack of books to be reviewed. But she admitted that reading books was now a "grinding effort," and that she "hated writing." The longer she sat at her typewriter the more paralyzed she became. She said she accepted the verdict of time. "My verses are no damn good. Let's face it, honey, my verse is terribly dated—as anything once fashionable is dated now." She added a mordant postscript: "I gave it up, knowing it wasn't getting any better, but nobody seemed to notice my magnificent gesture." She was able to finish an introduction to a book of James Thurber's cartoons, *The Seal in the Bedroom and Other Predicaments*, written because she needed the money, but also because the book evoked her sympathy for Thurber's odd men and women, "who seem to expect so little from life," and who "remember the old discouragements, and await the new."[4] She felt she was back home. "You just don't know how I love it," she told an interviewer; "how I get up every morning and want to kiss the pavement."[5] She moved into the Volney Hotel on East 74th Street, only a few minutes' walk across town from the neighborhood she had grown up in. The Volney was filled with women like her, women with few means, few friends, without anything in particular to do. Dorothy had epitomized a Manhattan life of frantic sociability, and now she lived a life of pervasive loneliness.

She collaborated on a play, *Ladies of the Corridor*, an acerbic depiction of the lives of women living alone in a hotel very like the Volney. Reviewers were very respectful. George Jean Nathan, the venerable critic who went back to the days of Dorothy's youth, called it the best play of 1953. The public thought it too grim. Asked to lighten the tone of writing that meant a great deal to her personally—"the only thing I have written in which I had great pride"—Dorothy adamantly refused. The play closed after forty-five performances. In 1956, she was able to return to Hollywood to work on a remake of *A Star is Born*, the film she had won plaudits for twenty years earlier, but no other film work was forthcoming. That year, a sympathetic interviewer heard Dorothy pass her final judgment on Hollywood. "I can't talk about Hollywood. It was a horror to me when I was there and it's a horror to look back on. I can't imagine how I did it. When I got away from it I couldn't even refer to the place by name. 'Out there,' I called it."[6] She also found Alan Campbell again, and they moved in together. She did book reviews for *Esquire* magazine, with a prominent byline: her name still had some resonance. But writing was agony and she was unprofessional, missing deadlines, sometimes not finishing her reviews. The editors were extraordinarily patient; but after seven years, forty-six columns, and two hundred and eight book reviews, she was finished.

Modest honors came to her: the Marjorie Peabody Waite Award for fiction and poetry; induction as a member of the National Institute and American Academy of Arts and Letters; Distinguished Visiting Professor of English at California State College of Los Angeles (which was not a success). Her drinking was now such a problem that she frequently appeared drunk in public and had to be taken home. Leonard Bernstein asked her to work with the poet Richard Wilbur on a lyric for his opera *Candide*, an adaptation of Voltaire's satire. Bernstein said of her: "very sweet," adding, "very drunk, very forthcoming, very cooperative. I expected it would take weeks of visits and phone calls to get the lyric, but amazingly, we had it next day."[7] Madame Sofronia's lament was the last verse she wrote and might very well have served to describe her personal situation.

Gavotte

I've got troubles, as I said.
Mother's dying, Father's dead.
Though our name, I say again, is
Quite the proudest name in Venice,
Our afflictions are so many,
And we haven't got a penny.

On the afternoon of June 14, 1963, Dorothy returned to the apartment she shared with Campbell and found him lying on the floor, dead, with sleeping tablets scattered around. The coroner listed his death as a probable suicide. Dorothy insisted that it was an accident. She was stunned by what had happened, but even that cannot explain the brutality of her response when a friend asked how she could help. Without a flicker of emotion, Dorothy replied, "Get me a new husband," and when the friend rebuked her for the tastelessness of such a wisecrack at that time, she said, "I'm sorry. Then run down to the corner and get me a ham and cheese on rye. And tell them to hold the mayo." [8] Campbell was buried in the family plot in Virginia. Dorothy didn't attend the funeral.

Friends were appalled to see how frail and wasted she was. A woman who came to interview her described her as "a bird in hiding. As I was leaving and going to the elevator. I could still see her peeking around the door." Dorothy refused to deny the truth. "People ought to be one of two things, young or old? No! What's the good of fooling? People ought to be one of two things, young or dead."[9] She couldn't rid her mind of remorse at the triviality of what she had written as an Algonquinite and in the years that followed. "We were a sort of Ladies Auxiliary of the legion of the damned. And boy, were we proud of our shame. We stayed young too long."[10]

The last thing she wrote was about New York City, captions for paintings of the city published in *Esquire* magazine in November 1964, almost fifty years since she had begun her journalistic career writing captions for *Vanity Fair*. The paintings produced in Dorothy a "dreamy longing" for the New York City of her childhood, the era of Henry James and Edith Wharton, and led her to characterize the prototypical New York hour as twilight. "As only New Yorkers know, if you can get through the twilight, you'll live through the night." Her last year was all twilight punctuated by her sobbing, "I can't write, I can't write." [11] Dorothy Parker died on June 7, 1967 of a heart attack alone in her room at the Volney.

She had said that there was not to be a funeral service; nevertheless, one was organized at which one of the speakers captured the true Parker spirit: "If she had her way, I suspect she would not be here at all." [12] There were extensive tributes in the papers but nothing more to the point than Somerset Maugham's judgment of a quarter of a century earlier in his introduction to *The Portable Dorothy Parker*. "Admirable as are Dorothy Parker's stories," he wrote, "I think it is in her poems that she displays the quintessence of her talent." Celebrated for their corrosive sarcasm, the poems had a special quality that has kept them in people's memories far longer that she would ever have imagined. That special quality, as Maugham discerned, was wit and pathos intertwined. "She had made little songs out of her great sorrows." [13]

3. Louise Bogan

Louise Bogan's later years "envelop her in full ciaroscuro,"[1] and yet she remained highly disciplined, followed a firmly established routine in her work. A photograph taken in the mid-1960s is, except for the passage of time etched on her face, virtually indistinguishable from one taken in the 1930s: sitting at her desk, writing her poetry reviews for the *The New Yorker*. Two omnibus reviews each year and many short notices; there were reviews and essays for other magazines, occasionally a poem for a future collection. And then the atmosphere darkened.

Rightly, she took pride in the hard-won emotional stability that enabled her to meet her obligations. There were no emotional explosions or displays of ego, no artistic "temperament," no missed deadlines, no failure to deliver copy to her editors who, recognizing her value, worked harmoniously with her. Widely read, a formidable autodidact, Louise didn't limit herself to criticism of poetry. She expressed her growing appreciation of the talents of English novelists, Dorothy Richardson, Elizabeth Bowen, Viola Meynell, and perceptively responded to French writers too, Colette, Flaubert, Gide.

Many of her reviews were of poetry by women. She was well aware of the formidable obstacles still faced in her day by women artists, but she was no respecter of reputations based on gender and didn't think female sensibility was something different from that of men. She intensely disliked the tone and manner of Virginia Woolf's fiction and criticism, recognizing that in the intensity of her response there was an element of class and cultural resentment by the Irish girl from Roxbury. She had no use for the New Criticism that became the most influential mode of academic criticism in these years. She held her ground with haughty literature professors, though she had denied herself, years before, more than one year of college, a lack she regretted. In this respect, Edmund Wilson's writing was encouraging; he was scathing in his dismissal of academic pedantry and pretensions.

IN 1951, AFTER three decades of thinking and writing about poetry, Louise published *Achievement in American Poetry, 1900–1950*. Slim, restrained, uncombative, the book remains indispensable reading for anyone interested in the subject and the period. In it, she developed an interpretation of the historical role of American women poets, contradicting the assumption that it was not until the advent of Modernism in the late 1910s that one could find a flourishing poetry culture. (And it was that book which, many years later, stimulated the writing of this one.)

The introductory chapters sketched the background of poetry in 1900 and the role of newspapermen and bohemians in sustaining an interest in poetry. In the third chapter, she identified writers, from Emerson to Frost, who represented New England town and rural culture and who, however else they differed from each other, represented "the line of truth," that is, literary realism and psychological truth. In contrast to that tradition, she identified one which revived a "warmth of feeling in the poetry of the early twentieth century," a task accomplished "almost entirely by women poets through methods which proved to be as strong as they seemed to be delicate." Much of this work and feeling was intuitive, but whatever its sources, "the line of poetic intensity which wavers and fades out in poetry written by men, on the feminine side moves on unbroken."[2] It was true, she recognized, that in the ninetieth-century women poets had contributed heartily to the saccharine sentimentalizing of American poetry; but after the Civil War the tone and subject matter of poetry written by women changed dramatically. It became ardent. It dealt with "love between the sexes." It was Ella Wheeler, Lizette Woodroth Reese, Louise Imogen Guiney whose work refuted the notion that the American poetic picture had been a blank canvas. "Freshness and sincerity of emotion, and economical directness of method" were the hallmarks of this poetry of love.[3]

In chapters four through six, Louise discussed many of the women who appear in these pages, paid tribute to the little magazines and their editors and to Modernist poets who helped liberate verse from Victorian mannerisms. Chapter seven is dominated by T.S. Eliot. She very wittily captured his spirit. "Pound was forced to discover modernity. Eliot was modern from the beginning."[4] Two chapters, "Ideology and Irrationalism, 1930-1941," and "Poetry at the Half Century," concluded the survey.

Her judgments about the poetry of some of her contemporaries are candid, firm, perceptive. She praised Amy Lowell for recognizing that "In any growing art every line must be explored to its end; all manner of temperaments and of stylistic variation must be given room." She admired Sara Teasdale's successful determination to free her work of traces of romantic vocabulary and tone and achieve poems "so naturally put together that they seem to be spoken, rather than written—spoken at the direct urging of passionate impulse." Teasdale's work became "increasingly lucid and tragic," achieving "classic depth and balance." Elinor Wylie brought to the lyric "emotional richness, as well as an added brilliance of craftsmanship." At first overwhelmed by her own virtuosity, "she became more tellingly controlled as time went on. Her work as a whole was far more complex than that of any feminine predecessor." Louise's estimate of Edna Millay (dead only one year) is extraordinarily balanced. Millay "took no part in the revolt against style. Her lyricism expressed itself in forms straight out of the Keatsian convention; and her modern mixture of abandonment and disillusion was almost always accompanied by classical ornament." But at her best, she could "cut into the center of complicated emotion with sharpness," though at her worst she fell victim to sentimentality and the dangers of self-pity and self-regard. She belonged to a generation "filled with genuine feminist and liberal idealism" and "formulated for a new generation of young women a standard of sexual defiance and 'heroism'…which was marked by truth and pathos." That she was, "by nature, a lyric poet of the first order, is an incontestable fact." Having frequently reviewed Marianne Moore's poetry, there was no need for Louise to elaborate on her achievement but rather to characterize it. "Her idiosyncrasies were from the beginning of her career her own." She combined "odd but striking attributes of the naturalist," with those of a "philosophic moralist" and her insights "struck close to the heart of things."[5]

Louise had always admired Léonie Adams's work and now, looking back, praised it in particular for having "completely escaped from the atmosphere of modishness" in the poetry of Millay and Wylie; and as well, she admired Adams's gift for having "sensitively interpreted nature…thought, and feeling," but her praise was tinged with disapproval of "an intensity which often seems to slip over into mystic vision." Louise mentioned, but did not evaluate the work of H.D., and didn't even mention Parker and Taggard. We know her personal opinion of Taggard's later poetry. They had been friends when associated with *The Measure*, but they became estranged and were increasingly politically antipathetic. Louise's final personal judgment was that Taggard was "no good" as a poet, a comment which infuriated Theodore Roethke. "Damn her, anyway," he said to Rolfe Humphries, "she and her Irish digs."[6]

Praise for *The Achievement* from her peers was followed by a succession of honors and awards. In 1952, she was elected to the National Institute of Arts and Letters. In 1954, her *Collected Poems, 1923-1953*, was published, and, in 1955, Louise and her friend Léonie Adams shared the Bollingen Prize for poetry. In the same year, her *Selected Criticism, Poetry and Prose* appeared. Marianne Moore wrote to her. "This book, nutritious and at the same time a source of pride, helps me to feel that life is worth while. Its associative creative insights, unfrivolity, and humor certainly fortify my courage."[7]

Her life was steady and sane, but diminished, detachment achieved at the cost of anticipating any joy. She traveled to England and responded deeply, as she had in Vienna three decades before, to a culture so rich with the forms of civilization. Back home, one evening in the spring of 1963, Edmund Wilson brought Léonie Adams by for an evening of talk and reminiscence. That same year Theodore Roethke died. Rolfe Humphries had moved to California. Invited to teach for a semester at Brandeis University, Louise spent several months in New England, a gloomy disappointment. She wandered the streets of her childhood in Roxbury, but much of what she remembered was dilapidated or had disappeared.

In mid-decade she plummeted again into breakdown, fearful of aging and of death. "I felt the consuming, destroying, deforming passage of time: and the spectacle of my family's complete helplessness, in the face of their difficulties, swept over me." At the heart of her slipping down into protracted depression were "anger and mourning" so deep that for a whole year she could not even listen to music. At the same time, she regretted that she had been living so isolated a life. She saw other old people on the streets. "People keep hopeful and warm and loving right to the end—with much more to endure that I endure...they are not 'depressed.' They gossip and laugh...Where has this power gone, in my case? I weep—but there's little relief there."[8] The unbearable loneliness of love forever lost is unforgettably captured in the poem "Little Lobelia's Song."

Louise was hospitalized twice but somehow she surmounted this breakdown as she had the previous ones. She returned to her apartment and to her work. Her publishers urged a new edition of her collected verse, and in 1968 she produced *The Blue Estuaries, Poems: 1923-1968*, a final summing up. She sternly cut out a number of fine poems from her previous collections, poems with which she had never been quite satisfied. She knew this was her final book. She dedicated it "To the memory of my father, mother and brother," a dedication that "acknowledged the bridge between her life's work and her love for her family."[9] There were twelve new poems, varying in mood and subject, some of them poems she had been working on for two decades or more, most written during and after the breakdown of the mid-Sixties. One of the poems,

"The Meeting," a dream song, captures the elusiveness of love. A man, a "gentle and plausible" man, like a "faithful brother," appears to her, smiles, holds her hand, and then dissolves and returns to a place Louise could not go.

The avalanche of books tumbling into *The New Yorker* to be read and reviewed was increasingly exhausting. "Her doubts mounted: her morning tears continued."[10] In September 1969, Louise retired from the magazine. Even that didn't free her of feelings of guilt about work unfinished and projects abandoned. Her health deteriorated rapidly. The few remaining friends who got to see her recognized that she was giving up the incessant struggle. One them who went to her apartment on February 4, 1970, found her lying in front of her bed, dead for many hours, probably of a heart attack sometime in the night.

There was a memorial service. Among these who spoke were W.H. Auden and two friends from those Columbia University days of half a century earlier, Margaret Mead and Léonie Adams. They articulated an artistic achievement which combined knowledge and a discerning imagination. And then, with eloquent appropriateness, the service concluded with a sonata by Mozart.

WRITERS WHO FAILED to gain a substantial audience in their day have responded to this painful experience in various ways. Stendhal was confident that his novels would find their proper readers a century after his death. Emily Dickinson accepted that she would sing her songs for herself alone. What of Louise Bogan? One of her poems suggests an answer. It grew out of that meeting years before with T.S. Eliot, an occasion that had moved her deeply and had an important sequel. Eliot's presence generated something in her at a time when she had been unable to write. She then gathered her notes from an unfinished lyric she had set aside for years, sat down, wrote out a draft, and the long barren spell came to an end. The poem looks forward to a time when, the life voyage concluded, the poet may proudly proclaim one thing left behind of enduring value; that where there is love—full, all-embracing love—the poet's song will be heard.

Song for the Last Act

Now that I have your face by heart, I look
Less at its features than its darkening frame
Where quince and melon, yellow as young flame,
Lie with quilled dahlias and the shepherd's crook.
Beyond, a garden. There, in insolent ease
The lead and marble figures watch the show
Of yet another summer loath to go
Although the scythes hang in the apple trees.

Now that I have your face by heart, I look

Now that I have your voice by heart, I read
In the black chords upon a dulling page
Music that is not meant for music's cage,
Whose emblems mix with words that shake and bleed.
The staves are shuttled over with stark
Unprinted silence. In a double dream
I must spell out the storm, the running stream.
The beat's too swift. The notes shift in the dark.

Now that I have your voice by heart, I read.

Now that I have your heart by heart, I see
The wharves with their great ships and architraves;
The rigging and the cargo and the slaves
On a strange beach under a broken sky.
O not departure, but a voyage done!
The bales stand on the stone; the anchor weeps
Its red rust downward, and the long vine creeps
Beside the salt herb, in the lengthening sun.

Now that I have your heart by heart, I see.

4. Marianne Moore

T HE EARLY 1950S were triumphant years for Marianne Moore. In 1951, her *Collected Poems* was published. "Best Living Poet," *Newsweek* magazine proclaimed her, and Louise Bogan in the *The New Yorker* attested to her preeminence, "a naturalist without pedantry and a moralist without harshness."[1] In 1952, there was an avalanche of recognition and praise: The Pulitzer Price, the National Book Award, the Bollingen Prize. The National Institute of Arts and Letters presented her with its Gold Medal for lifetime achievement in 1953, and in that same year Bryn Mawr College awarded her its M. Carey Thomas award, especially cherished by Moore and previously given only to Jane Addams and Eleanor Roosevelt. The year 1954 saw the publication of her translation of *The Fables of La Fontaine,* and in 1955 came the appearance of *Predilections,* a volume of prose pieces. In those years, she received honorary degrees from eight colleges and universities.

This recognition of thirty-five years of unflagging commitment to austere aesthetic ideals was immensely gratifying for a writer who had never achieved popular success and could never hope to do so. "It is hard for an exacting mind to be popular,"[2] she noted. That she personified the artist too rarefied and difficult to be popular turned out to be the precondition for a development that was wildly surprising.

In the mid Fifties and into the Sixties, she became a New York City public figure and then a national celebrity, the creation of the mass culture of post World War Il. Edna Millay and Dorothy Parker had also achieved national recognition; but there was a fundamental difference between their fame and Moore's. Millay and Parker wrote poems that were easy to remember. Their poetry represented feminist attitudes and values. By contrast, Moore's poetry never became familiar. Her poetry was not quoted in the stories about her and was rarely even referred to. Marianne Moore became newsworthy as a "character," a "personality." A grandmotherly type, a deadpanned eccentric, an implausibly amusing figure, whose image was played off against her unquestioned reputation as a formidable highbrow. This Marianne Moore disarmed populist minds deeply suspicious of intellectuality and of art. And she happily and no doubt genuinely played her role in this popular culture story. When she said of her verse, "I don't know why my work should be called poetry except that there is no other category in which to put it," she pacified the potentially hostile, who surrendered unconditionally when she added, "Anyone could do what I do."[3]

Marianne didn't contrive this kind of celebrity, but she enjoyed it. And it was permitted now because of the absence of the mother/censor who would have been appalled by it. She wore funny hats. She went to baseball games and took part in publicity stunts such as throwing out the first ball at Yankee Stadium to begin the baseball season.

Marianne Moore

She went to Belmont Park to see the horses run and was photographed there intently engaged in a close textual analysis of the *Daily Racing Form*. She exchanged autographs with Muhammad Ali at Toots Shor's saloon. She had written about the Brooklyn Dodgers and when they moved to Los Angeles, supported the Mets. One much-reproduced photograph was amusing in its own right, with splendidly-hatted Marianne intently conversing with manager Casey Stengel (with the Mets' owner in the middle). It was also a bit of an inside joke, for those who knew something of both septuagenarians, the garrulous manager exchanging insights with the incomprehensible Modernist.

Whatever the situation or company, Moore was good-spirited, likeable. Poets were not thought of in that way. Imagine the passionate Millay, the feisty Parker, the haughty Wylie, the anguished Bogan. Who would be intimidated or put off by Great Aunt Marianne? This was captured on the cover of *Esquire* magazine, which featured eight likeable celebrities. "In a time when everybody hates somebody, nobody hates ... 'The Unknockables'"[4] Joe Louis, Helen Hayes, Jimmy Durante, Eddie Bracken, Kate Smith, John Cameron Swayze, and Marianne Moore, who is holding the hand of Norman Thomas—given Thomas's socialism, an unlikely pairing.

She went to her desk each morning, drawing on the clippings and phrases she had stored up. What she had to say reflected her wider and more eclectic social life. In 1956 came a new collection, *Like a Bulwark*, another of her slim volumes. This collection and the two that followed have been the subject of considerable critical disagreement. Some have seen these poems as no more than "a variety of thinking out loud, a kind of verbal doodling." For others they are simply light verse adapted to the subjects of mass culture. Marianne was sixty-nine when *Like a Bulwark* appeared. Whether or not her newly achieved popularity was a factor in how she was now writing, it is likely that she could not have written as she once had, even if she wished to do so. And apparently she didn't wish to. "She was now a trapeze artist floating above the mundane."[5]

The title poem is paradoxical. There are phrases and images associated with power; power pent-up, constrained but also released, "affirmed," in human action, "tempest tossed." Is it a response to her critics?

Like a Bulwark

Affirmed. Pent by power that holds it fast—
a paradox. Pent. Hard pressed,
  you take the blame and are inviolate.
   Abased at last?
   Not the tempest-tossed.
Compressed; firmed by the thrust of the blast
  till compact, like a bulwark against fate;
   lead-saluted,
    saluted by lead?
though flying Old Glory full mast.

O To Be a Dragon (1959) was the next collection. The title poem, another of her creatures, is utterly charming—and deceptively simple. It is a poem about "problems of identity" and expresses "the wish to have, like the dragon of Chinese legend…the ability to infuse the world with moral and spiritual strength." It is also the humorous rearrangement of traditional dragon attributes and the variations in rhythm corresponding to these patterns." [6]

O to Be a Dragon

If I, like Solomon,…
could have my wish –

  my wish…O to be a dragon,
a symbol of the power of Heaven – of silkworm
size or immense: at times invisible.
  Felicitous phenomenon!

There was another charmer in the collection, a poem written in 1909 but never included in any of Marianne's books over the previous half-century. It appeared under its original title.

Progress

If you will tell me why the fen
appears impassable, I then
will tell you why I think that I
can get across it if I try.

Brooklyn and Manhattan had furnished Marianne with indispensable intellectual nourishment to such an extent that she recognized one could become an arrogant "ruffian" about living in a big city, "boasting to those at a distance of the pleasures of town life." Her town life had become so hectic that it threatened to exhaust her. A friend urged her "to put an ocean between you and New York."[7] She needed no encouragement since she had been from her early years a transatlantic person intellectually. In 1962, she traveled to Greece and Italy. In 1964, she went to Ireland, where she was pleased to find the house in which her grandfather had been born. At the same time, she was a resolute Anglophile; she and her mother had avidly followed the fortunes of the British royal family. Her reputation in England was very high. While there, she renewed contact with her old friend Bryher and with the much admired T.S. Eliot.

In 1965, she experienced a different change of scene. Life in her Brooklyn neighborhood had become dangerous. There were break-ins and muggings. This was not the Brooklyn of 1929. She was persuaded to move back to Manhattan, to the Village, to 35 West Ninth Street. A newsworthy event. The *New York Times* devoted considerable space to Brooklyn's loss of its "last" gem. For many who knew nothing of her early Village years, she had been entirely identified with Brooklyn. The Village had also changed but she still liked walking around in it as much as she could. Her health had begun to deteriorate.

In 1966, Marianne published *Tell Me, Tell Me,* a book which included poems about an amusement park, baseball, a horse named "Blue Bug," the Brooklyn Bridge, and the effort to save Carnegie Hall from being torn down. As well there was another of her tributes to an Englishman she admired, Walter Savage Landor (1775–1864), a natural eccentric who combined a literary life with martial manners and was as modest as he was accomplished.

W.S. Landor

There
is someone I can bear-
 "a master of indignation...
meant for a soldier
 converted to letters," who could

throw
a man through the window,
 yet, tender toward plants, say "Good God,
the violets!" (below).
 "Accomplished in every

style
and tint" – considering meanwhile
 infinity and eternity,
he could only say, "I'll
 talk about them when I understand them."

Honors continued to flow to her: a book of critical essays to mark her seventy-fifth birthday (1965), the Poetry Society's Gold Medal (again), and an honorary degree from Princeton University. She grew steadily weaker but was strong enough to appear on a popular evening TV show. In the summer of 1969, she suffered a stroke, spent more than a month in the hospital and after that was never again able to write.

She died in her sleep on February 5, 1972.

EZRA POUND OUTLIVED her by only nine months, so these heroes of Modernism left the scene at virtually the same time and, after years of separation, had been briefly together before Marianne's stroke. In the summer of 1969, Ezra returned to the United States to attend a meeting of the American Academy of Arts and Letters. Marianne was also there and able to greet the man who was among the first to notice her poetry and to sense a remarkable talent. She had also been intrigued by his poetry from early in his career. Critical as she was of some of his views and of his combative temperament, she had defended him in the years immediately after World War II.

When they met, the poetry controversies of the 1910s and Twenties had long since faded, passing into the hands of scholars. Their most celebrated contemporaries were dead. All that remained was for Marianne to say, "Oh, Ezra," and for Ezra to reply, "Oh, Marianne." And then they touched hands.[8]

Notes

Epigraphs

T. S. Eliot, *The Sacred Wood: Essays on Poets and Criticism*, preface to the 1928 edition (London, 1928), viii, ix

Louise Bogan, in Ruth Limmer, ed., *What the Woman Lived: Selected Letters of Louise Bogan, 1920-1970* (1975), 22

PART ONE: ROADS TO ROME

*Place of publication is New York unless otherwise indicated.

1. Dorothy Parker

Biographies: Leslie Frewin, *The Late Mrs. Parker* (1980); John Keats, *You Might as Well Live: The Life and Times of Dorothy Parker* (1970); Arthur F. Kinney, *Dorothy Parker Revised* (1998); Marian Meade, *Dorothy Parker: What Fresh Hell Is This?* (1989)

Criticism: Barry Day, ed., *Dorothy Parker in Her Own Words* (Baylor 2004); Kevin C. Fitzpatrick, *A Journey Into Dorothy Parker's New York* (Berkeley 2005); Rhonda Pettit, *A Gendered Collision: Sentimentalism and Modernism in Dorothy Parker's Poetry and Fiction* (Madison 2000); Rhonda Pettit, ed., *The Critical Waltz: Essays on the Work of Dorothy Parker* (Madison 2000); Marion Capron, Dorothy Parker in Malcolm Cowley, ed., *Writers at Work: The Paris Review Interviews* (1958)

1. Meade, *What Fresh Hell*, 8
2. Frewin, *The Late Mrs. Parker*, 5
3. Capron, *Writers at Work*, 72-87
4. Frewin, *The Late Mrs. Parker*, 7
5. Frewin, *The Late Mrs. Parker*, 6
6. Meade, *What Fresh Hell*, 13
7. Meade, *What Fresh Hell*, 15
8. Frewin, *The Late Mrs. Parker*, 8
9. Keats, *You May as Well Live*, 25
10. Keats, *You May as Well Live*, 24
11. Capron, *Writers at Work*, 12-13
12. Frewin, *The Late Mrs. Parker*, 18
13. Frewin, *The Late Mrs. Parker*, 10
14. Keats, *You Might as Well Live*, 34-35
15. Frewin, *The Late Mrs. Parker*, 18
16. Keats, *You May as Well Live*

2. Sara Teasdale

Biographies: Margaret Haley Carpenter, *Sara Teasdale, A Biography* (1960); William Drake, *Sara Teasdale, Woman Poet* (San Francisco 1979); Carol Schoen, *Sara Teasdale* (Boston 1986)

1. Drake, *Teasdale*, 22-23; Schoen, *Teasdale*, 5-6
2. Drake, *Teasdale*, 8; Carpenter, *Teasdale*, 15-18
3. Drake, *Teasdale*, 9
4. Schoen, *Teasdale*, 6-8; Drake, *Teasdale*, 10
5. Drake, *Teasdale*, 29; Schouen, *Teasdale*, 9-12; Carpenter, *Teasdale*, 14-47
6. Schoen, *Teasdale*, 8-9; Drake, *Teasdale*, 24; Carpenter, *Teasdale*, 78-84
7. Schoen, *Teasdale*, 17-23; Drake, *Teasdale*, 25
8. Drake, *Teasdale*, 54; Schoen, *Teasdale*, 30-33, 76; Carpenter, *Teasdale*, 115-123

9. Drake, *Teasdale*, 64; Schoen, *Teasdale*, 53-55

10. Drake, *Teasdale*, 66; Carpenter, *Teasdale*, 139-143

11. Drake, *Teasdale*, 68; Schoen, *Teasdale*, 56

12. Drake, *Teasdale*, 69

13. Schoen, *Teasdale*, 66; Drake, *Teasdale*, 87

14. Drake, *Teasdale*, 108; Schoen, *Teasdale*, 76

15. Drake, *Teasdale*, 105

16. Drake, *Teasdale*, 100; Carpenter, *Teasdale*, 163-219

17. Schoen, *Teasdale*, 76-77; Drake, *Teasdale*, 116-117

18. Drake, *Teasdale*, 145; Schoen, *Teasdale*, 77-78; Carpenter, *Teasdale*, 320-248

19. Schoen, *Teasdale*, 78

3. Edna St. Vincent Millay

Biographies: Elizabeth Atkins, *Edna St. Vincent Millay* (1964); Norman Brittin, *Edna St. Vincent Millay* (1962); Anne Cheney, *Millay in Greenwich Village* (1975); Daniel Epstein, *What Lips My Lips Have Kissed* (2001); James Gray, Edna St. Vincent Millay (University of Minnesota Press (1967); Miriam Gurko, *Restless Spirit: The Life of Edna St. Vincent Millay* (1962); Nancy Milford, *Savage Beauty, The Life of Edna St. Vincent Millay* (2001); Toby Shafter, *Edna St. Vincent Millay, America's Best-Loved Poet* (1975); Vincent Sheean, *The Indigo Bunting, A Memoir of Edna St. Vincent Millay* (1951), Allan Ross MacDougall, ed., Letters of Edna St. Vincent Millay (1952).

Criticism: Diane P. Freedman, ed., *Millay at 100: A Critical Reappraisal* (Southern Illinois University Press 1995), William B. Thesing, *Critical Essays on Edna St. Vincent Millay* (1993).

1. Frewin, *The Late Mrs. Dorothy Parker*, 19

2. MacDougall, ed., *Letters*, 176

3. Milford, *Savage Beauty*, 14

4. Thurman, *Siren Songs, The New Yorker*, 9/3/01, 86

5. Cheney, *Millay in Greenwich Village*, 76

6. Epstein, *What Lips*, 23

7. Milford, *Savage Beauty*, 76

8. Milford, *Savage Beauty*, 109

9. Milford, *Savage Beauty*, 87

10. Milford, *Savage Beauty*, 92-93

11. Milford, *Savage Beauty*, 107

12. Milford, *Savage Beauty*, 94

13. Milford, *Savage Beauty*, 131

14. Milford, *Savage Beauty*, 108

15. Haight, *Vincent at Vassar, Vassar Alumnae Magazine*, 5/51

16. Milford, *Savage Beauty*, 96

17. Milford, *Savage Beauty*, 92; Wetzsteon, *Republic of Dreams*, 247

18. Milford, *Savage Beauty*, 137-138, 114

19. Epstein, *What Lips*, 82

20. Milford, *Savage Beauty*, 130

4. Marianne Moore

Biographies: Bernard F. Engel, *Marianne Moore* (1964); Charles Molesworth, *Marianne Moore, A Literary Life* (1990); Robin G. Shulze, *Becoming Marianne Moore* (2002); Laurence Stapleton, *Marianne Moore, The Poet's Advance* (Princeton 1978)

Criticism: Harold Bloom, ed., *Marianne Moore: Modern Critical Views* (1987); Bonnie Costello, *Marianne Moore: Imaginary Possessions* (Cambridge, Massachusetts 1981); Margaret Holley, *The Poetry of Marianne Moore: A Study in Voice and Value* (1988); Robin G. Shulze, *Becoming Marianne Moore* (Berkeley 2002); John Slatin, *The Savage's Romance: The Poetry of Marianne Moore* (University Park, Pennsylvania 1985); Laurence Stapleton Laurence Stapleton, *Marianne Moore: The Poet's Advance* (Princeton 1978); Laurence Tomlinson, ed., *Marianne Moore: A Collection of Critical Essays* (New Jersey 1969); Patricia Willis, ed., *Marianne Moore: Woman and Poet* (1990)

1. Tomlinson, ed., *Marianne Moore, A Collection of Critical Essays* (Englewood Cliffs, New Jersey, 1969), 23
2. Phillips, *Marianne Moore, Dictionary of Literary Biography*, 45, 280
3. Costello, ed., *Letters*, 178
4. Costello, ed., *Letters*, 57-58
5. Costello, ed., *Letters*, 62
6. Costello, ed., *Letters*, 75-77
7. Costello, ed., *Letters*, 74; Molesworth, *Marianne Moore*, 109
8. Costello, ed., *Letters*, 981
9. Costello, ed., *Letters*, 122-123; Tomlinson, *Marianne Moore*, 25;
10. Friedman, *Hilda Doolittle H. D., Dictionary of Literary Biography*, 45, 120
11. Friedman, *H. D. Dictionary of Literary Biography*, 45,121
12. Friedman, *H. D. Dictionary of Literary Biography*, 45,122
13. Doolittle, *Marianne Moore, The Egoist*, 8/16, 111; Costello, ed., *Letters*, 113
14. Costello, ed., *Letters*, 103
15. Costello, ed., *Letters*, 104
16. Costello, ed., *Letters*, 112

5. Louise Bogan

Biography: Elizabeth Frank, *Louise Bogan: A Portrait* (1986); Ruth Limmer, ed., *What the Woman Lived: Selected Letters of Louise Bogan 1920-1970* (1973)
Criticism: Martha Collins, ed., *Critical Essays on Louise Bogan* (Boston 1984); Mary Kinzie, ed., *A Poet's Prose: Selected Writings of Louise Bogan* (Ohio University Press 2005)

1. Frank, *Bogan*, 42
2. Frank, *Bogan*, 7-10
3. Frank, *Bogan*, 11
4. Frank, *Bogan*, 21
5. Frank, *Bogan*, 20
6. Frank, *Bogan*, 35
7. Frank, *Bogan*, 26
8. Frank, *Bogan*, 31
9. Frank, *Bogan*, 26
10. Frank, *Bogan*, 42

6. Elinor Wylie

Biographies: Judith Farr, *The Life and Art of Elinor Wylie* (Louisiana State University 1983); Evelyn Helnick Hively, *A Private Madness: The Genius of Elinor Wylie* (Kent State University Press 2003); Nancy Hoyt, *Elinor Wylie: The Portrait of an Unknown Lady* (1935); Stanley Olson, *Elinor Wylie: A Life Apart* (1979)

1. Stein, *Elinor Wylie, Dictionary of Literary Biography*, 45, 441
2. Hively, *Madness*, 14-16
3. Hively, *Madness*, 14
4. Farr, *Life and Art*, 23
5. Hively, *Madness*, 28
6. Hively, *Madness*, 29
7. Hively, *Madness*, 34
8. Olson, *Elinor Wylie*, 297
9. Hively, *Madness*, 33
10. Hively, *Madness*, 29
11. Olson, *Elinor Wylie*, 152
12. Olson, *Elinor Wylie*, 153
13. Olson, *Elinor Wylie*, 180

14. Olson, *Elinor Wylie*, 182
15. Olson, *Elinor Wylie*, 183

PART TWO: MANHATTAN, 1917–1921

1. Overview: The Village and Feminism

1. Wetzsteon, *Republic*, 6
2. Cheney, *Millay in Greenwich Village*, University of Alabama Press, 1975, 37
3. Stansell, *American Moderns: Bohemian New York and the Creation of a New Century*, 2000, 264-265
4. Stansell, *American Moderns*, 273
5. Stansell, *American Moderns*, 246
6. Bogan, *Achievement in American Poetry: 1900-1950*, Chicago, 1951, 22

2. Sara Teasdale

1. Drake, *Teasdale*, 215; Schoen, *Teasdale*, 95; Carpenter, *Teasdale*, 234
2. Drake, *Teasdale*, 168; Schoen, *Teasdale*, 99-104; Carpenter, *Teasdale*, 232-242
3. Drake, *Teasdale*, 173; Schoen, *Teasdale*, 105
4. Drake, *Teasdale*, 145
5. Drake, *Teasdale*, 178
6. Drake, *Teasdale*, 193-204; Schoen, *Teasdale*, 111; Carpenter, *Teasdale*, 243-248
7. Drake, *Teasdale*, 200; Schoen, *Teasdale*, 111-121
8. Drake, *Teasdale*, 168
9. Drake, *Teasdale*, 205; Schoen, *Teasdale*, 123; Carpenter, *Teasdale*, 252-255

3. Edna St. Vincent Millay

1. Macdougall, ed., *Letters*, 81, 73-74, 83

2. Macdougall, ed., *Letters*, 69-71

3. Milford, *Savage Beauty*, 147

4. Hart, *Edna St. Vincent Millay, Dictionary of Literary Biography*, 45, 268

5. Milford, *Savage Beauty*, 148

6. Cheney, *Millay in Greenwich Village*, 111

7. Milford, *Savage Beauty*, 148

8. Wetzsteon, *Republic of Dreams*, 249; Epstein, *What Lips*, 125-127; Milford, *Savage Beauty* 154-156; Cheney, *Millay in Greenwich Village*, 64

9. Cheney, *Millay in Greenwich Village*, 104-107; Milford, *Savage Beauty*, 158

10. Milford, *Savage Beauty*, 191

11. Wilson, *Epilogue, 1952: Edna St. Vincent Millay, The Shores of Light, A Literary Chronicle of the Twenties and Thirties*, 1952, 751

12. Milford, *Savage Beauty*, 194

13. Milford, *Savage Beauty*, 192

14. *New York Times*, 10/16/21; Thesing, *Critical Essays on Edna St. Vincent Millay*, 1993, 118

15. Macdougall, ed., *Letters*, 102

16. Macdougall, ed., *Letters*, 106

4. Dorothy Parker

1. Keats, *You Might as Well Live*, 35

2. Meade, *What Fresh Hell*, 40

3. Keats, *You Might as Well Live*, 37; Frewin, *The Late Mrs. Parker*, 23-30

4. Meade, *What Fresh Hell*, 46

5. Meade, *What Fresh Hell*, 44-45

6. Dorothy Parker, *Constant Reader*, 67, 114

7. Frewin, *The Late Mrs. Parker*, 46

8. Frewin, *The Late Mrs. Parker*, 106

9. Meade, *What Fresh Hell*, 89

5. Overview: Modernism

1. Macdougall, ed., *Letters*, 35-36; Damon, *Amy Lowell, A Chronicle*, Boston 1935, 194-195

2. Bogan, *Achievement in American Poetry 1900-1959*, 1951, 29

3. Limmer, ed., *Letters*, 49; Costello, ed., *Letters*, 123,128

4. Costello, ed., *Letters*, 123

5. Costello, ed., *Letters*, 162

6. Amy Lowell

Biographies: S. Foster Damon, *Amy Lowell: A Chronicle*, (Boston 1935); Horace Gregory, *Amy Lowell, Portrait of the Poet in Her Time* (1958); Adrienne Munich and Melissa Bradshaw, *Amy Lowell: American Modern* (Rutgers University Press 2004).

1. Damon, *Amy Lowell*, 88

2. Damon, *Amy Lowell*, 76-98

3. Damon, *Amy Lowell*, 148

4. Damon, *Amy Lowell*, 190

5. Healey, *Amy Lowell, Dictionary of Literary Biography*, 54, 254

6. Bradshaw and Munich, eds., *Selected Poems*, xix

7. Amy Lowell, *Men, Women and Ghosts*, 1916, Preface, ix

8. Friedman, *Hilda Doolittle, H. D., Dictionary of Literary Biography*, 45, 125

9. Damon, *Amy Lowell*, 257

10. Anderson, *My Thirty Years War, An Autobigraphy*, 1930, 60-62

11. Gregory, *Amy Lowell*, 159

12. Amy Lowell, *Pictures of the Floating World*, 1919, Foreword, viii

7. Marianne Moore

1. Costello, ed., *Letters*, 122

2. Frank, *Brogan*, 49

3. Costello, ed., *Letters*, 123, 128, 125

4. Molesworth, *Marianne Moore*, 316

5. Costello, ed., *Letters*, 122-123

6. Costello, ed., *Letters*, 123; Bogan, *Achievement in American Poetry*, 64

7. Costello, ed., *Letters*, 75

8. Molesworth, *Marianne Moore*, 192

9. Costello, ed., *Letters*, 119

10. Schulze, ed., *Becoming Marianne Moore*, 285

11. Costello, ed., *Letters*, 181-182

12. Costello, ed., *Letters*, 100

8. Louise Bogan

1. Frank, *Bogan*, 43

2. Frank, *Bogan*, 47

3. Frank, *Bogan*, 55

4. Frank, *Bogan*, 42

5. Frank, *Bogan*, 44-45

6. Frank, *Bogan*, 90

7. Frank, *Bogan*, 45

PART THREE: MANHATTAN, 1921–1925

1. Elinor Wylie

1. Olson, *Wylie*, 173-179

2. Olson, *Wylie*, 212; Hively, *A Perfect Madness*, 109

3. Wilson, *The Twenties*, Leon Edel, ed., 1975, 78

4. Olson, *Wylie*, 144

5. Olson, *Wylie*, 184-185

6. Wylie, *The Collected Prose of Elinor Wylie*, Preface by Carl Van Vechten, 1933, 8

7. Hively, *A Private Madness*, 162

8. Olson, *Wylie*, 214-215; Hively, *A Perfect Madness*, 98

9. Olson, *Wylie*, 216-17

10. Olson, *Wylie*, 190-191

11. Hively, *A Perfect Madness*, 20; Olson, *Wylie*, 262-263

12. Olson, *Wylie*, 243-244, 254, 256; Hively, *A Private Madness*, 133-134

13. Olson, *Wylie*, 249, 251-253, 265; Dorothy Parker, *Willow, Willow, Waley, The New Yorker*, 3/7/28, 34

14. Olson, *Wylie*, 262

15. Olson, *Wylie*, 263

2. Marianne Moore

1. Costello, ed., *Letters*, 142

2. Costello, ed., *Letters*, 128

3. Costello, ed., *Letters*, 152, 144, 121

4. Costello, ed., *Letters*, 188

5. Molesworth, *Marianne Moore*, 147

6. Molesworth, *Marianne Moore*, 147

7. Tomlinson, *Critical Essays*, 36

8. Marianne Moore, *The Sacred Wood, The Dial*, March 1921, 336-339

9. *The Dial*, Announcement, 78, 1/25, 89

10. Schulze, ed., *Becoming Marianne Moore*, 27-38

11. Molesworth, *Marianne Moore*, 202-202

12. Molesworth, *Marianne Moore*, 192

3. Edna St. Vincent Millay

1. Macdougall, ed., *Letters*, 124

2. Macdougall, ed., *Letters*, 136, 143, 139

3. Macdougall, ed., *Letters*, 130

4. Milford, *Savage Beauty*, 209

5. Macdougall, ed., *Letters*, 137; Milford, *Savage Beauty*, 222-227

6. Milford, *Savage Beauty*, 231-234

7. Milford, *Savage Beauty*, 235-237

8. Milford, *Savage Beauty*, 250

9. Milford, *Savage Beauty*, 253

10. Milford, *Savage Beauty*, 258

11. Milford, *Savage Beauty*, 260

12. Milford, *Savage Beauty*, 260

13. Milford, *Savage Beauty*, 273

4. Louise Bogan

1. Frank, *Bogan*, 52

2. Frank, *Bogan*, 53

3. Frank, *Bogan*, 53

4. Frank, *Bogan*, 46, 114

5. Frank, *Bogan*, 74, 73, 57

6. Frank, *Bogan*, 82

7. Frank, *Bogan*, 89

8. Frank, *Bogan*, 75

9. Frank, *Bogan*, 88

10. Ashbel Green, ed., *My Columbia: Reminiscences of University Life* (Columbia University Press, 2005), 122

5. Léonie Adams

1. Mead, *Blackberry Winter, My Earlier Years*, 1972, 102, 106-108

2. Limmer, ed., *Letters*, 24; Meyers, *Edmund Wilson, A Biography*, 1995, 103-104

3. Mead, *Blackberry*, 107

6. Genevieve Taggard

1. McCann, *Genevieve Taggard, Dictionary of Literary Biography*, 45, 376; Berke, *Women Poets of the Left: Lola Ridge, Genevieve Taggard, Margaret Walker*, University Press Florida, 30

7. Dorothy Parker

1. Capron, *Writers at Work*, 72-87
2. Frewin, *The Late Mrs. Parker*, 78-79
3. Capron, *Writers at Work*, 72-87
4. Mead, *What Fresh Hell*, 141
5. Frewin, *The Late Mrs. Parker*, 103

8. Sara Teasdale

1. Drake, *Teasdale*, 238
2. Drake, *Teasdale*, 254, 235-236; Schoen, *Teasdale*, 150-153
3. Drake, *Teasdale*, 214; Hively, *A Private Madness*, 97-98
4. Drake, *Teasdale*, 206; Schoen, *Teasdale*, 124-126; Carpenter, *Teasdale*, 252-254
5. Drake, *Teasdale*, 214-215
6. Drake, *Teasdale*, 214-215; Schoen, *Teasdale*, 132
7. Drake, *Teasdale*, 221; Schoen, *Teasdale*, 122, 126
8. Drake, *Teasdale*, 223
9. Drake, *Teasdale*, 222

9. Amy Lowell

1. Damon, *Amy Lowell*, 515, 100
2. Damon, *Amy Lowell*, 664
3. Damon, *Amy Lowell*, 548
4. Damon, *Amy Lowell*, 654
5. Damon, *Amy Lowell*, 619
6. Redford, *A Transatlantic Affair, Amy Lowell and Bryher*, Munich and Bradshaw, *Amy Lowell, American Modern*, Rutgers University Press, 2004, 47
7. Damon, *Amy Lowell*, 318, 479
8. Damon, *Amy Lowell*, 352, 358
9. Damon, *Amy Lowell*, 643

10. Damon, *Amy Lowell*, 644

11. Damon, *Amy Lowell*, 661-663

12. Damon, *Amy Lowell*, 646

13. Damon, *Amy Lowell*, 648-649

14. Damon, *Amy Lowell*, 184

15. Damon, *Amy Lowell*, 442

16. Lauter, *Amy Lowell and Cultural Borders*, Munic and Bradshaw, *Amy Lowell, American Modern*, 5

17. Damon, *Amy Lowell*, 431-432

18. Damon, *Amy Lowell*, 696

19. Damon, *Amy Lowell*, 699

20. Damon, *Amy Lowell*, 701

21. Marianne Moore, Comment, *The Dial*, July, 1925, 87-88

PART FOUR: DIVERGENCE, 1925–1929

1. Marianne Moore

1. Costello, ed., *Letters*, 224

2. Tomlinson, *Critical Essays*, 37

3. Costello, ed., *Letters*, 218

4. Whitemeyer, ed., *Selected Letters of Ezra Pound and William Carlos Williams*, 1996, 40

5. Costello, ed., *Letters*, 235

6. Costello, ed., *Letters*, 219

7. Costello, ed., *Letters*, 234, 223

8. Costello, ed., *Letters*, 122

9. Costello, ed., Letters, 233

10. Costello, ed., *Letters*, 234; Molesworth, *Marianne Moore*, 224

11. Whitemeyer, ed., *Selected Letters of Ezra Pound and William Carlos Williams*, 1996, 91

12. Costello, ed., *Letters*, 245

13. Molesworth, *Marianne Moore*, 244

2. Dorothy Parker

1. Kinney, *Dorothy Parker*, Keats, *You Might as Well Live*, 118; Meade, *What Fresh Hell*, 177-178
2. Meade, *What Fresh Hell*, 178
3. Pettit, *A Gendered Collision*, 68
4. Meade, *What Fresh Hell*, 188
5. Frewin, *The Late Mrs. Parker*, 139-140
6. Meade, *What Fresh Hell*, 191
7. Day, ed., *Dorothy Parker in Her Own Words*, 2004, 118

3. Louise Bogan

1. Limmer, ed., *Letters*, 30
2. Frank, *Bogan*, 90
3. Frank, *Bogan*, 86
4. Limmer, ed., *Letters*, 16
5. Limmer, ed., *Letters*, 22-23
6. Frank, *Bogan*, 96
7. Limmer, ed., *Letters*, 38-39
8. Limmer, ed., *Letters*, 28-29
9. Limmer, ed., *Letters*, 35-36
10. Frank, *Bogan*, 101-102
11. Limmer, ed., *Letters*, 50
12. Limmer, ed., *Letters*, 37
13. Limmer, ed., *Letters*, 37
14. Frank, *Bogan*, 91
15. Frank, *Bogan*, 105
16. Frank, *Bogan*, 105

4. Léonie Adams

1. Bawer, *Leoni Adams, Poet, The New Criterion*, 10/88, 23; Redd, *Léonie Adams, Dictionary of Literary Biography*, 3-9, 48

5. Louise Bogan

No Notes

6. Genevieve Taggard

1. Ridge, *Miss Taggard Encircles the Metaphysical poles, New York Evening Post*, 4/5/30
2. Moore, *The Dial*, 4/29, 86, 345-346

7. Edna St. Vincent Millay

1. Macdougall, ed., *Letters*, 194-195; Milford, *Savage Beauty*, 276
2. Macdougall, ed., *Letters*, 215
3. Milford, *Savage Beauty*, 493
4. Milford, *Savage Beauty*, 289; Macdougall, ed., *Letters*, 231
5. Milford, *Savage Beauty*, 304

8. Sara Teasdale

1. Millett, *Contemporary American Authors*, 1944, 611
2. Teasdale, *The Answering Voice*, New Edition 1927, x-xi; Carpenter, *Teasdale*, 237
3. Drake, *Teasdale*, 240; Schoen, *Teasdale*, 174-176; Carpenter, *Teasdale*, 262-269
4. Drake, *Teasdale*, 252; Schoen, *Teasdale*, 154-155
5. Drake, *Teasdale*, 258; Schoen, *Teasdale*, 155-157; Carpenter, *Teasdale*, 286-287
6. Drake, *Teasdale*, 260; Carpenter, *Teasdale*, 288-289

9. Elinor Wylie

1. Olson, *Wylie*, 251

2. Hively, *A Private Madness*, 178

3. Olson, *Wylie*, 285

4. Olson, *Wylie*, 261-262

5. Hively, *A Private Madness*, 162-163; Olson, *Wylie*, 271-272

6. Olson, *Wylie*, 319-320

7. Hively, *A Private Madness*, 67; Olson, *Wylie*, 188

8. Olson, *Wylie*, 300

9. Farr, *Life and Art*, 22

10. Meade, *What Fresh Hell*, 111-112

11. Hively, *A Private Madness*, 96

12. Olson, *Wylie*, 280

13. Hively, *A Private Madness*, 99

14. Milford, *Savage Beauty*, 290

15. Milford, *Savage Beauty*, 293

16. Milford, *Savage Beauty*, 294

17. Milford, *Savage Beauty*, 302

18. Milford, *Savage Beauty*, 196

19. Hively, *A Private Madness*, 195

20. Olson, *Wylie*, 290-291

21. Olson, *Wylie*, 291

22. Olson, *Wylie*, 296

23. Olson, *Wylie*, 302

24. Olson, *Wylie*, 305

25. Hively, *A Private Madness*, 201

26. Olson, *Wylie*, 313, 319-320

27. Olson, *Wylie*, 317-318

28. Olson, *Wylie*, 310

29. Olson, *Wylie*, 310

30. Olson, *Wylie*, 326

31. Olson, *Wylie*, 330-331
32. Milford, *Savage Beauty*, 307

PART FIVE: AFTER: 1935

1. Overview: The End of the Roaring Twenties
No Notes

2. Dorothy Parker

1. Meade, *What Fresh Hell*, 203
2. Frewin, *The Late Mrs. Parker*, 144
3. Meade, *What Fresh Hell*, 239

3. Sara Teasdale

1. Drake, *Teasdale*, 270; Carpenter, *Teasdale*, 289
2. Drake, *Teasdale*, 273
3. Drake, *Teasdale*, 273; Schoen, *Teasdale*, 161-164; Carpenter, *Teasdale*, 308
4. Drake, *Teasdale*, 277; Schoen, *Teasdale*, 157
5. Drake, *Teasdale*, 290; Schoen, *Teasdale*, 170
6. Drake, *Teasdale*, 291; Carpenter, *Teasdale*, 319
7. Drake, *Teasdale*, 293; Carpenter, *Teasdale*, 324-325; Moore, *Poetry*, 4/33, 71

4. Louise Bogan

1. Limmer, ed., *Letters*, 56-57
2. Frank, *Bogan*, 137
3. Roethke, *The Poetry of Louise Bogan*; Martha Collins, ed., *Critical Essays on Louise Bogan*, Boston, 1984, 88
4. Collins, ed., *Critical Essays*, 93
5. Frank, *Bogan*, 189

6. Frank, *Bogan*, 202
7. Frank, *Bogan*, 225
8. Limmer, ed., *Letters*, 84-85
9. Limmer, ed., *Letters*, 132

5. Elinor Wylie

1. Limmer, ed., *Letters*, 44
2. Hively, *A Private Madness*, 29

6. Marianne Moore

1. Molesworth, *Marianne Moore*, 248; Willis, ed., *The Complete Prose of Marianne Moore*, 1986, vii
2. Costello, ed., *Letters*, 279, 298-299
3. Costello, ed., *Letters*, 319
4. Costello, ed., *Letters*, 251-252
5. Costello, ed., *Letters*, 317
6. Costello, ed., *Letters*, 329-330
7. Molesworth, *Marianne Moore*, 268
8. Costello, ed., *Letters*, 329
9. Costello, ed., *Letters*, 335

7. Léonie Adams

1. Redd, *Léonie Adams, Dictionary of Literary Biography*, 7-9, 48; Fowlie, *Remembering Leoni Adams, The New Criterion*, 1988, 16-20
2. Millett, *Contemporary American Authors*, 213

8. Genevieve Taggard

1. McCann, *Genevieve Taggard, Dictionary of Literary Biography*, 45, 379-380

9. Edna St. Vincent Millay

1. Milford, *Savage Beauty*, 398-399
2. Milford, *Savage Beauty*, 383
3. Milford, *Savage Beauty*, 335
4. Milford, *Savage Beauty*, 388; Limmer, ed., *Letters*, 38
5. Milford, *Savage Beauty*, 304
6. Milford, *Savage Beauty*, 312
7. Milford, *Savage Beauty*, 309
8. Milford, *Savage Beauty*, 316
9. Milford, *Savage Beauty*, 301
10. Milford, *Savage Beauty*, 294
11. Epstein, *What Lips*, 219
12. Macdougall, *Letters*, 244
13. Milford, *Savage Beauty*, 329
14. Tate, *Fatal Interview*, Sonnets by Edna St. Vincent Millay and Genevieve Taggard, Edna St. Vincent Millay in William Thesing, ed., *Critical Essays on Adna St. Vincent Millay*, 1993, 64, 137-140
15. Milford, *Savage Beauty*, 350, 358
16. Milford, *Savage Beauty*, 396; Macdougall, ed., *Letters*, 251
17. Milford, *Savage Beauty*, 388

PART SIX: AFTER: 1950

1. Louise Bogan

1. Frank, *Bogan*, 177-178
2. Frank, *Bogan*, 287
3. Frank, *Bogan*, 242
4. Frank, *Bogan*, 280, 301
5. Frank, *Bogan*, 231
6. Roethke, *The Poetry of Louise Bogan*, Collins, ed., *Critical Essays on Louise Bogan*, 87-96

7. Frank, *Bogan,*

8. Frank, *Bogan,*

9. Kunitz, *Land of Dust and Flames,* Collins, ed., *Critical Essays,* 64-65

10. Frank, *Bogan,* 308-309

11. Frank, *Bogan,* 327, 335

12. Frank, *Bogan,* 337-338, 348

13. Willis, ed., *The Complete Prose of Marianne Moore,* 1986, 367-369

14. Frank, *Bogan,* 348

15. Frank, *Bogan,* 343

2. Dorothy Parker

1. Kael, *For Keeps, 32 Years at the Movies, Part Four, Raising Kane from the Citizen Kane Book,* 1994, 235-325

2. Page, *Dawn Powell,* 1998, 145

3. Fitzpatrick, *A Journey Into Dorothy Parker's New York,* 2005

4. Meade, *What Fresh Hell,* 313

5. Meade, *What Fresh Hell,* 331

6. Meade, *What Fresh Hell,* 339

3. Marianne Moore

1. Costello, ed., *Letters,* 336, 339

2. Moore, *In Memory of Harriet Monroe,* 12/36, 155-156

3. Moore, *What Are Years,* Notes

4. Costello, ed., *Letters,* 449

5. Costello, ed., *Letters,* 444

6. Molesworth, *Marianne Moore,* 323

7. Costello, ed., *Letters,* 464

8. Costello, ed., *Letters,* 466

9. Costello, ed., *Letters,* 464

4. Léonie Adams

1.   Redd, *Léonie Adams, Dictionary of Literary Biography*, 8, 48

5. Genevieve Taggard

1.   McCann, *Genevieve Taggard, Dictionary of Literary Biography*, 45, 381

2.   Millett, *Contemporary American Authors*, 603

6. Edna St. Vincent Millay

1.   Milford, *Savage Beauty*, 403
2.   Milford, *Savage Beauty*, 410
3.   Milford, *Savage Beauty*, 419-423
4.   Epstein, *What Lips*, 250
5.   Milford, *Savage Beauty*, 427
6.   Milford, *Savage Beauty*, 439
7.   Milford, *Savage Beauty*, 487
8.   Epstein, *What Lips*, 264
9.   Epstein, *What Lips*, 268
10. Macdougall, ed., *Letters*, 367-368
11. Milford, *Savage Beauty*, 507

PART SEVEN: AFTER: 1972

1. Léonie Adams

1.   Redd, *Léonie Adams, Dictionary of Literary Biography*, 9, 48

2. Dorothy Parker

1.   Meade, *What Fresh Hell*, 339

2.   Cowley, ed., *Writers at Work: The Paris Review Interviews*; Capron, *Dorothy Parker*, 1958, 75; Keats, *You Might as Well Live*, 295

3. Cowley, *Writers at Work*, 80

4. Meade, *What Fresh Hell*, 222; Cowley, *Writers at Work*, 75

5. Meade, *What Fresh Hell*, 346

6. Cowley, *Writers at Work*, 79, 81

7. Meade, *What Fresh Hell*, 339

8. Meade, *What Fresh Hell*, 339

9. Meade, *What Fresh Hell*, 339

10. Frewin, *The Late Mrs. Parker*, 300-301

11. Meade, *What Fresh Hell*, 339

12. Petit, ed., *The Critical Waltz, Essays on the Work of Dorothy Parker*, Farleight Dickinson University Press, 144

13. Maugham, *The Viking Portable Dorothy Parker*, 1944, Introduction, 17-18

3. Louise Bogan

1. Frank, *Bogan*, 387

2. Bogan, *Achievement in American Poetry 1900-1950*, 1951, 22-23

3. Bogan, *Achievement*, 24-25

4. Bogan, *Achievement*, 67

5. Bogan, *Achievement*, 53-54, 78-80, 61-62

6. Frank, *Bogan*, 226; Bogan, *Achievement*, 80

7. Costello, ed., *Letters*, 513

8. Frank, *Bogan*, 398-399

9. Frank, *Bogan*, 400

10. Frank, *Bogan*, 410

4. Marianne Moore

1. Bogan, *The New Yorker*, 8/2/52

2. Molesworth, *Marianne Moore*, 353

3. Molesworth, *Marianne Moore*, 357

4. *Esquire* Magazine, *The Unknockables*, 6/66

5. Molesworth, *Marianne Moore*, 385

6. Nitchie, *Marianne Moore, An Introduction to the Poetry*, 1969, 157-158; Stapleton, *Marianne Moore, The Poet's Advance*, Princeton, 1978, 85; Engel, *Marianne Moore*, 1964, 141

7. Molesworth, *Marianne Moore*, 423

8. Molesworth, *Marianne Moore*, 447

TEXT CREDITS

Leonie Adams:
"April Mortality," "Those Not Elect," "Quiet," "A Wind of Fall," "Song," "Caryatid," "Kennst du das Land," "Alas, Kind Element," "The Reminder," "The Walk," reprinted with permission of Dr. Judith Farr, literary executor. All rights reserved.

Louise Bogan:
"To My Brother Killed: Haumont Wood: October, 1918," "Cassandra," "Hypocrite Swift," "Roman Fountain," "To An Artist, to Take Heart," "The Dream," "Song for the Last Act" from *The Blue Estuaries*, by Louise Bogan. Copyright © 1968 by Louise Bogan. Copyright renewed 1996 by Ruth Limmer. Reprinted by permission of Farrar, Straus and Giroux.

Edna St. Vincent Millay:
"Scrub," "Justice Denied in Massachusetts," "To Those Without Pity," "The Buck in the Snow," "On Hearing a Symphony of Beethoven," "Dedication of Fatal Interview, 1931, to Elinor Wylie," "Sonnet: ["Not in the silver casket cool with pearls"]," "Sonnet: ["Love is not all: it is not meat nor drink"]," "Childhood is the Kingdom Where Nobody Dies," "Spring in the Garden," "Huntsman, What Quarry?," and "Rendezvous" from *Collected Poems* (HarperCollins Publishers). Copyright 1923, 1927, 1928, 1931, 1951, 1954, © 1955, 1982, by Edna St. Vincent Millay and Norma Millay Ellis. Reprinted with the permission of The Permissions

Harriet Monroe:

Marianne Moore:

IMAGE CREDITS

Edna St. Vincent Millay:
Same credit for both photos:
Page 39: Billy Rose Theatre Division, The New York Public Library.
"Edna St. Vincent Millay" *The New York Public Library Digital Collections*
Page 394: Billy Rose Theatre Division, The New York Public Library.
"Edna St. Vincent Millay" *The New York Public Library Digital Collections*

Marianne Moore:
Page 377: Portrait: © George Platt Lynes, *Marianne Moore*, The Catalog of American Portraits, National Portrait Gallery, Smithsonian Institution Archives

Page 472: Baseball: © The Rosenbach Library

Dorothy Parker:
Page 126: Billy Rose Theatre Division, The New York Public Library. (1924). *Dorothy Parker in backyard of residence at 412 West 47th Street, New York City*

Page 353: Portrait: Courtesy Yale Collection of American Literature, Beinecke Rare Book and Manuscript Library, Yale University

Gertrude Stein:
Page 144: Henry W. and Albert A. Berg Collection of English and American Literature, The New York Public Library. (1937 - 1948). *Gertrude Stein and Pepe at Bilignin, June 13, 1934*

Genevieve Taggard:
Page 228: Portrait: Courtesy George Eastman Museum; © Nickolas Muray Photo Archives

Page 437: Outdoor photograph: Unknown photographer. *Genevieve Taggard,* Sarah Lawrence College Archives

Sara Teasdale:

Page 245: E.O. Hoppé, Sara Teasdale, 1925 ©Curatorial Assistance Inc. / E.O. Hoppé Estate Collection

Page 319: E.O. Hoppé, Sara Teasdale, 1928 ©Curatorial Assistance Inc. / E.O. Hoppé Estate Collection

Elinor Wylie:

Page 84: Oval portrait: Photographer unknown, courtesy Yale Collection of American Literature, Beinecke Rare Book and Manuscript Library, Yale University

Page 335: Portrait with hands clasped: © Nickolas Muray Photo Archives, courtesy Beinecke Library & Rare Book Manuscripts, Yale University

New Yorker Cartoon:

Page 333: Cartoon by Carl Rose, 1928, © Condé Nast, The New Yorker magazine

CPSIA information can be obtained
at www.ICGtesting.com
Printed in the USA
BVHW071329020619
549930BV00002B/149/P